Hot Air, Cool Music

Hot Air, Cool Music

Bruce Turner

Quartet Books
London Melbourne New York

First published by Quartet Books Limited 1984
A member of the Namara Group
27/29 Goodge Street, London W1P 1FD

British Library Cataloguing in Publication Data

Turner, Bruce
  Hot air, cool music.
  1. Turner, Bruce   2. saxophonists—
  England–Biography
  I. Title
  788′.66′0924   ML419.T8/

  ISBN 0-7043-2459-8

Typeset by MC Typeset, Chatham, Kent
Printed and bound in Great Britain
by Mackays of Chatham Ltd, Kent

Contents

Now I must . . . dodge
And palter in the shifts of lowness, who
With half the bulk o' the world played as I pleased

Antony and Cleopatra, Act III Scene 2

Intro

I have now been a jazz enthusiast for fifty years, and a professional musician for almost forty of those years. That is quite a long time. Naturally, as a musician, I would like to know more about the position of music and art in our lives. But I know I can get closer to the truth only by discussion with other musicians. A few of my own opinions may have slipped out in the course of writing this book. This was inevitable, but I am only offering a few tentative suggestions. Let's say they are the opening gambits in what I sincerely hope will be a much wider discussion.

Only on one point would I be prepared to claim a reasonable certainty. I believe that the performer in jazz is bound to know more about his art than the non-playing pundit, and that his opinions are the ones which will count in the end. So it is up to the people who make jazz to guide it forward to better things.

I also hope that the reader will forgive me if I have talked rather a lot about myself. This is not conceit, but an attempt to show what happens when an adolescent misfit finally discovers an idiom in which he can express himself. During the thirties, it wasn't easy for a confused teenager to find his way to jazz, mesmerized as he was by the innocuous, mass-produced dance music of that time. He either had to reject the Establishment to some extent, or to be rejected by it. I suppose I fell into the second category. Like so many kids of my generation, I grasped at music as a form of escape – and then found that the greatest music is not an escape at all. It is an expression of warm reality. It was just that none of us quite realized this at the time.

Bruce Turner
1984

1 Background Music

Some are born musical, but I had music thrust upon me along with the nappies and the baby food. By the time I was only a few months old, Chopin and Beethoven were sounds I had become accustomed to, like the chatter of human voices or the distant hum of traffic. Mum was one of those compulsive pianists who can never keep away from the keyboard for long. She never was one for the household chores. As far back as I can remember, we had to bring in kitchen-maids and part-time cleaners to attend to even the simplest tasks. Don't ask me how we were able to afford this luxury. We were just an ordinary, lower-middle-class family, and lived in a smallish terraced house in the plainest of streets in Saltburn, north Yorkshire. But the domestics had to be taken on, or nothing would have ever got done. Mum was good with her hands, but only as long as they were poised over piano keys.

This background music was strangely comforting -- a soothing voice that told me life was proceeding as normal. And it was always on tap. To obtain the best listening, all I had to do was follow my mother into the drawing-room. This room nearly always smelt of fag-ends and bad air. Even with the windows open you were likely to get a noseful of these stale tobacco fumes. In various nooks and alcoves, the remains of strong tea grew cold and sloppy in tiny porcelain cups, until the servant managed to break in, invading the private sanctum and rescuing them all in one great swoop.

The floor was littered with crumpled sheets of manuscript paper and thick Beethoven scores with tea-stains on their outer covers. Through the haze, I could just about discern the small dark-haired woman at the piano, haloed like a genie in swirls of greyish-blue smoke. Anguished cries came from the pursed lips, and she glared at the sheet music as if she expected it to pounce upon her at any moment. A really difficult passage would be greeted with a muffled curse or two. Then would come the theatrical discord. Splayed fingers would come crashing down, in a fine display of exaggerated pique. It might have relieved *her* feelings in some way, but to me it was all very like watching a horror movie. Just as everything was nice and peaceful, you had one of these dramatic displays. I concluded that music was an intense sort of experience. Certainly there was no dozing off when she was at the keys. You sat the thing out in awed silence until the last note.

My mother's family was not only musical but very talkative. Aunts and uncles came round to discuss opera or the latest West End show. Conversation became rather animated at times. I used to stand and wait for a slight pause in the ceaseless flow of sound. After a while, although I had been christened Malcolm Bruce, my mother decided to call me 'Souris', which is French for 'mouse', because for years I just stood about waiting for a gap in the conversation which never came. My brother and sister were soon precocious enough to add their voices to the general clamour, cutting down my chances even further. Uncle Tren and Uncle Julian made a fuss of their nice quiet nephew and started slipping pennies into my hand whenever the conversation eased off slightly. They looked and talked exactly like Mum. It was like having a trio of mothers, two of them taking the harmony parts.

My father was never around much in those days, and I saw him only in passing, a shadowy figure. He was tall and muscular, with a jagged Scottish accent you could have drilled holes with. His face usually seemed to wear a fierce expression when he was talking to me, and this scared me for a number of years. I think he scared the uncles and aunts too. Dad wasn't at all fond of music, and as soon as he showed up people had to pretend to be talking about something else. It was as if a non-believer had entered the sacred precincts. This made for a somewhat strained atmosphere in the home. Saltburn was where my mother's folk lived, and whenever we went to stay with Dad's family in Scotland, it was Mum's turn to feel ill at ease. The two tribes had about as much in common as the Montagues and the Capulets.

Dad's work took him all over the place. He was a college professor and lectured in different areas at different times. It was like belonging to a nomadic tribe. At one time we were moving house every few months. At the age of three I was living in Chester, at four I was in Baroda, in northern India, and after that we moved back to Saltburn. We also spent some time in

Scotland, with Dad's family, and as my sixth birthday came up we moved to London. By the time I was going to school in Twickenham, I had done more mileage than most people do in a lifetime.

At Twickenham I started to feel that my world was built upon shifting sand. I was now going to school with kids who had strange, unfamiliar accents. The place unnerved me. Still, it was no more than just another stopping-off place. Soon I would be staring out of that train window again, wondering what our next 'home' would be like.

It was in Twickenham that I managed to see my father more often than hitherto, and began to get to know him better. We went for walks together and had contests to see who could eat the most ice cream. I believe he thought of me as a moody, introverted child. He blamed the music – that stuffy, indoor music that he had never been able clearly to understand. Every time one of us sat down at the piano or started listening to some music on the radio, he suggested a long walk. Fresh air and exercise were his cure for all the ills of mankind.

Outside in the open, he became like a benevolent PT instructor. 'Swing those arms, Soory,' he bellowed at me. 'Deep breaths, chest out! Get those shoulders back!'

The rest of his words would be lost to me as he went pounding off into the distance. Passers-by simply dived for cover as this human steamroller trundled by. In the busy London suburbs he never stopped behaving as though the wild Scottish lowlands were around him on all sides.

My mothers's own musical talents he thought of as charming and essentially feminine. He liked to see her at it, and I think he was proud of her musical ability. The sound of frenzied Beethoven continued to seep through from the drawing-room.

'Why doesn't Dad like music?' I asked her one day.

'It's the Scotch,' came her unexpected reply. She wasn't talking about his drinking habits: a pet theory of my mother's was that Scottish people had no feeling for music and absolutely no sense of humour. A sweeping generalization; but it did have to be admitted that Father could often keep both music and humour at arm's length. Yet he did have a wonderful sense of the absurd. That is the only way I can describe certain eccentric displays – one of which I will now offer as a brief example.

In Twickenham, we bought our groceries from a bearded and extremely deaf old man in the High Street. One day, my father took me and my sister into the shop, strode up to the counter, and solemnly chanted: 'Bearded man, bearded man – a pound of sugar if you can.'

The old fellow was so startled by this form of address that he fiddled with his deaf aid for what seemed an eternity, my father all the while repeating his incantation in the same theatrical tones, refusing to alter his demeanour with so much as a smile.

Presently we were off again to our next address. This time it was a large detached house in Hastings, on a steep incline on the Old London Road. I complained bitterly when told about the move. I had only just settled in at the old address, and started to make some friends at school. Why couldn't we stay in one place like everybody else I knew?

Mum told me that we were shortly to be enjoying a higher standard of living than before. Father had been offered an important position in India, as headmaster of one of the big colleges.

'Is Hastings in India?' I asked her, perplexed.

'Of course not, dopey. Hastings is where we will be staying until your father sends for us. It might take some time.'

'Then why can't we just stay here? I don't know anyone in Hastings.'

'We can't afford to go on living in London. Surely you don't want to go on living in rooms.'

'Won't there be any rooms in the Hastings house? Fine sort of house that is – without any rooms!'

'Souris, my head is beginning to ache slightly.'

The new house was said to be in a very convenient position, close to a school. I soon found out what this meant, and my heart sank. 'Laurelhurst' was close to a school all right. The school was right next door, on the other side of our garden fence. It was also a *girls' convent*!

'No! No!' I screamed, 'you're not going to send me *there*!'

'It will only be for a short while,' explained my mother. 'It's just that the place is so handy, and as Ruby will be going there . . .'

As a matter of fact, there were several other six-year-old boys at the convent, pathetic little sods who, like myself, had older sisters at the school. The place certainly took some getting used to. Instead of the usual line in teachers, we had black-robed figures gliding about. At the entrance to each classroom a tiny container was built into the wall. Before going through, we had to dip one finger into the bowl and make the sign of the cross.

Our family wasn't even Catholic. The first time my finger made contact with the holy water I felt a shiver run down my spine. It was my very first experience of religious mysticism. Supposing I forgot, one day, and went in without making the sign! I had unshakable visions of a dark pit waiting to engulf me if the thing ever slipped my mind. Since then, submissive worship has never seemed attractive to me. Nowadays, if I go on my knees, it is to find something on the floor. The closest thing to heaven, for me, is the Django Reinhardt chorus on 'Japanese Sandman'.

Ruby and I never found out why we were sent to this place, since there hadn't been any religious fervour in our family for years. I still believe my mother's motives had been coldly practical from the start. Here was this nice house going cheap, and how very useful that there was some sort of school right next door!

My sister thought the whole thing an excellent joke. Unlike me, she had a dominating personality and was held in awe by the other kids. They treated her with a kind of open-mouthed respect, while tending to ignore me altogether. I very much liked being ignored, and tried to make myself as unobtrusive as I could. In playtime, while the girls were forming a respectful circle around my sister, I often climbed through the fence so that I could sit at home, even for a few minutes. Every moment away from the convent was time well spent.

After school, I had to tag along with Ruby and her gang, as I was considered to be too young to be let loose on my own. We rang doorbells and then ran off, or we grimaced at lorry drivers from the safety of our front-garden wall. I was nearly always the one who got caught, having forgotten to run for safety.

Already my sister was mocking at the establishment and developing a very cutting sense of humour. She was good at mimicry, and so was I. We vied with each other in cruelly impersonating people who happened to have odd mannerisms. It was thought that I might grow up to be an impressionist or a stand-up comic. If we were taken to the cinema, I never found the films boring. If there were corny scenes, I looked on them as potential comedy – especially the heavy, melodramatic bits. Once we were taken to see *King of Jazz*. It featured Paul Whiteman's Band, with some big-name jazz musicians, but all I was interested in was the romantic lead, a Mr John Boles. His ardent love-making scenes were very funny to me. I memorized as many of them as I could, so that I could amuse the family later on, with my parody of the Great Lover.

Jazz was just a word, currently being bandied around. In this country we still took it to mean any kind of fast, noisy American music. At this time, 'Rhapsody in Blue' was being passed off as a jazz work.

The Hastings sojourn could have been pleasant, if only I had been sent to a normal school. It is an endearing town, and in the late twenties it hadn't yet been vulgarized along part of its seafront. Even now the place has a lot of character and quiet charm. In those days it seemed to me to consist entirely of steep pathways up to the East and West Hills, tiny shops where you could buy quite a lot for only a halfpenny, and a perfectly marvellous beach. The convent loused it up for me. Hemmed in on all sides by girls and devout nuns, I had no chance of forming any normal friendships, or living a natural life. When I heard of the move from Hastings, I wasn't sure whether to cheer or feel very wary indeed. What new horrors did Fate have in store?

Mother then imparted the news that I would not be seeing her for quite a long time – maybe even a couple of years. She tried hard not to make it sound dramatic, but that was the way it hit me. It had been bad enough with only one parent on the scene – I somehow couldn't imagine what it would be like without either of them. Was it something I'd said, or what? Then she told me that she was off to India to join Dad, and that as soon as there was enough money coming in, then the three of us would be sent for. Meanwhile Tren and Ruby would be at boarding-school, and I would be sent to stay with my grandparents in Scotland. During the long wait, Mum and Dad would be sending sporadic words of encouragement from a place on the other side of the globe. It all sounded rather depressing to me. I had stayed with the Castle Douglas crowd before, but hadn't been able to understand a word they said. Now I was to be stranded there for almost two years!

The worst thing about this next period was that the background music wasn't there any more. Not that I'd ever really understood all those sonatas and things – but now there was an uneasy silence that hadn't been there before. It left an enormous gap. The Scottish folk were extremely kind, but if there was one thing they were *not,* it was musical. There was also the language difficulty. Granny did her very best to make me feel at home, but my accent clearly presented her with a problem. She listened carefully to all that I said, but her brow furrowed with the effort of concentration.

Right from the start, she fell into the habit of saying

everything twice for my benefit – first in careful English and then in her normal voice. 'You're at home now,' she pronounced slowly on my arrival. Then came a gruff: 'Yer at hame the noo!' accompanied by a fond embrace that seemed to crack several of my ribs. I felt sometimes as if I were two separate individuals – one of them a rather refined sort of chap who had to be deferred to, the other a robust Scot.

Grandad was toothless and almost completely deaf. He never said very much, but sat rocking in a corner and smiling at us all – a nice old man. Then a smattering of some old folk ballad would wander into his head.

'Toum toum ti toum toum,' he would go, scaring away the silence. We would all jerk our heads round, locate the disturbance, and then go on with what we were doing. This was the only live music I managed to hear during my long stay. We did have a wireless set, but it was really just a piece of antique furniture. If you were rash enough to turn it on, it was likely to make odd spluttering noises interspersed with faint melodies, just discernible if you kept your ear close to the tiny speaker. The big hits were 'Lady Play Your Mandolin' and 'Shepherd of the Hills'. I clutched at these trite melodies as a drowning man grabs at a piece of driftwood, Things were slightly better at school. There we had to learn some of the good old Scottish ballads that lie somewhere in between real folk song and light concert pieces. The two I liked best were 'Braw Braw Lads from Yarrow Braes' and 'Along with My Love I'll Go'. They really must have made an impression, as I can still remember them clearly after a lapse of fifty years!

At Castle Douglas I was able to find out more about my father. He wasn't such a great ruffian as I had imagined. Old Granny put some of the missing pieces into place for me. Dad had risen from being a simple country boy to a position of some prominence in the world of letters. For no apparent reason, and almost overnight, he had begun to take a passionate interest in the poems of Walter Scott and Robbie Burns. He had bludgeoned his way through all the necessary exams, finally emerging as Professor William Turner, MA, lecturer at Edinburgh University and quite an authority on the subject of Elizabethan drama. At present he was something big in the educational life of Hyderabad – but where that was I had no idea at all.

'Oor Wully,' explained Auntie May with panache, 'went oot and stuck tae his wurrk. A fine mahn, Malcolm and, ye ken, we're a' lookin' tae you ta gang oot an' dee the same.'

I could understand some Scottish by this time, so I made some suitable reply, promising to do my best at school. Auntie May spoke in a stream of gutturals, like a distraught lemming coming up for the third time. When she became emotional I could follow her only with difficulty. She was proud of her brilliant younger brother, and wanted to be equally proud of me. The problem was that I had none of my father's red-blooded determination to get on. At school I was handicapped by a painful shyness, and paid no attention at all to my lessons. The only thing that interested me in class was the clock on the wall.

Sigmund Freud might have had a few words to say on the subject of all this deep-seated insecurity. Around this time, I went in for a spot of bed-wetting too, and old Sigmund would probably have understood about this – but he wasn't in the neighbourhood. In any case, he couldn't have helped. The simple fact was that there was nothing about my upbringing that was in the least solid or consistent. It wasn't just the absence of any feeling of 'home', but that my existence wasn't even rooted in a particular *class*. I hovered somewhere in between Mum's urban lifestyle and the small-town peasant community I had now to adjust to. There wasn't time to make the adjustment properly. The social groups remained completely outside my ken, whether scholastic, rustic, proletarian or genteel middle-class. No matter where I ended up, it was sure to be some place where I didn't quite fit in.

What I missed most of all was the background music that used to seep through the walls. I wanted to find my way back to that smoky room, with its aura of splendid disarray.

Miss Fergusson, my teacher at school one day gave me a perfectly routine telling-off. I was white and trembling when I arrived home. The aunts made a great fuss up at the school, after which Miss Fergusson hardly dared to address me other than in a polite undertone.

It looked as though I needed bringing out of myself. Grandad suggested taking me on a hunting trip. This sounded good to me, so off we went through the green fields. I hadn't the faintest idea what we were supposed to be hunting, and kept looking apprehensively over my shoulder. The old man led me to a place where he had set traps the night before. Some of the rabbits were still not quite dead, and the ones that were had obviously spent a rough night first. I never went on any more hunting trips after that. The family told me I was silly to be upset, because Nature was like that. Whenever we had rabbit stew for dinner, they had to try and pretend that it was something quite different. I will never forget those rabbits, and the blood on their beautiful soft fur.

The Castle Douglas folk were a warm-hearted crowd. They did everything they could to get me into a happier frame of mind. My closest friend was Aunt Bessie, who had been confined to a wheelchair since birth. She laughed and joked all the time. Once when I asked her about her infirmity she answered me by making a big joke out of the whole thing. Most people had funny legs anyway, she said. We found some drawing paper, and Aunt Bessie made some sketches of other people's legs – all different shapes and sizes. Fat legs, skinny legs, hairy legs. When Aunt May walked in, she found us both doubled up with laughter – but later the drawings were tactfully destroyed.

The year was 1932. Stanley, my Scottish cousin, had discovered the word 'jazz', which he used liberally in conversation. He was enthusiastic about the Paul Whiteman Rhythm Boys, and had a friend who knew someone who had once heard the Original Dixieland Jazz Band. Auntie May was continually shouting at him for trying to find dance music on the radio, and then turning the volume up as loud as it would go. If it was harsh and syncopated, it was jazz, and Auntie May felt obliged to frown upon it. Jazz was something anti-social and vaguely irreligious – not the sort of thing for decent law-abiding folk.

Much of the day's commercial music was still based on comic song and quasi-opera. Evidently there wasn't anything wrong with tunes like 'Daisy, Daisy' or 'Drink Brothers Drink', but as soon as syncopated rhythms were detected Auntie May pursed her lips and said she didn't know what the world was coming to. How could she possibly have known that we were all living in an artistic vacuum? It was as certain as anything could be that this vacuum would soon have to be filled by something genuinely expressive of the popular mood.

Millions of inhabitants of the modern cities, finding themselves cut off from folk song, would at last try to find a music of their own. At first there would be raw, grating sounds, but then the idiom would take shape. When the new music finally emerged, no power on earth would be able to check the flow of it into every corner of our impoverished lives.

My mother showed up after an eternity. It felt as if I were

being released from prison when she walked in. With the callousness of youth, I quickly forgot the kindness and care with which the simple Scottish family had looked after me. I had been left to rot in this dungeon for about a year and a half, but now everything was fine. Mother and I took a long walk and discussed the bright future.

'You look as if they've been feeding you, anyway. I suppose you've been getting plenty of porridge and haggis – or whatever they live on up here.'

'The food was all right, but they kept giving me far too much. And once I found a needle and thread in my dinner. I could have been killed. Gran is quite a good cook. I hate Scotch broth, but she makes all kinds of scones and baps and home-made jam. And there's a thing called queen's pudding . . .'

'I'm sure they did their best. Of course, in India we have a qualified chef. Just wait until you taste the food out there.'

Apparently, Dad was now on a good salary, which was why I was at last to be taken out there. I had been to India once before, when I was very small, but I didn't remember much of this earlier visit. In Baroda there had been plenty of curious pleasures to delight the soul of a four-year-old. I'd had my first taste of mangos and guavas, and chicken pillau heaped high upon the plate – but these were faint memories indeed. The servants had watched these orgies with what seemed a special intensity, following each mouthful as it disappeared down my delighted throat. I supposed then that it gave them a lot of pleasure, watching the small white sahib enjoying himself.

So now all that was in store for me again, only this time we had climbed a rung or two up the social ladder. I would have to try to find room for even bigger helpings of everything.

My sister and I, Mum assured me, were in for a pleasant surprise when we arrived.

'My friend Albert,' I told her dubiously, 'doesn't think it is safe out there. He says they keep on having wars. At school, they play a game called the Chinks and the Japs . . .'

'That's somewhere else. Don't worry – Indians aren't allowed to have wars. The British government wouldn't hear of it.'

From now on, life would be one big chicken pillau. I was already pushing the brief Scottish episode to one side, as if it had been a depressing dream.

In retrospect, I can think of these as the good times, compared to what came later on. The house in Oakwell Road was where I had a glimmering of what it is like to be with one's own family, and to belong somewhere. I liked roaming about in the fields right opposite to our house, and to watch the cattle trucks being shunted back and forth on the track that lay just beyond these fields. It was also good to paddle in the winding burn, or to roll dilapidated car tyres along the quiet country lanes, in the company of Albert Bryden and Dougie McNought. But I didn't get particularly misty-eyed about these things until a long time after this chapter in my life had come to an end.

Soon I was gliding across the Mediterranean, bound for the mysterious East. In those days it took three weeks to get a passenger ship from the London docks to Bombay. It seemed to me as if the SS *Mongolia* was just one more temporary address – rather more luxurious than most. Tren was staying behind at boarding-school. We never did seem to have the whole family assembled under one roof. This was a disappointment to me, because he had always led the way when it came to discovering new and exciting pastimes. But for him, I might never have discovered treacle tart, Sandy Powell, or a boys' paper called the *Wizard*. All of these things had given life an extra sheen.

My sister and I did nothing but argue, and make fun of one another's mannerisms. I had started to speak in a monotone, devoid of all expression. This was probably due to the dizzying succession of local accents I had been subjected to over the years. My speech sounded as if I were reciting from the Book of Psalms. Ruby lost no time in aping this doleful sound, much to my great chagrin at the time.

The *Mongolia* stopped briefly at Gibraltar, Naples, Marseilles, Port Said and Aden. Even my philistine soul was stirred by the sight of Arabia in the dusk. We came to the Suez Canal at a very early hour, and I dressed and went up on deck before any of the other passengers had roused themselves. I had the ship's rail to myself for a few precious moments, as we slid past the shoreline only a few feet away. Robed figures on the backs of camels gazed back at me, simply clad but bearing themselves likes sultans as they watched the great symbol of Western civilization go by. It was one of those moments that remain clearly in the mind, thrilling to recall. Next moment, the deck was swarming with noisy Europeans, and the spell was broken.

After the silent splendour of Suez at dawn, India appeared to be all smells and squalor. Bombay lay scorching under its sun, displaying its millions of scurrying, dispossessed citizens. When we arrived in Hyderabad it was the same depressing mélange, only on a slightly smaller scale – pitifully overcrowded cities, the vast population seeming to be huddled into every available inch of living space.

It is a squalor even more sickening when you are looking over your shoulder at it, entering the palaces of the rich. My father had a large white bungalow in the lawned gardens of Nizam College, where he had now become principal. He had three serving men and a cook, not to mention the private chauffeur who drove us from the station in a large open car.

Not that I was capable of being sickened by very much in those days, except perhaps a third helping of pudding at the end of a meal. That evening, Dad was doing everything he could to impress us with his new position. Special drinks had to be brought in, and when the servant brought them in the wrong glasses my dad shied one of them straight at his head. The patient and inoffensive Matiala just managed to duck down in time, and the glass shattered to pieces against the wall behind him. Dad then looked very sheepish and pretended he had only meant it in fun.

As a rule, he liked to appear overtly democratic in front of the hired help, chatting and joking with them for all the world as if he felt they were his equals. It was just that he had this rather explosive temper. Unlike most of his friends, Dad was no racialist. He would throw glasses at just about anybody, if the fit was on him. When the Indians took their country back from us after the war, he chose to stay on. The place had become his adopted homeland by that time. He loved everything about it, and looked on the Indians as his own people.

Dad occasionally behaved like the White Raj, but I believe he was acting a part that had been foisted on him. It was the same with Ruby and me. We were expected to live by certain rules of conduct that had been laid down, not by our parents, but by the regime. You didn't get into conversation with the natives, unless you wanted to order something. Otherwise, you kept them at arm's length. This meant that we could speak only to white kids of about our own age – but there was a problem.

These white children were snobbish and 'upper-crust', as likely as not. They could tell from our faint Teesside accents that we were not out of the top drawer. So they tried talking down to us – and we just weren't having any of that.

'Mummy and Daddy,' drawled one of these little horrors, 'are frightfully well awf. Tell me, how well awf are *your* parents?'

'Oh, fraitfully!' replied my sister, copying the other girl's inflections with merciless accuracy, whereupon the two of us broke into a fit of giggling in front of the wretched child. This poor girl then tried to impress us with some more boasting, her face frozen in an expression of self-righteous scorn. Each time, we gasped theatrically and said that she must be 'tirribly, tirribly well awf'. Perhaps all this was rather discourteous of us, but rather than seek out this vapid company we preferred to keep to ourselves.

Mother, too, was an inveterate snob, but in her case it had nothing to do with class or social position. She simply held that the world was divided into those who appreciated great art and those who didn't. The artists were the true aristocrats – the chosen few. Working people were ill-bred, not because they dropped their 'aitches', but because they didn't understand Brahms. She had just as little respect for the upper-class twit who measured everything in terms of material wealth. Some of this arrogance rubbed off on me, I'm afraid. I began to think the Turner blood must be in some special category, and that most of the visitors to our home were brought there so that I could do impersonations of them all the next day.

Some of these visitors were pleasant enough, but reminded me of characters I had seen in West End farces. There always seemed to be at least one Ralph Lynn among the guests, or a Claude Hulbert with big floppy ears and a stutter. Mum tried hard not to be amused at these comic impressions of her regular guests.

'Don't let your father hear any of this,' she warned me. 'He won't think it so very funny. These are friends of his, and besides, you know the Scots. No sense of humour at all.'

One thing about Dad's rich friends though: they certainly knew how to put on a spread. There were garden parties all the year round, and outdoor functions of various kinds. I soon found myself living in a dream world of gateaux and chocolate buns – a schoolboy's idea of heaven. All around the big, spacious lawns, under gaily coloured awnings, the Master Race stuffed itself until it could eat no more. Tables fairly groaned under the weight of assorted goodies. My parents would arrive at one of these functions, dump me at a table, and then go off to socialize, leaving me to guzzle undisturbed. Occasionally I might have to be sent for, if some Very Important Personage had arrived, and there were formal introductions to be performed. Maybe it was the Viceroy and his wife to whom I was obliged to offer my sticky paw; or perhaps it was the Nizam of Hyderabad's turn – minor distractions anyway, in between mouthfuls of cake.

My father had a special word to describe my reluctance to make polite conversation. He complained that I was 'jungly'. He meant that I was outside the realm of normal good manners. This obviously had him worried. First of all he hired a private tutor to visit me for a couple of hours every day. Miss Strettle was young and attractive, with oriental eyes. Obviously this wasn't helping me to concentrate on my lessons, so we had to think of something else. My parents decided on a full-time governess, who would live in and exert discipline generally. Ruby and I hastily planned our counter-attack. The new governess scarcely knew what hit her from the moment she first set foot inside our door. Ruby had the voice off in no time, and the odd mannerisms. Mrs Gay was a large, beefy woman of fair complexion, but with an Anglo-Indian accent which stuck out a mile. She wore her topee in all weathers, used phrases like 'We English' and was studiedly rude to the servants. My mother was not sure what to make of the stranger in our midst; Mrs Gay's ancestry became of paramount interest to her. The mousy-coloured hair just did not seem to go with the sing-song voice and the quaint choice of words. It was really too bad of Mrs Gay to be neither one thing nor the other.

'If you want my opinion,' said Mum, as if diagnosing an illness, 'she is one of those half-castes.'

This racialism of my parent was not vicious but, I believe, largely a result of perplexity. To be an Indian was just damned bad luck, but to be only *half* Indian was somehow underhand.

The new governess worked hard to keep her nice, cosy job but we gave her a hard time. Discipline broke down completely after the first few weeks. Mrs Gay was no fool, however. She took it all with a fixed smile, and then reported it to my father. He swore at us steadily for at least ten minutes, after which the lessons became rather more orderly – but then came the unfortunate business at the riding school. My sister had started riding lessons, and so I had to tag along. I never was even remotely interested in horses. I started those riding lessons completely against my will, and was delighted when I didn't have to go any more. What happened was that Mrs Gay took her attention off me for just a moment, long enough for my horse to take fright and start racing off towards the distant horizon. I heard my sister shouting instructions at me, and our distraught governess raising hell with the stable-boy who ought to have been holding the reins. Then it was just me and the horse, speeding through the fields – what an unpleasant sensation – I never want to go through *that* again!

The way I remember it, although it seems like one of those tall stories, I stayed on that animal's back right to the end. It wasn't until it came to some loose gravel, and went into a bit of a skid, that both horse and rider came crashing down simultaneously. How I managed to get away with only minor injuries I will never know; the horse also managed to survive the fall. I was badly shaken, but Mrs Gay was in for an even rougher time. She had to explain things to my father. I didn't have to go to any more riding lessons after that, and Mrs Gay suddenly wasn't around any more.

Next a pathetic figure shambled into our lives. Mr Clark had once been a schoolmaster, but he had a serious drink problem. My father told him that he had one last chance to kick the habit, and then we were placed in his care. We had a lot of fun destroying this poor tragi-comic man. Our impersonation of Mr Clark trying to say 'mathematical method' was one of our best efforts. His boozing soon became more frequent, and at last he was given notice to quit. Too late, we discovered we had killed the goose that laid the golden eggs: not long after this we were packed off to school.

Those months of aimless freedom hadn't done a thing for me. I was 'jungly' all right, and getting worse all the time. No one could get me to carry on a normal conversation – all I could summon up was a string of pseudo-funny sayings, platitudes and inanities that were my substitute for communication. I didn't want to communicate. I wanted a defensive screen behind which it was possible to hide away from the necessity of being serious – what other people thought of as serious, anyway. My idea of profound experience was to eat myself paralytic on cakes and ice cream.

Music? There was plenty of that about, but I'd heard it all so many times before. There is a limit to the number of times one can hear the 'Moonlight Sonata' without suddenly wanting to scream. I discovered that much of the fierce pleasure that my mother derived from these pieces lay in the execution of them, the gradual mastery over interpretation and technique. What if I learned to play some piano, to make my own sounds? It might at least save me from the awful frustration of being in this huge, fascinating country while remaining chained to the ennui of a small, parasitic white community. My mother finally did teach me a few simple pieces. Armed with 'Liebestraum' and 'Melody in F' I could now show off in front of the weekend guests. There would be the usual request for her to play some of her set pieces, and then I would come on with my 'Liebestraum' by way of a little comic relief.

Mother deserved a more discerning audience than this crowd of polite lame-brains. To these dreary middle-class bores, music was just another side-show. After five minutes of it, you could see them becoming restless. The only music they understood was the rustling of chequebooks and the merry tinkling of gold coins.

My escape-hatch, when visitors were at the door, was the flat roof of our bungalow. Up there I could fly kites, play with our bull-terrier pup, or shoot at vultures with a small air-gun. I was also keen on tennis, but it is hard to play this on your own unless you are Speedy Gonzales. Dad was glad to hear that I had taken some interest in a healthy outdoor sport. He promptly assigned one of his star pupils to me as a private coach. Najabeth Ali was the brightest student and all-round athlete at the college, yet here he was, following me around like a personal valet. This star pupil, who looked rather like a teenage Henry Fonda when I knew him, was the closest thing to a friend I ever had in India. He not only showed me how to hold a tennis racket, but what sort of things to say when confronted by an attractive girl. His studies kept him away for much of the time, which was a pity.

My own studies had to be considered too. A suitable school was decided upon, and Ruby and I were kitted up with the necessary clothing. The long holiday was now over. The Brigade School was some distance from our home, entailing a car journey and a packed lunch. We found ourselves stuck in a rather unfriendly atmosphere each day, impatient to get back home. The other pupils were nearly all Indians and Anglo-Indians whose fathers were minor officials, or junior officers in the army. Once again we had become trapped between the upper and lower strata of society. It wasn't one of the select, pukka establishments, for that would have been rather beyond our means. But we were never accepted at the Brigade School for one very important reason. Father was the school inspector. He also had a seat on the local committee. As soon as we arrived, we could sense that we were separated from the other pupils by a great gulf. It wasn't anything you could put into words. We just had the feeling that everyone wanted us to be alone: two privileged white kids who had things the easy way. Some of the teachers didn't exactly help matters, by behaving as though it was a great honour to have us at their humble little school. The English mistress liked to read our essays to the class as examples of correct English, while we sat trying to avoid the other kids' stares.

The MCC were touring India round about this time. I had never been to a first-class match, but very much wanted to go. Hearing that there was to be a match against Hyderabad State, I asked if I could go along.

'Since when have you been interested in cricket?' Dad wanted to know.

'Najabeth has been showing me how to bowl.'

'Oh, he has, has he? What happened to the tennis?'

I explained that Najabeth had been giving me information about all kinds of things. I didn't mention that we talked about girls for most of the time.

Then Dad said: 'Just let me think,' and proceeded to do so. I waited for the verdict, wondering what there was to think about. I mean, *one* day off school!

'It wouldn't be fair,' he said at length, 'just you going, and nobody else. No, there's only one thing for it – I'll give the whole damned school a day off.'

I didn't know what I had let myself in for, until the headmistress assembled us all next morning for a special announcement.

Speaking in a flat, sepulchral voice, the headmistress informed us that there would be no school on the day of the MCC match. She had been prevailed upon to grant a school holiday, so that anyone wishing to attend the match would be free to do so. A few of the older boys gasped, and some of them made approbatory noises.

'Oh don't thank *me*,' replied the lady, fixing me with a stare that would have doused a forest fire at twenty paces, 'thank the Turner children.' And she stalked angrily out of the room, leaving a charged atmosphere in her wake. Now things were even more strained than they had been before.

The MCC match was followed by a dinner in honour of the visiting team. I don't remember a great deal about the cricket, but that dinner was an occasion long to be remembered. There I was, in a roomful of cricketing legends, taking in every word and gesture of the great players. Verety and Bakewell devoured their meal in silence, but Nichols and Ken Farnes talked cricket all the way through dinner and at one point even used the salt and pepper pots to demonstrate a fielding manoeuvre. I was so enthralled that I even said no to a second helping of fruit tart.

A couple of days later I was introduced to Jack Hobbs at one of the local cinemas. It was during the interval, and my father had gone to speak with two men who were seated a few rows in front of us. When he came back, he asked me casually: 'How would you like to meet Jack Hobbs?'

I glanced across increduously, and the greatest cricketer in the world was grinning back at me and beckoning me to a seat next to his. Hobbs was travelling with the English team as a journalist. I treasure this memory of my encounter with the great man. A few days later I met Hobbs again, at one of the garden parties, and beat him at tennis. I don't think he was trying very hard. I actually managed a sort of conversation with him. It was easier than talking to people in the ruling junta. The man was completely down-to-earth – no side at all about him. He somehow put me at my ease from the very first.

Then came my memorable encounter with the Indian jazz band. Well, not a jazz band, exactly – more of an itinerant dance band, whose members had been skilfully lassoed by my mother and forced back to our house for tea. Two of them were shapely young women, and this caused me to gulp a little during the introductions. They were called, respectively, Miss Partridge and Miss Reporter. All of these musicians spoke with that slick self-assurance that showed they had been around Westerners for quite some time. Then I noticed the saxophone. It was a shiny, golden creation of brushed lacquer and mother-of-pearl. It nestled in the hands of a chubby young man who introduced himself to me as Jamshid Munshi. Munshi could see at once that I had become spellbound by the sight of his alto sax. Instead of doing the sensible thing, and shoving it hastily back into its protective case, he held it out to me, inviting me to touch it.

'Go on,' said Jamshid encouragingly, 'take it. No – fingers . . . there, like so.'

I took hold of the proffered sax, hardly able to believe all this was happening to me.

'Now then,' said Jamshid, helpfully, 'deep breath, and . . . blow down here.'

I gulped in as much air as I could. I blew down there, and the sound came out like a chair-leg grating against the floor. For some reason, I wasn't much interested in blowing into it after that. I had fallen in love with the saxophone for its looks, long before the urge to play music on it occurred to me. I just stood there with it in my hands, gazing down upon it as if I had been handed some rare art treasure. If it had been mine instead of Jamshid's I would probably have kept it in a vault somewhere, to be taken out and gloated over at regular intervals.

The meetings with Hobbs, and then the musicians, had been all very well, but at other times I was becoming very morose, and I was losing weight too. Dad saw that the hot weather wasn't helping either. Sometimes we went for walks together, but I ended up crawling several yards behind him and grunting like a pig. What I liked best was to be taken to the cinema. Dad loathed these cinemas, where the residents' wives habitually turned up to gossip with one another before, after and all too often during the film. He preferred taking me with him to his club in Secunderabad. Here he could deposit me in the reading-room and then go off and play bridge.

There was a large sweet shop next to the reading-room, where I was allowed to run up a bill, if he was away a long time. One time, Dad came back earlier than usual. I was sitting quietly in a corner, apparently immersed in *The Times*. He came up behind me on tip-toe, and took a look over my shoulder. There, nestling inside *The Times,* was a copy of *La Vie Parisienne,* with its pictures of curvaceous females in various stages of undress. I started up to find him towering over me, his face wearing an expression I had never seen before. I took it to be wild rage. There was a fearsome silence while we studied each other. All the walls and background shapes seemed to be spinning round before my eyes. Then he threw his head back and roared with laughter. 'You're not quite ready for all that, Soory,' he chuckled. 'That comes later.'

For days, Dad went around the club, recounting the incident to his friends. So I was not such a backward child after all, eh? *La Vie Parisienne!* And right in the middle of the club's reading-room! After this small incident, Dad seemed to regard me with a new fondness, as if I had become a man in his eyes.

But I was still only a child – and a rather puny one at that. I was wilting visibly in the heat, so when school holidays came around he drove us all into the cool Nilgiri Hills. We spent several weeks in a climate which is not all that different from an English one, and soon I was looking and feeling a lot better. Once back in Hyderabad, however, I started wilting all over again. There was nothing for it but to ship me back to England, where I could be sent off to one of the public schools. The idea was that plenty of fresh air and rugger would soon set me right.

India hadn't been much fun for me, but I loved the place for all that. The truth is that once you've lived there it is almost impossible to get the sounds and scenes and smells of it out of your system. It is a magnificent land, and the people deserve far more than history has endowed them with up to now. If it were somehow possible to go back with the aid of a Time Machine, I would feel that I had an awful lot of apologizing to do. Not for myself, for I was too young to know any better, but for the parasitic class of empire-builders to which our family – thank the heavens – never really belonged. It was so easy to fool ourselves that we were not parasites at all, but in some way 'benefactors'. By 1946, not many people believed that any more.

My father had less to feel ashamed about than most. At least he went there to teach literature to the young, and was not out to make vast profits from the plight of the most underfed large nation in the world. It was sad to be leaving *him* again, but as for the regime – I couldn't get away from that quickly enough.

We returned to England on the *City of Paris,* a small but comfortable liner. On the way out, on the *Mongolia,* I had spent a lot of time reading boys' comics and playing deck quoits. Now, two years older, I was lolling by the swimming pools, pondering on the magic appeal of Sex. Why was it that the female leg had become a thing of exquisite beauty? And why hadn't I noticed this before?

Music, too, was becoming a bit of an obsession. I was finding out that certain tunes were becoming strongly associated in my mind with the places where I had listened to them, and that these tunes were often not erased with the passage of time. Even now, fifty years later, whenever I hear Edward German's 'Shepherd's Dance' I get something like total recall. I can almost *smell* India, where I heard this piece so many times on the lawns of the ruling élite. On the way home, I simply couldn't get the Edward German tune out of my mind, and it couldn't have been nostalgia, at that tender age. I needed music to emphasize certain feelings about places and happenings that I couldn't locate by any other means.

My brother was waiting to meet us as the ship docked. He had much interesting news to impart, but the thing he talked about most was music. He had discovered something called 'jazz'. Wasn't that the stuff Jack Hylton played, I enquired, not all that concerned. I knew some of the vigorous little tunes of the period, tunes such as 'Lost', 'Lullaby of the Leaves' and 'You're So Delish-ee-us', but I wouldn't have thought they were worth getting burned up about.

'No,' said Tren, 'jazz is a thousand times better than any dance music you ever heard.'

I didn't understand, and it didn't seem important anyway. Being back home again was the important thing, even though 'home' simply meant a number of transitory addresses scattered about Britain.

'You'll like it when we move to Finsbury Park,' said Mum, as soon as we were disembarked. 'It's a very nice flat. You can see the trees and flower gardens from our front window. The drawing-room is immense, and of course you will have a bedroom of your own.'

'How long will we be staying there?' I asked, cautiously.

'About four weeks. After that we're moving to Bedford, where Tren's school is. You'll be going to the same school for the time being – won't that be nice? You'll really like Bedford.'

I agreed that, for the time being, I probably would.

2 Portrait of a Jazz Fan

Nineteen thirty-four was a good year for jazz in Britain. If you were an enthusiast of the new sound, almost every one of the great players would be available to you on record. It was true that only a few works had been released for the British market, and each of these lasted no more than three and a half minutes. But the avid listener treasured his small collection and played each tiny masterpiece over and over again.

What was happening was that a new era of self-made music was opening up. Millions of people who had never learned even the rudiments of musical theory were now able to buy saxophones, cornets or guitars. And then, they hoped, a lot of expressive music would come gushing forth. Unfortunately, it wasn't quite as simple as that. In Britain, we had to break out of the old ways of thinking, in order to embrace the new.

In Bedford, we had records of all kinds of music. Works by Alban Berg nestled up against the latest dance hits by Harry Roy's band; Fats Waller releases were squeezed in beside the comic songs of Mr Sandy Powell. My own preference was for cheerful vocals with an easily recognizable tune. This put Berg at rather a disadvantage.

One day my brother came back from the shops brandishing a package. He had just been to a record store, and was in a state of agitation over someone called Fletcher Henderson. Tren was a devout jazz fan. He was always trying to explain to me the difference between the new idiom and ordinary dance music, but as yet my ear wasn't able to detect these subtleties. I preferred the dance bands, for their arrangements sounded smoother and they sometimes featured comic vocalists. Tren hastened to put his new record on to the turntable. Then he turned to me and called out, before I could get out of the room: 'How would you like to earn sixpence, Malcolm, for doing absolutely nothing at all?'

'What's the catch?'

'All you have to do is listen to this piece of music all the way through.'

'Not *all* the way through! Ugh. How about tuppence for just the beginning?'

'No, come on. I tell you, you'll enjoy this. Henderson has probably the greatest band in the world. You can't possibly not like it. Just give it a chance.'

I had already started to back off towards the door. Then he changed his line of approach. Delving into his shopping-bag, he pulled out a large treacle tart, and proceeded to break off a generous portion. Well, what could I do? I was on that stuff at the time.

Tren beckoned me to a seat next to him. He had put 'I've Got to Sing a Torch Song' on the turntable. The treacle tart lay ostentatiously between us on the arm of his chair. As the urgent tones of a tenor saxophone filled the room, my brother was in rapture, his eyes closed. When he opened them again, at the end of the record, the piece of tart was gone – and so was I.

All I wanted was to hear funny singing, but my brother went on fighting the good fight. He couldn't understand my imperviousness to good jazz.

I'd call out: 'Play the one called "Hot Feet". It has a great scat vocal.'

'Never mind the vocal. Listen to the trumpet and trombone solos. Superb!'

I hardly noticed the jazz instrumentation. Music was again having to be thrust upon me, while I tried to push it into the background. Other things, I thought to myself, are more important than music: like food, radio comedians – that sort of thing. You really had to keep a sense of proportion.

Bedford Modern School was the place where Tren had been handed in, like a piece of left luggage, when Mum and Dad first went to Hyderabad on their own. Now I was to join him there for about three school terms. I saw it as a cut-price Eton College, the smaller boys having to wear enormous stiff collars like harnesses around their scraggy necks. Authority sported the cap and gown, and canes were swished threateningly to discourage the evil-doer. The school song began with the inspiring lines:

Splendid the school with tradition behind it,
Gained and upheld by proud fathers of yore.
We rise to our duties like sons of our fathers

To see and to do them as they did before . . .

Tren told me it wasn't such a bad old place as long as one behaved. I wasn't planning to kick anyone in the shins. Anything for a quiet life, I thought.

We were staying with a family in Bedford, in a couple of large rooms plus access to the lounge. The son of the house, Kenneth George Dinsdale, was around Tren's age and was a pupil at Bedford Modern. I was furious when he started to monopolize my brother, discussing music with him in what I considered to be an affected and pompous manner. I was feeling left out in the cold.

One day they took the portable gramphone down to a hut at the bottom of the garden. Dinsdale told me to keep out, protesting that I always made too much noise. The two of them had become very solemn in their listening habits, crouching over the machine as if every note had to be carefully weighed.

'Sorry, Malcolm, we don't want you in here' said K.G., noticing that I had followed them down to the hut, 'we don't want you fidgeting about. Go away.'

I made off to the house, lusting for revenge. There was a small water-pistol on the kitchen table. I filled this at the sink, crept back to the hut, and let fly at Dinsdale from a small window in the roof. Spluttering with rage, he chased me back into the house – but I had made my point. No one was going to exclude *me* from the music group.

Tren, five years my senior, wasn't able to pay much attention to me at school. Sometimes we talked about jazz on the way home. I wasn't able to follow it all.

'Who on earth is Big Spider?' I wanted to know. 'How can anyone be called Big Spider? And why does a sax player call himself Frankie Trombone?'

'No, no. I keep telling you – it's Trumbauer. Bix Beiderbecke and Frankie Trumbauer. I do wish you'd listen.'

There were further problems. The most widely respected figure in all jazz appeared to be a gentleman known as 'The Duke'. In Duke's band there were some even stranger names. Two trumpet players called Bubber and Cootie – even a man who called himself Tricky Sam. I could never get used to anyone being called Tricky Sam, especially when his name was Joe.

Jazz was clearly a strange new territory, peopled by the most extraordinary beings. They were the great masters of a respected form, yet they had names of the kind that cropped up in gangster movies. There was a Spike, several Reds, even a Hot Lips. Later a sensational girl singer joined the Chick Webb band. I thought for several months that she was named Elephants Gerald, and was even a bit disappointed when I found this not to be the case. As for Lucky Millinder, for years the name conjured up visions of someone who had inherited a hat business.

My brother's record collection was already full of good things by Ellington, Henderson and Trumbauer, to mention but a few. With absolutely no guidance, but only a pair of ears, he had discovered for himself the supreme masters of jazz. It wasn't always plain sailing. Reginald Forsyth's New Music was at first mistaken for advanced jazz, rather in the Ellington class, but never mind that. The voyage of discovery went on, with me tagging along in the rear.

For a long time my two favourite jazz records were 'Rosetta' by Earl Hines's orchestra and 'Crazy 'Bout My Baby' by Fats Waller. I loved the infectious singing, but didn't notice the superlative piano playing until much later on.

My real conversion to jazz came quite suddenly. The record was Ellington's 'Hot and Bothered'. It made my feet tap, and I felt as if I wanted to shout for joy. I'd never felt that way about a piece of music. I believe I even crouched forward a little, head bowed in an attitude of respectful attention. If someone had taken the cellophane off a box of chocolates, I would very likely have told them to keep the noise down. I don't know what first attracted me to this particular Ellington record. Perhaps it was the extraordinary 'chase' sequence. After the ensemble, trumpeter Bubber Miley swaps phrases with a singer called Baby Cox. The Cox interjections sound remarkably like another trumpet, not at all the way one expects a human voice to sound.

We played this record to one of Tren's schoolfriends, a chap by the name of Lucas. He had thick glasses and one of those chunky, immobile faces. When we came to the 'chase', Lucas became a man transfixed. He fairly quivered behind his glasses, and was at first bereft of speech. Then he managed to find voice. 'Marvellous!' he enthused. 'It does everything but get up and talk.'

Lucas, in his error, had probably just defined jazz for all time. Here you have a music where trumpets sound as if they are 'singing', and the singer takes off as if playing upon a horn.

Whichever way it is, the music 'talks'. Maybe it is this vocalized sound that lies at the very heart of jazz.

I was thirteen when we moved to London and I became a pupil at Dulwich College. This turned out be a large public school, more prestigious than Bedford Modern, with somewhat vaster buildings and higher fees. I arrived with a tuck box crammed with goodies, mostly an assortment of carbohydrate foods.

'But didn't anyone tell you?' enquired one of the other boys. 'This is autumn term. All the boarding-houses are in training. This means no sweet things, so if a prefect catches you with this little lot, you're for it. Better get rid of it as fast as you can.'

I got rid of most of the food by using what seemed to be the most direct method of all. I found a quiet corner and started eating. By the time I had finished, my stomach looked as if I was in the last stages of pregnancy. That left a few tins and packets that could be smuggled out later and taken home. It was just as well that I'd taken the precaution. Blew House was run by five giant prefects called Gibson, Williams, Chatten, Talya Khan and Agazarian. They took their sports seriously, and were determined that we should beat the Ivyholm fellows next door. Ivyholm, our main rivals, had the young Trevor Bailey, and other promising sportsmen in embryo. I must have spoken to Trevor several times while I was at the school, little realizing that he was soon to become a giant of Test cricket. He was just one of 'that Ivyholm lot'.

When Dad first mentioned sending me to boarding-school I had made a terrible fuss, thinking that I was to be cut off completely from home life. The situation wasn't as bad as all that. My mother was now living in the south of London, or perhaps it would be more accurate to say that she was on tour in that area. We had addresses in Sydenham, Norwood, Forest Hill and West Dulwich, before she finally settled on a large flat in Blackheath Village. At each of these places I spent weekend leaves or brief Sunday visits. If Tren was about, we mulled over the latest jazz-record releases, crouching a great deal. In the summer we played cricket on the heath, or in the long hallway of the Blackheath flat. There were rapturous visits to Lord's and the Oval, to watch local heroes like Patsy Hendren and Alf Gover in action. Our family also went to the cinema about once a week, and to the occasional theatre show. My Uncle Tren was working in the chorus of 'OK for Sound', with the Crazy Gang. Watching one's uncle cavorting on a stage, even in a minor capacity, was quite an event.

West End shows were a rare treat to be looked forward to. I was too young to understand the sophisticated patter, but I relished the feeling that I was in some way partaking of the 'forbidden fruit'. There would be reports of a show being risqué, unsuitable for the young mind. Somehow this didn't seem to apply to our family. We prided ourselves on being virtually unshockable. The sight of Ralph Lynn de-trousered, or Tom Walls finding a strange girl in his bed was smart comedy and I didn't connect it in my mind with sex.

Back at Blew House I was conscious of a more puritanical view of things. Our house master, the Rev H.H. Dixon, was a soft-spoken, meticulously correct sort of chap. The only time he gave permission for a group of us to visit a cinema, it was *Snow White* . . . He wasn't taking any chances with our impressionable young minds.

I never quite came to accept some of the routines at public school. For one thing, I couldn't get used to small boys addressing one another by their surnames: 'I say, White, have you seen anything of Turner? I believe he is wanted in Gibson's study,' was always a bit rich coming from the mouths of boys aged twelve and upwards.

Then there was the seniority, which had to be strictly observed at all times. If I walked into a room ahead of Taylor or White, I was in for it. If Cue walked into a room ahead of me, *he* was in for it. You could get into a terrible tangle in doorways. Everyone was expected to remember his 'place'. We filed in and out of rooms in this exact order: Pennel, Genders, Cole, White, Taylor, Cue, Lord, Royle and de Hoxar. There wasn't anything lower than de Hoxar.

Unless you counted the day-boys. The lowliest of juniors at Blew House was still vastly superior to the day-boys, as everyone knew. A day-boy was a chap whose father had not been able to afford the extra fees, or to be sure he would have sent his son to Blew House or Ivyholm.

For the first two or three terms, I sat next to one of these unfortunates in class. Roland George Duckworth was a day-pupil, but when I went to tea with him during the holidays I discovered his home to be quite palatial. Duckworth and I had much in common, as we soon found out. We both hated lessons, and we both worshipped the bandleader Harry Roy. It was probably the infatuation with Roy that made us so bad at our lessons. But for this distraction, we may both have had a chance of becoming great scholars. I turned my back on deep learning in order to persuade Duckworth, if I could, that Harry Roy was no jazz musician, though a supreme entertainer in his own way. At the end of each term Duckworth came bottom of the class and I came bottom but one.

My exam results became so bad that in the end I was sent for by the form master and given a pep talk. 'I'm not surprised at Duckworth,' he confided in all seriousness, 'but you – a Blew House chap. You'll have to do better than this!'

My father flew in for a brief visit. He was not overjoyed with my progress at public school. Dad warned that unless my standard of work improved I might have to take extra tuition during the holidays. He raged at me for a while, but never carried out his threat. My reports were getting to be so bad that I believe he came to think of me as beyond redemption.

I never could explain to my parents just how I felt about public school. It is a sure thing that I would have worked harder if I had been living at home. Boarding-house was sapping my confidence by the minute; in particular the fagging system and the whole mentality upon which it was based. Boys being subservient to masters was bad enough; boys being subservient to other boys was especially hard to take. Sometimes the reverberating cry of 'Junior' issuing down from the prefects' studies was enough to set my heart pounding up against my ribs.

In answer to this summons, the junior who was nearest to the common-room door was supposed to sprint up those stairs in double-quick time. I always tried to keep away from that door. I didn't fancy spending my leisure time cleaning some prefect's rugger boots or tidying up his study. It was at times like these that one envied the day-boys. They were at home with their families and no doubt enjoying their moments of freedom. I decided one day that I was not going to accept the fagging system any more. I would go slow, and make a hash of every job I was given, until I became known as the most inefficient of all the juniors, who wasn't to be trusted with even the simplest of jobs.

Rather to my surprise, the thing worked. 'No, not you, Turner. Go and send up someone else,' was the usual cry, as soon as I appeared, 'I want this job done properly. Oh, and – Turner. Brace up, for Christ's sake!'

This made life easier to bear. It didn't get me out of the usual whackings, however. These were delivered with a large slipper, across the seat of the pants. You wouldn't think a slipper would hurt very much, but if a prefect ran at you along the corridor, he could get up quite a bit of steam by the time the blow fell. The slipper was administered for such minor crimes as being caught coming out of the sweet shop while the House was 'in training', coming in late for a meal, being caught out of bounds, or simply for failing to pass a Colours Test. These Colours Tests were sprung on us unexpectedly, and the idea was to make sure that the smaller boys were taking a healthy interest in the school. They usually occurred in the middle of 'prep' – the supervised period for homework. While we were sitting round the common-room table, wrestling with algebraic equations or French verbs, the prefect would come in, glaring at us for a moment in silence. Then it would be: 'All right, you fellows – Colours Test!'

I had absolutely no interest in the school sports events. First question: who is the present captain of Little Sides? (I hadn't even *heard* of Little Sides.) Next question: how many trees are there in the Clump? (The Clump was a cluster of trees in the centre of the playing fields, but I'd never inspected them very closely.) After marking our papers, the prefect would order me to take off my slipper and hand it to him. I had the largest foot in the common-room, and he wasn't going to wear out his *own* leather on our backsides.

Three or four terms went by, and I had the sensation that I was mentally opting out. Perhaps I could stick it out somehow, but only because I was even more scared of my father than I was of the school.

Certain of the other pupils depressed me. They reminded me too much of the pampered sons of the White Raj I had met in Hyderabad. There were some more likeable types, I am pleased to say, and the two I found particularly amusing were Montague and Street. The three of us found that we had common interests, but the rest of the inmates bored me not a little. I even invented my own patent conversation-killer, to get me out of having to talk with them. It went something like this:

'Turner, you can't possibly wear that shirt – it's off-white.'

'Yep.'

'But what will Gibson say? We're supposed to wear white shirts.'

'Nope.'

'Well, he'll only get into a rage. I'm just warning you.'

'So am I.'

By this time, with any luck, the other fellow is clutching his head and not able to continue the conversation, which is perfectly all right with me. Bob Montague and Pat Street were both jazz fans, so as long as they were discussing jazz I could lend an attentive ear. As soon as they went on to other topics I immediately slipped into my 'yep' 'nope' routine. This must have been quite infuriating, I suppose.

One evening during prep, one of the juniors came up to see me. I had just been promoted to the senior common-room, which meant I now had my own small cubicle on the first floor. This skinny junior had exercise books under his arm, in which he had carefully copied down the personnels of some leading jazz bands. I put him straight on who played bass with Fats Waller's Rhythm, after which we became close friends. Nevil Skrimshire and I quickly founded a jazz-records society at the school. In its heydey it must have had at least seven members. We took our gramophone to remote corners of the playing fields, or down to the Clump. Nobody was counting trees. We fairly steeped ourselves in *le jazz hot*, playing our Bixes and Venuti-Langs under the reproving glare of any masters who happened to pass by. Heated discussions took place, after and even during each playing of a cherished record. Far more important than the square on the hypotenuse was the question as to whether Frank Teschemacher or Pee Wee Russell had taken the clarinet solo on 'Basin Street Blues' by the Louisiana Rhythm Kings.

Bob Foskett was always mispronouncing the names of some revered players. He spoke of 'Bix Beidy-becke', 'Bubbly Miley' and 'Muggy Spaniel', and could never seem to get the names right. He was a day-boy, and didn't know any better. Bob was always greatly impressed by visual performance of jazz. The facial contortions and glistening foreheads were a final proof that something desperately urgent was going on. All of us had seen brief glimpses of the swing musicians who appeared in some Hollywood musicals. Cavorting figures pointed their horns dramatically heavenwards, or interspersed their performances with ecstatic cries of 'Yeah!'. This became too much for Foskett, who began to measure each recorded solo in terms of blood, sweat and tears. Bob was an endearing character and an amusing companion. After the war, he showed up at some of the jazz clubs, and had a few cutting things to say about the incursions of 're-bop'. Then he simply disappeared, and none of us has heard a word from him since.

Montague and Street had a friend called Johnny, who cried

real tears when any record by the Ellington band was being played. Opinion was divided as to whether this was genuine emotion, or whether it was an effect he managed to achieve by biting his own tongue. It was impressive, anyway. Johnny always did go in for the extravagant gesture. At the peak of any recorded performance he would clutch at his heart or begin sagging at the knees, to show that the music was really getting to him. Soon we were all striking dramatic postures around the gramophone, as if scarcely able to cope with it all.

Our attitudes were raw and simplistic. Jazz was 'sincere'. The opposite of this was 'commercial', a shameful thing for any music to be. Sincere music pitted itself against vested interests and the scurvy businessmen raking in their profits behind the scenes. The 'sincere' jazzman was a heroic figure – not among the common run of men. All this, of course, was partly true but also our naïve oversimplification of a complex problem. And our conclusions were hopelessly wide of the mark. Jazz came from somewhere 'out there'. One had to be exceptionally gifted in order to play it, so any outsider who had a go at it was liable to make himself look rather silly. This gave the jazzman a certain glamour – like a young hussy let loose in the reading-room of an exclusive men's club. Only much later did an alternative view present itself. Jazz was nothing to do with favoured genetic types after all, but only with ordinary men and women expressing themselves. At last the idea of a people's music began to dawn.

By this time my brother had become engrossed in Bruckner and Mahler, although he still liked to put on the occasional Ellington record. Imagine my surprise and delight when he suddenly handed over his entire jazz-record collection to me. I was like someone who had won the Pools. There were almost three hundred of these precious 78s, now in my keeping. What I'd listened to before as an outsider, I now found myself to be completely involved in. This wasn't all. A year later Tren handed me his clarinet as well. He had been given this clarinet as a birthday present, but hadn't given it a great deal of attention. He had fooled around with it for a few weeks, and then gone back to his symphonic records. After that I had gradually taken the thing over.

At last the clarinet found its way into Blew House, where I was allowed to go and practise upon it for a few hours a week, in a deserted music-room. The way I learned to play tunes on it would have horrified most classically trained musicians. I simply fumbled away for hours on end until the sound came. Trial and error showed me where I had to place the fingers and what lip pressure would result in the most satisfactory sound. To say I was self-taught would be an understatement. For about three years I played only in the low register, for it took me about that long to discover the register key. As this key is situated a quarter of an inch away from the left thumb, in the playing position, you could say I was unobservant.

The last thing that entered my head was that I might learn quicker by taking lessons. It was part of the fascination of music that I could make up my own rules. 'Hot' style, as it was then called, was not what many legitimate music teachers would want to teach their pupils – far from it. They would think it was their solemn duty to take out such 'impurities' as a fast vibrato, or a tendency to pep up a written melody with passing notes. A music teacher would have set me to the task of learning the accepted rule book. He would have armed me with techniques for playing other people's music, accurately and with the prescribed classical tone. That wasn't what I had in mind at all.

I just went on trying out ideas until they came out right. This was about as near to practising as I ever came. I also knew I could improve by listening to the great players. In 1938 I went with Skrimshire and Fleming to a Coleman Hawkins concert at the Phoenix Theatre, in Victoria. Hawkins was at the peak of his form then. It was my first experience of live jazz, and what an experience it was! Fats Waller had already appeared in this country as a variety act, singing and playing piano to some torpid crowds who seemed to have expected him to be a slapstick comedian. I'm afraid I was one of them, but that later concert by Hawkins really made an impression.

In those days I had started to fantasize a great deal. I liked to imagine myself becoming a big-time jazz musician and playing in front of large crowds. The trouble was, I *identified* this as fantasy, rather than as part of any ambitious plans for the future. It was just fun thinking about it. My other big obsession was girls, and it was fun thinking about them too. As long as I was simply using my imagination, and giving reality a wide berth, I didn't have to plan any concrete moves. This dream world was a nice safe place where one could hide away from decision-making. It was a convenient shell into which one might withdraw at certain opportune times – like in the middle of a dull physics lesson, or fielding at deep third man.

In order not to be disturbed in these reveries, it was necessary to get far away from the school. If I couldn't manage a weekend leave, I would settle for a Sunday pass, mainly for the opportunity this afforded for walking around Blackheath in a daze. Once I had arrived home, I wasn't able to get away quick enough on my ethereal jaunts. Mother came to expect the ritual.

'Hello, everybody,' I would call out on arrival, 'any grub yet? No? Well anyway, I'm just off for a bit of a stroll. Back at eight.'

At eight, there was a meal on the table for the tired traveller, accompanied by the usual complaint that I was never around unless food was being proffered to me as an enticement. All this was perfectly true, I'm afraid.

In retrospect, I can see that I was in retreat from just about everything in the mundane world – the school, my fellow-students and even my own family. It wasn't a very healthy state of affairs. Soon the outer husk of me would be striding off towards Greenwich Park, while on an entirely different plane I would be leading my own band at the Café de Paris, or having breathtaking experiences with a chorus girl. As sheer escapism it was better than anything that had ever been thought up by Walter Mitty or the Bulpington of Blup.

Psychiatrists know this as introversion, and warn that it can lead to serious neuroses if something isn't done about it. The danger is that an introvert is *happy* with his fantasy world, and the last thing he wants is to be disturbed by reality. So in the end he gets further and further away from the rational universe. The dream situations take precedence over real ones – you get to meet a better class of people.

Sometimes I spent entire Sundays alone in the Blackheath flat. If Mother was not going to be at home, I would write and say that I was coming anyway. All I asked for was a cold meal to be laid out on the sideboard, and a key left under the mat. There was something exhilarating about the thought of empty rooms, a whole day of being left entirely alone with my thoughts. There would be the usual long walk, with its accompanying mental images and extravagant dreams, then about three hours of jazz records before the return journey to Dulwich. Sometimes I would leave early, pocketing the bus fare and seeing if I could walk the entire distance without running out of time.

During the holidays I noticed that Mum was staying up later than usual, and putting away some considerable quantities of booze. This wasn't at all her usual style. It was, I think, the behaviour of a woman trying to get an unsuccessful marriage out of her system. The separation wasn't yet definite, but Dad was settled on remaining in India, whatever happened. He no longer felt at home in this country, and in any case a doctor had warned him that the Scottish winters might be too severe for him from now on.

At Blackheath, I slept in a small boarded-off anteroom next to the lounge. I could hear the noisy and brittle laughter as guests came and went during the late evening. There was a boozy ex-actress who had a flair for the dramatic. When she was holding forth, small ornaments came crashing down from the mantelpiece. Then there was a man called Felix, whose whole attitude to life placed him slightly to the right of Ghengis Khan. He wore hideous plus-fours and sported an evil-looking military moustache. When he spoke it was in a series of staccato barks, like an enraged bull terrier, He had once met my dad in the Indian army and never stopped reminding me of the fact. 'I knew your father . . . at Nigg . . . fine officer . . . no nonsense with *him*, by God . . . great life, that . . . man's life . . . wish I was back there now.' And he would begin swishing at imaginary wogs with his walking stick.

Felix was indignant at the sight of my brother wasting his time with classical music. This was not a manly preoccupation, in his view. 'Look at him, Malcolm, just look at him – he's at it again!' he would rasp, during one of these drink-ins. I would turn to him enquiringly, to find him pointing scornfully across the room at my brother. All I could see would be Tren sitting innocently on the sofa, humming to himself.

'At what?' I would enquire, mystified.

'Eh? But dammit, can't you see? He's thinking of Bruckner!'

This was the unpardonable crime. In other respects, though, Felix was more inclined to take a tolerant stance. One day he took me to one side and whispered this advice hoarsely in my ear: 'Just a friendly word, old son . . . older than you . . . you know what I'm talking about . . . I know you do it . . . *all* boys do it . . . thing is, know when to stop . . . keep it within reason . . . I always do.'

Felix and his friends were coming round at all hours, to lap up the free whisky. One night, I was roused from sleep by angry noises coming from the lounge. Mother was way under the influence, roaring away at the unwanted guests. I lay there savouring every word, for it was my contention that Felix had

had this coming to him for a long time. From that moment the spongers came round only occasionally, which made the place seem more like home.

Back at college, it was the old routine all over again. It was impossible for me to keep my mind on any of my studies, since lessons had become for me a brief, uneasy respite from the fagging system. I always seemed to be either bored to distraction by lessons or harassed by the house prefects. On my return from the holidays Montague and Street, suave men of the world, started to cross-examine me about what I'd been doing. Surely I had a girlfriend by now or was I, after all, just a baby in these matters? This time I produced a photograph of a pretty brunette, claiming that she was Milly, the girl back home. She wasn't, of course. I had dug up the photo from a pile of old snap-shots I'd found in one of Mum's old trunks. The photo was about ten years old. I hoped that none of the other chaps would notice the out-of-date clothing and hair-do.

Nevil, Bob and Maurice often came round to discuss jazz and its origins. We had long since decided that much of what the writers believed was nonsense. It was best to use one's own ears, surely. But things that are obvious now were not yet clear to us.

'Listen to this, chaps,' someone would cry out in great glee, holding up a jazz magazine. 'It says here that the Mills Brothers are a *jazz group*. It actually says it here. Look – a *jazz* group. Isn't that priceless!'

'Well, but hold on a minute. They *are* negroes.'

'So is the Emperor of Abyssinia.'

After more arguing, we would agree that the Mills Brothers, though fine artists in their own way, were certainly not a jazz contingent. Billie Holiday on the other hand was the very epitome of what jazz singing is all about.

'It's all a question of impro-vation,' – this from Foskett, who had picked up the word after reading Panassie's *Le Jazz Hot*, and then mislaid some of it in his head.

'Hold on, Foskett. People have been improvising for hundreds of years. Jazz has only been going on for – what – twenty years or so.'

'Rot. You show me a musician who's been improvising for hundreds of years.'

'Don't be so dense. Anyway, Billie Holliday doesn't improvise. The words are all written out for her.'

'Yes, I suppose so. But it's something to do with

the *way* she sings the words.'

And so the tiny fragments of crystallized truth continued to build up. It was a painfully slow process, this business of learning to recognize a jazz performance from a plausible imitation. But at least we didn't have the Pundit to contend with. He came along later.

I had by now made some progress on the clarinet, upon which I had even learned to get through two well-known dance tunes in the open key. These were 'Whispering' and 'Red Sails in the Sunset'. I was perfectly all right with these two, as long as I was clinging to the melody for dear life. If I then went in for a spot of 'impro-vation', the whole thing was liable to collapse.

The other problem was that I didn't know how to get rid of the Squeak. When you are learning to play a clarinet, the Squeak is never very far away. Just as you think you have conquered it, back it comes. It is all to do with faulty embouchure and not covering the holes properly with the fingers. To the casual listener it often shows up as a rather absurd mannerism, like a nervous laugh. The music is no longer to be taken seriously. One end-of-term, I was asked to play my clarinet on a house concert. I was happy to oblige, but during rehearsals the Squeak started to take over. The prefect in charge told me not to worry – he thought it would be best if we simply turned my clarinet spot into a broad comedy routine: 'Every time it happens, simply start looking around you, as if you can't think where the sound's coming from, Everyone will split their breeches.'

'But Lees, I think I can play better than this. If I could just go and buy some more reeds.'

'Not worth it, old son, Hell, it's only a bit of a lark.'

So much for my serious contribution to the house concert.

A few weeks before the big event, Montague and Street had sent me off to Catford, where I had seen two cheap guitars in a shop window. On my return, they grabbed the guitars and proceeded to twang away on the open strings. I could see that they had no intention of learning to play chords. The approaching concert was threatening to become a fiasco. We had more rehearsals, during which time a small birdlike child by the name of Cue added himself on mouth organ. In 'Red Sails' he kept missing two beats in the second bar, throwing everything out of step.

'Play it for laughs,' reiterated Lees, who would have been happy if we'd scrapped the music and simply thrown custard pies at each other. As the day drew nearer, I wondered if we shouldn't have postponed things for at least two years.

I needn't have worried, because the concert was a great success. I squeaked six times in 'Whispering' and about the same number of times in 'Red Sails' while merry peals of laughter came from all sides. For the record, I didn't once look under my chair, or alter my expression from one of blank terror. The house hadn't laughed so much in years. Next term we were begged to do a repeat, but this time it wasn't all that funny. The act had definitely lost something. What had happened was that I had improved my playing, to the extent that I was able to get through a chorus of 'Whispering' without squeaking at all. My playing was no longer hilariously funny, but only bad.

When yet another term drew towards its close, I wasn't asked to play my clarinet this time. The Rev Dixon wanted to know if there was anything else I could do to entertain the house. I offered to write a serious play, and he thought it might be a good idea. I came up with a ghastly piece of hokum about a mad scientist. At the end, the house went so wild that we had to keep taking curtain calls. The general consensus of opinion was that this play was even funnier than the Squeak.

I had never been more popular at the school. A number of people now looked on me as a brilliant satirist, who only *pretended* to be stupid. It was like this for a few weeks, and then the awful thing happened. I became involved in a bit of a row at school, culminating in a severe caning from the Master of Dulwich College.

It all started in Ernie Tapper's class. I was not following the lesson at all, in fact Ernie might have been talking to us in Swahili for all the sense I could make out of him. I was bored, so I thought I would amuse myself by sharing a joke with the boy sitting directly behind me in class. I jotted down some rude words on an order form. These were forms we made out when we needed certain items from the school bookshop, such as writing materials, etc. Perhaps my little joke wasn't all that funny. I handed this list of 'items' to the other boy, and then pointed to Ernie Tapper. I pretended I was going to ask Ernie for his signature. The list was handed round, there were a few quiet chuckles, and the matter should have ended there. But it didn't.

The list of words had raised a few smiles, and now it was gone from my mind. It now lay on the side of my desk, totally erased from my thoughts – but then a hand snaked out from nowhere, and there was Ernie running his eyes down the list. Then he screwed it into a ball, and tossed it on to his own desk without saying a word. I still didn't grasp the significance of what had taken place.

Next morning I was sent for by the Rev Dixon, who was more than a little ruffled. He had the list of naughty words in his hand, and when he spoke it was as though a terrible thing had happened at the school. There followed an inquisition which lasted for several days, and at the end of it I was given this awful thrashing. I still have no idea what there was about this stupid prank of mine that caused several masters at Dulwich to have something like apoplexy. I had copied some words out of a dictionary, and now people were telling me I had brought Smut and Filth to the school. And just as I was feeling a little bit more friendly towards the place. It certainly caused a load of confusion in *my* mind. For a time, I believed they were thinking of expelling me, and this gave me a nice, warm feeling inside – but it never came to that. All that happened was that relations between me and the school became very badly strained. I now retired almost completely into my fantasy world.

If anyone is looking for a blatant form of escapism, he can't do much better than go to the movies – and then keep on going. I had discovered Hollywood films a long time ago, but now I became something of a fanatic. Cinema-going became a pernicious drug to be taken at regular intervals. Seated in the dark auditorium, I could forget the college and its austere rules of conduct, at least for a time. But I needed money to pay for my 'fix'. During weekends at home, I filched coins from my mother's handbag, and crept away to my illicit joys. At school, the nearest cinema was in Norwood, which was strictly out of bounds. We had only once been allowed to go there – and that under the supervision of a prefect – to watch the Crystal Palace on fire. I now went out of bounds at least once a week to visit the cinema, enjoying the sensation of stolen freedom.

Hollywood was like a huge repertory company, with its stock character actors appearing and then reappearing in successive plots. Guy Kibee was the prototype for fat, jittery businessmen, Alan Mowbray the irate head-waiter type, Franklin Pangborn the desk clerk or department-store chief, while Runyonesque heavies were played by Warren Hymer, Edward Brophy and Nat Pendleton. I had the time of my life in movieland, but there was always the grey, problematic world to contend with afterwards. The same old dreary situations had to be picked up again where they had left off.

Europe teetered on the brink of war, but I was innocent of political thoughts. Tren occasionally talked about the approaching crisis, while I tried to switch the conversation round to something more cheerful. Once he even suggested that I ought to be supporting one or other of the major political parties, since it was the apathy of masses of people that had led us into the mess we were in. I had a quick think about it, and then asked him: 'Is there a party that says people should be left alone? Is there one that believes in everyone doing just what they like, and nobody interfering?'

'I suppose the closest to that would be the Conservatives.'

'That's the one for me. How do I join?'

Hitler's advance through Europe was a nuisance, for it was causing me no end of personal inconvenience. After the fall of the Sudetenland, the entire school was evacuated to Gloucestershire. I didn't notice that the countryside near Cinderford was ravishingly beautiful, but only that there was no gramophone in our new premises. I found a small record shop nearby, purchased a Wingy Manone record for a shilling, but then found there was nothing to play it on. What is more, there would be no more getting home on Sundays, and even weekend leaves would now be difficult. Those Nazis had no idea of the trouble they were putting me to.

As it happened, we were all taken back to Dulwich within only a few weeks, after the betrayal of Czechoslovakia and the subsequent short-lived easing of tension. It was back to the old classrooms again, and the old routines, but even these were welcome to me after the Cinderford makeshift. It would be hard to describe the tense atmosphere that now prevailed. Politicians had made their reassuring noises, but war was still in the air. Mr Rubie, our chemistry teacher, was gloomily predicting war long before it happened. To him, the First World War was 'the last, and lesser, war' – a phrase which he even made us copy down into our exercise books, with reference to some scientific data. Even when Mr Chamberlain returned from Munich with his absurd scrap of paper, Mr Rubie had continued to talk about 'the last and lesser war' and was not exactly a laugh a minute. Soon we were all trying on gas masks and doing field drill with the Officers' Training Corps. I told Skrimshire I was blowed if I would go into the army, as I couldn't bear the thought of having to wear puttees.

Later it looked as if the war might be on after all, since Hitler was not satisfied. In 1939, the summer holidays were held in an atmosphere of rising tension, as the Nazis mustered for the attack on Poland. There was talk of the school being evacuated yet again. I wondered if it would be possible to take a portable gramophone this time.

We were on holiday in Devon during those last tense weeks. I remember wandering around Ilfracombe in a depressed state, munching brazil-nut chocolate as if my life depended on it. It wasn't just the war that bothered me. A dentist in Lewisham had expressed a great urge to pull out one of my front teeth. I would soon be walking about with an unsightly gap showing every time I opened my mouth.

This would spell out the death sentence on my love life even before it had begun. My age group was sensitive about these things. Teenagers were just as self-preoccupied in my time. It is only the fashions that have changed.

In my time, long hair and 'effeminate' clothing were out. Any young man who showed up looking like that would have been ostracized. What *we* took as our model was the typical transatlantic wise guy. Hair was not only kept very short, but was glued on to the head with an oily substance that glistened horribly. Suits were heavily padded to give the impression of giant strength, and the upper lip was sometimes adorned with what looked like a third eyebrow. This would complete the picture of a self-assured city slicker who knew all there was to know about life.

I still have some pictures of myself taken as a teenager, and quite terrifying they are too. The face that leers back at me from these photos is distorted into a sinister expression, left eyebrow raised disdainfully and the shoulders braced in what is supposed to be an aggressive stance. If anything like that came at me in a dark side street I would be tempted to turn and run.

My idol during the war years was Victor Mature, an actor who played tough, sardonic heroes who were never at a loss with women. I wanted to be like Mature but my own build was not quite the same as his. I was shaped rather like an animated bean-pole, and knew it. It was no use wearing suits with padded shoulders, since my own shoulders couldn't support the weight. Often I stood in front of a mirror and grimaced, in the way I had seen Mature grimace on the screen.

'Do stop pulling those awful faces,' said my mother one morning, 'you look exactly like Max Miller.'

It was in Ilfracombe that I first spoke to a girl. To be more exact, she did most of the talking, while I stood speechless, making strange clucking sounds. Mr Mature would not have been proud of me. Confronted at last with a real-life situation, I made the awful discovery that I couldn't communicate. It was as if I had found myself face to face with some strange alien being. The girl was friendly and talkative, and tried me again the next day. Again I couldn't think of a thing to talk about. I just stood there, spluttering away. This attractive wench, whose name was May, was certainly no quitter. A day or so later, I was greeted yet again, with the same cheery flow of talk. It must have been like talking to a perambulating road sign. I then went home and became very morose, cursing my incredible shyness and imagining suave sentences that I might have used, if only I'd thought of them in time. I also played a certain record over and over again, because it reminded me of the girl. The record was Django's 'Souvenirs'.

Django Reinhardt's music was unashamedly tender, at times rather sentimental, but I never thought of it as anything but authentic jazz. Those critics who patronized Django as a 'pretty' player, not quite in the idiom, were displaying certain narrow concepts about jazz being an American music. The sound of his guitar on 'Souvenirs', 'Black and White' and 'Nuages' is one of the most powerfully expressive sounds in all jazz, and places Django up there with the very top men. I was spending a great deal of my pocket-money on records by the Quintet of the Hot Club of France in those days. Sometimes I would take off one of these records and then go and laugh at myself in the mirror, having been moved to tears by the guitar solo. It wasn't easy to see why some short passages of improvisation by a Belgian gypsy guitarist should have this disconcerting effect.

We were living in a desolate-looking house perched on top of a hill. From a bedroom window we could see Ilfracombe strewn untidily at our feet. Two of the rooms had packing-cases of items that hadn't even been unpacked yet. Paint pots and rolls of underfelt lay about on the bare floorboards. Then, right out of the blue, Mum announced that we were leaving.

'What! But we've only been here a few weeks!'

'I know. It was a mistake coming here in the first place. Your father kept on at me to get out of the London area, in case the bombers came. Now it looks as though we'll all die of boredom.'

'It is pretty gruesome. I think it's the black-out – other places will be just as bad.'

'I can think of a few places that aren't. Hyderabad, for one.'

Mother had bought the house on one of her sudden impulses. Now she was just as impulsively getting ready to leave. The small seaside town had seemed like a good idea at first, but now everyone was thinking that even a German air-raid might not be such a bad thing after all. It would at least liven things up a bit. Ilfracombe, on the eve of a world war, was taking on the appearance of an outsize churchyard. Black-out restrictions, and the tendency for local inhabitants to go about with very sombre expressions, didn't contribute towards a cheery frame of mind. So we moved to Exeter which, by comparison, was almost a bustling metropolis.

My brother and I were playing tennis in Exeter when the war started. We missed the radio announcement, but saw it in the stop press. The nation was at war.

'If the war goes on beyond Christmas of next year,' said Tren dramatically, 'you and I will have to go into the army – and most probably get killed. The world seems to have gone raving mad.'

'They won't get *me* in the army,' I told him defiantly. 'Nobody is going to get *me* to wear puttees.'

3 Looking for Turner

We stayed in a large board residence for what turned out to be a very long time – by Mother's standards at any rate. For nearly two years I had a small attic bedroom at this place in Longbrook Street, Exeter. The establishment was run by a jolly, apple-cheeked woman called Mrs Sercombe. The other occupants were a group of characters who, mainly due to infirmity or middle age, would sit the war out in relative comfort.

The stars of this little company were two gentlemen called D'Arcy and Bates. The first-named was a senile and bloated Tory who looked as though a cartoonist on the *Daily Worker* had just thought him up. The other man was a blunt northerner who opted for social reform. The two of them did nothing but hurl insults at one another from dawn till dusk, or so it appeared. They did this in such strident tones that the rest of the company had no option but to sit back and enjoy the show.

Not that I had the faintest interest in their political harangues. I was more intrigued by a certain Mr Bennett. This was a rascally sort of fellow who claimed to know a great deal about nightlife. Winking lewdly, Mr Bennett told me of a way the opposite sex could be got hold of at any time and with a minimum of fuss. There were things called dance halls. All you had to do was buy a ticket and walk in. Before you knew it, you were shuffling about the floor with a woman in your arms. I had never dreamed that meeting girls could be so incredibly simple.

'There's only one problem,' I said, 'I can't dance.'

'You can walk, can't you, old boy?'

'Of course.'

'Then you can dance. It's very much the same.'

Soon I had become an ardent pupil of the Bennett Method. I followed the middle-aged roué into one dance hall after another, closely studying his movements. With him, walking and dancing were *exactly* the same. If he wanted to change direction, he executed a sort of skipping movement, like an army recruit changing step. Otherwise he just slithered about the room. After only a few visits to dance halls, I was doing the same. My usual haunt was a place called the St James's Institute, where I spent a lot of time clasping females in my arms and asking them whether they came there often. Back in 1940, I supposed this to be nightlife at its most depraved.

Henry Setter led the band at St James's. It was usually a three-piece front line with two saxes and Henry leading on trumpet. For much of the time they had their eyes glued to the standard arrangements – things like 'Franklyn D. Roosevelt Jones' and 'You Can't Black Out the Moon'. But Henry had evidently heard some Louis Armstrong. Towards the end of an evening, if the cider was in him, he would let rip with one of the swing numbers currently in vogue. His own solo was likely to contain several wrong notes, but certainly never lacked verve. One evening I was so interested in what the band was playing that I sat in front of the bandstand all evening, drinking it all in. In the interval, Henry stopped in front of me and remarked chattily:

'What's the matter tonight? No dancing partner?'

'Oh, I just felt like listening. You sounded like Louis in that last one.'

'Louis who?' I thought he was serious, and started to explain, but now Henry was all smiles.

'We swing about four numbers during an evening, if we get the chance. The best time is right at the beginning, when nobody is here – or right at the end, when nobody is sober. Otherwise, we play for dancing. Have to.'

I told Henry I played clarinet, but only in the easy keys. I had been making conversation, but then he said: 'Bring it with you next time. You could join us in the last set. Tell 'em at the ticket desk that you're with the band.'

From that moment onwards I was able to come to the institute free, and also to a larger place right above Dellers Café in the town centre, whenever Henry's band was there. The boys in the band told me I sounded just like Goodman. This was surely no more than polite small-talk, I decided. But then everyone took to calling me 'Benny', inviting me to play with the band whenever I felt like coming along. They were a warm, friendly bunch of guys, with none of the condescension I might have expected from such hardened semi-pros.

It was all most encouraging from my point of view, for at the boarding-house I was made to feel decidedly small. Mr D'Arcy and Mr Bates, though they disagreed about most things, were in close harmony when it came to condemning me. I was considered to be a lazy young oaf, who ought to have joined one of the armed forces by this time. Too young, was I? Then at least I should be out doing *something* for the war effort.

At the end of the summer holidays, I had flatly refused to go back to the college when the time came, I had had quite enough of the life there, and on no account would I agree to return. And that, I insisted, was final.

Mum surprised me by readily accepting the situation, though warning me the news would not do Dad's blood pressure any good. So now I was loafing around Exeter during the first months of the war, getting in everybody's hair.

This wouldn't have been so bad, only I looked considerably older than my years. One day as I was roaming the streets, humming the solos from Carter's 'When Day is Done', an old lady and her middle-aged companion happened to be coming towards me on an otherwise deserted stretch of pavement. The old lady brandished her umbrella in my face and demanded to know why I wasn't wearing a uniform. Her companion became very embarrassed and whispered audibly: 'Hush, dear. The young gentleman's probably in munitions.'

Neither of them had been aware that I was at least a year below the call-up age group. As far as I was concerned, though, age didn't matter a damn. It was all I could do not to shout after these two women something or other to the effect that they could stuff their ridiculous war. If some myopic brass-hats in England and Germany wanted to fight each other, it was all right with me – but it was certainly not *my* war. This was the anarchist view, based on some rather muddled thinking – though in my own case I am afraid it was based on almost no thinking at all.

In case he could throw any light on all this insanity, I even discussed the war with Tren. I hated all the talk about politics, but what I badly needed to know was whether there was a chance we could somehow get out of having our limbs blown off.

'Don't worry, I've worked out a plan,' was his reply. 'What we'll do is this – we'll apply for work on a merchant ship heading for Venezuela. Washing the dishes, scrubbing floors – anything will do. Then, as soon as we get to the other side, we'll desert ship, and stay in Venezuela for the duration.'

It sounded like something out of a boy's magazine. Was my

brother serious, or simply trying to keep my spirits up, or what? Next day he went out and bought a copy of Hugo's *Spanish Course*.

'We'd better start learning the language,' he said. 'There isn't much time to lose. Later, I'll make some enquiries about merchant steamers.'

So it was on after all. Within three weeks I had started on some of the irregular verbs, conscious that things had taken a dramatic turn. Tren believed at first that the war was a dispute between rival groups of businessmen over how to divide up the world. Maybe it was, at first. Later it became clearly a war of survival against an unspeakable Fascist tyranny. Tren had second thoughts about Venezuela. The whole scheme was too complicated for words. It was so much simpler to put on a uniform and get blown to bits.

Anyway, even a bumbling and outmoded democracy was better than none at all.

Tren went into the army when his time came, and I was on my own.

Music had become easily the most important thing in my life by this time. It had taken precedence over the pursuit of young girls and even over confectionery, to the point where I had to play clarinet regularly in order to find any outlet for my feelings at all. Henry Setter wasn't in any position to feed this urgent desire of mine to blow a stream of jazz solos whenever I had the message. These sedate wartime dances were run by non-musicians who only wanted to get people on to the floor with nice respectable waltzes and fox-trots, interspersed with old-time medleys for the aged and infirm. Swing was tolerated in very small doses, if it managed to stop the patrons from actually falling into a deep sleep.

I was fortunate enough to meet a tall, affable Yorkshireman who played drums in his spare time. John Watkinson was crazy about Goodman, Krupa and other artists of the swing era, and he was interested in forming a group based on the music of the Benny Goodman Trio. His brother, Len, played some piano and they had already lined up a bass player. Why didn't we form a quartet which could present whole evenings of jazz for dancing? We would show the Exeter folk that jazz could be just as entertaining as any other kind of dance music – and about a hundred times as exciting to listen to.

As soon as I had joined the Watkinson Four, we were able to find work playing at small functions and private parties in the area. This gave me back a little of the confidence I had lost under the puritanical glare of the senior citizens at Longbrook Street. At least I was doing something – if not for the war effort, at least for my own self-esteem. It also felt good to be paid something at the end of the evening, although this money was the kind that chinked rather than rustled. John was also a good friend. It was as though he sensed that I had just lost the support of an elder brother, and needed some kind of guiding hand in my life. We talked a great deal about the importance of revitalizing the dance-band scene with a more virile and meaningful music, to replace mass-produced commercial noise. John knew as well as I did myself that jazz was putting real heart into popular music, and that for the next generation of listeners this would become a crying need.

Any Louis Armstrong record bore witness to this fact. Louis had been the key figure in the great musical upheaval, and after him nothing had remained the same. He altered the rules of the game. It is tempting to talk about a genius years ahead of his time. This could be misleading, because great music reflects its time. Louis was no ivory-tower dreamer, but a man of the people. Everything he did was worldly and intimately in touch with life. Still, it was forward-looking, as genuinely popular music tends to be. 'Potato Head Blues' is not the music of dreams, but of throbbing human activity.

Louis crystallized human change. He was the greatest of all jazz performers, but this is not to place him on some lofty pedestal, or to endow him with special magic. What he really symbolized was the man in the street finding a voice at last. The new music shows us how to replace sickly escapist fantasy with something profoundly truthful and real.

John Watkinson and I shared a *Melody Maker* every week. He paid for it, and I examined it for the amusing bits. In one feature article, Benny Goodman was dismissed as a pallid imitation of the New Orleans clarinettist Jimmie Noone. This was funnier than watching the Crazy Gang. What could you do with a self-appointed 'expert' who chose to malign Goodman? You could only make the remark that was once made at a Yorkshire v. Lancashire cricket match, to a noisy Londoner complaining of the slow scoring rate: 'Shut mouth – it's nowt ta do wi' thee!'

The Watkinson Four played Goodmanesque music for dancing. We played at small private parties and at some functions where they couldn't afford to hire real musicians. I revelled in this situation, but at the same time I was aware that it was turning me away from the unpleasant fact of war. I was trying hard to ward off the odious business going on hundreds of miles away. When I did allow myself to think about the war, it was with an airy disdain. My brother had lent me a book called *Social Chaos and the Way Out* – a ranting piece of anarchism which he had thought might amuse me. Instead I made the wretched thing my bible and even learned some of the more pungent phrases by heart. I always made sure the D'Arcys and Bateses would know what I was reading. The exasperated clicking of their tongues, as they peered at it over my shoulder, was music to my ears. Perhaps it would shake them out of their complacency just a little.

One morning we had a very unpleasant scene at Mrs Sercombe's. It was during breakfast, and it all started with Mr Bates walking in and mumbling against people in high places. Usually Mr D'Arcy was there to oppose him, with the customary good-natured quips – but this time he wasn't in the room. Instead of the usual snappy dialogue, what we had was Mr Bennett leaping into the fray. Mr Bennett's debating technique consisted almost entirely of patriotic slogans, delivered in a high-pitched scream.

'How dare you!' gabbled Mr Bennett. 'Stabbing our boys in the back . . . defending freedom with all our might . . . democratic way of life . . . you come along, criticizing the war effort . . . ought to be taken out and shot . . .'

'Calm down, Bennett – and don't give us all that crap about *your* war effort. You spend half your time in dance halls.'

'Good mind to report you . . . going around making trouble . . . all you Reds . . .'

'All right, I'll keep quiet – just for you. Just one question, though. If we've got no freedom, how can we defend it with all our might?'

At about this juncture, I looked round at the other guests, and found to my amazement that they were smiling fondly upon the perspiring Bennett. When this gentleman roared out that Mr Bates was a traitor to his country, which seemed a bit strong to me under the circumstances, there was a general murmur of approval, and when Mr Bates retaliated by emptying a jug of water over the other man, I could see that this mildly liberal reformist didn't have a friend in the place. Both men were now swishing water at each other, while everyone in the room appeared to be mouthing banalities and waving the flag. To make the situation even more confused, a lot of the water went over the innoffensive Mr Hill, who was sitting at the same table. War jitters had evidently come to 82 Longbrook Street in a big way.

I felt disgusted and went out the next day to find myself a job. It was clear to me that even work would be better than hanging around with this crowd of stiffs. My good friend John Watkinson immediately rallied round. He was working at a wireless repair shop run by a man called Fildew. John gave me a big build-up and got Fildew to hire me, as extra help in the shop.

'Sort of make yourself generally useful,' said Fildew. 'Keep an eye on the place when I'm not here, sell a few records – that sort of thing.'

It sounded complicated, but I promised to try. My mother proudly announced at breakfast that I had at last found myself a job. Doing what? enquired Mrs Paine, who was a sort of falsetto version of the obese D'Arcy. Selling records, I replied. The other lodgers exchanged supercilious glances and went on with their breakfast. I could see that my status was exactly as before.

A new lodger came to stay. He was a young man with golden locks and a permanent sneer. He was about my age, but unlike me in just about every way. He worked in an armaments factory, earned a good regular wage and spoke very highly of the war. Mr D'Arcy beamed upon the newcomer, and was heard to whisper something about a refreshing change. Within hours of his moving in, this teenage Fauntleroy had become everybody's adopted son. It was nice, anyway, that the other guests had stopped giving me withering glances. Now they didn't even bother to look at me at all. Then, when I was least expecting it, some of them decided to have a go. Up to then, most of their criticism had been levelled at my evident reluctance to go out and kill large numbers of Germans. Now people became heavily sarcastic about my musical tastes.

'When are you going to grow out of all that jazz nonsense and give us all a rest?', bellowed someone.

I promised to stuff something down inside my gramophone to deaden the noise. I was all for a policy of live and let live, where music was concerned.

'It isn't that your records are too loud,' was the reply, 'just damned annoying. Why can't you put on something that has a tune?'

The new boy said he liked tuneful music himself. In fact, he had quite a collection of really pleasant, listenable records at home. He promised to go and get some of them, and bring them to the boarding-house.

'What are you going to play them on?' I enquired pleasantly.

My blood was really up by this time. Then my mother told me I would have to share my bedroom with the new lodger. She didn't like him much either, but there was an accommodation problem all over the town. Another bed was moved into my room. There we were, two absolutely opposite types, forced on to one another by the exigencies of war.

After the first few days, we had hardly spoken to each other. As soon as he came in from work, I pretended to be hurrying away on a date. There was something about the newcomer that didn't seem right. It wasn't long before my suspicions were shown to be well-founded. He came down to breakfast one morning looking all burned up, fumbling around in his pockets and peering about the room. 'I had this pound note in my pocket, see – just before I went to bed. Can't think where it can have got to.'

Everybody turned and looked in my direction. This was too much. I snorted in disgust and stamped out of the room, but next morning I was to find out exactly what was going on – only it was a little late to do anything about it. My own pockets had been picked clean! A few days earlier, Mum had handed me four one-pound notes – in full view of the new boy – so that I could take a coach down to London and spend the weekend with my pal Fleming. Now they weren't in my pocket. A simple trick, but an ingenious one. First put your room-mate under suspicion, then lift his wad – and then see if he has the nerve to go downstairs and report the theft. Of course, everyone would laugh themselves silly if I now reported something missing – after Fauntleroy had already made his move.

Mum knew me well enough to know I was speaking the truth. All the same, she didn't think it would be any use blurting out my story in front of all the other lodgers. Nobody was likely to take the word of a chap who went around reading *Social Chaos and the Way Out*. After considering the matter carefully, she thought it best if we wrote off the four quid, but naturally I would have to sleep with my loose change under my pillow until she was able to persuade Mrs Sercombe that the sleeping arrangements would have to be changed.

We even held a council of war with two of the other lodgers,

Mr Hill and a dour Aberdonian called Jock, who believed everything we told him after learning that there was Scottish blood in our family. They agreed that the Golden Boy had been too clever for words. All that remained was for me to keep the rest of my money in a safe place, and my nerve steady.

'Who's nervous?' I thought, 'just don't rustle anything.'

That night I put all my loose change under my pillow, but I couldn't get off to sleep. With my eyes closed I heard my room-mate come in and prepare for bed. Then I must have dozed off, for the next thing I knew was that a lot of activity was going on underneath my pillow. There was something else under there besides my loose change, and I was soon able to identify this as a human hand. On the other end was the Golden Boy, trying to pretend he had lost his way in the dark. Next morning Mum and I insisted that the kleptomaniac would have to find somewhere else to sleep, but Mrs Sercombe remarked that some people didn't understand there was a war on.

It was a relief to get away from Exeter for a couple of days. Maurice Fleming lived in Victoria, and had arranged for me to do a private recording with piano and drums on the second day. On the first day, Fleming and I were in Piccadilly as the sun was sinking below the roof-tops. It was just as we were wending our way homewards that I noticed the women. They were posted along the narrow pavement at regular intervals, plying their trade. In fact, the friendly cry of: 'Short time, dearie,' was audible from all sides. My school chum wasn't paying much attention to all this, but I was. An idea was forming in my mind. Later that evening I would think of an excuse for slipping away on my own. I had made a note of the street name – 'Lisle Street' – and could be back at this same spot in no time at all. At the age of nineteen, I still knew almost nothing about women, except that they were the ones who danced backwards. For years my education had made scarcely any progress at all, but now I intended to go on a crash course.

All I had was a pound note in one pocket, and my return ticket in the other. It was all changed when I found my way back to Lisle Street. The place now looked deserted, except for a few hurrying figures. I was determined to get myself accosted, do the foul deed, and be back at Fleming's in time for supper. I wasn't out for any thrills, either, only the reassurance that I was adult, male and in reasonable working order. I wanted to get the experience over and done with, safely tucked away in the past.

One solitary figure was now to be seen, parading up and down at the street corner. She must have been at least thirty-five, which would make her twice my age. I scanned her for some compensating feature, such as good looks, but without success. Not that it mattered. I was about to have a lesson in life, and you don't expect teachers to look like Rita Hayworth.

An hour and a half later, I was back at Maurice's place, minus my pound note. I hadn't been able to accomplish a damned thing, although the lady had persevered. So much, I thought, for the Mystery of Sex. The only mystery was why anyone should want to go in for it in the first place.

Maurice Fleming had booked a small studio in Bond Street, where I would cut four sides with piano and drums. Bob Farran was the pianist and Jack Mold the drummer on this session, of which I am inordinately proud. The four titles were 'Sugar', 'Someday Sweetheart', 'Honeysuckle Rose' and 'Bond Street Blues'. On the second and third titles I had a go at playing a battered C Melody sax, which I'd managed to buy very cheap. Considering our lack of experience and even greater lack of rudimentary technique, the session wasn't all that bad.

'Not a bad noise,' was Fleming's verdict as we packed up to leave. 'You were not too horrifying on the C Melody – sort of a cross between Chu Berry and Bud Freeman. By the way, who *were* you trying to sound like?'

'Funny thing is,' I replied, 'the place made me so nervous – I forgot all the phrases I'd worked out. I just stood there and blew.'

'A novel approach. Wonder if it'll catch on.'

Maurice and Bob Farran wanted to visit the Bag O' Nails on that last evening to attend a meeting of the Number One Rhythm Club. They also talked me into taking my clarinet along. The idea was that I would sit in during the final jam session and cover myself in glory. It didn't work out quite like that.

'George Shearing has just walked in,' whispered Farran. 'He's sure to take over on piano. Go on, show him what you can do.'

We all took up our positions around the small microphone. Shearing, the big star, beat us in for the first number. Soon all the front-line men had taken solos – except me. I stood up and launched into one, but at that very moment George had decided to take one on the piano. The two of us battled it out, hoping the other would give ground. The Bag O' Nails was beginning to sound like a rehearsal studio with thin walls.

Usually, when this sort of thing happens, somebody has to give way. In this instance, it should certainly have been me, but I was past making rational decisions. The room was swimming before my eyes. People in the front rows were putting their hands over their ears, as piano and clarinet battled for supremacy. At last George decided to give me the floor, which by this time I prayed might open and swallow me up. Most inconsiderately, it did not.

I never tried sitting in at rhythm clubs after that. I had found out why it is that some people play with their eyes closed. It isn't ecstasy after all – they just can't stand seeing the expressions of horror on the faces of their friends.

Meanwhile, my call-up was coming closer with every day that dawned. On my return, Mr D'Arcy greeted me with the exact number of weeks he thought I still had coming to me, before the army came to take me away. He must have had a good time working it all out and rubbing his hands together.

There had to be a way I could avoid this contingency – and then a faint possibility did present itself. One of the guests at Mrs Sercombe's who for some strange reason was on speaking terms with me, thought he knew of a way. He had a friend who owned a farm in Tiverton, and this man was desperately short of help. If I went to work on the farm there was always a chance that this might be construed as 'essential war work' when the time came.

I agreed to give it a try. It wasn't long afterwards that this man fixed it with the farmer and I was asked to start right away.

The news that I was about to become a farm labourer gave much pleasure to Mr D'Arcy. He wanted to take bets on whether I would last about four or five days, or even six if you stretched a point. He wasn't even close.

When I arrived on the farm, everyone was nice and friendly. There was a hot meal waiting for me when I came down after tidying myself up. The farmer and his family sat around the table laughing and joking. I couldn't understand one of the jokes. The farmer's wife said she would not call me until six on the first morning, so that I could have a lie-in, Four-thirty or five was the usual time I should expect to be roused. Very obscure, some of this rustic humour.

By seven that first morning, I was cleaning out cow sheds by the pale glow of a lantern. After that, one of the old hands would show me how to pitch hay. This sounded like fun. In romantic fiction, the country boy pitches hay with a merry song on his lips, stopping occasionally to chat up dairymaids. All I could manage, after the first few minutes, was a series of agonized grunts. Hay isn't all that heavy until you get a pitch-fork to it – then it's almost impossible to lift it off the ground.

After the midday meal I went upstairs for what was supposed to have been an hour's rest. Instead, I scrawled an apologetic note and left it on the bed. Then I tip-toed down to the front door, opened it quietly – and fled. I didn't stop running until I came to the bus stop at Tiverton. The old folk at Mrs Sercombe's enjoyed the sight of their farm labourer limping home, defeated, after one morning's work. The only person who wasn't amused was Mr Moor, who had recommended me for the job on his friend's farm. I was in disgrace – no doubt at all about this. The general consensus, though, was that it didn't matter all that much anyway. Pretty soon they would be coming to take me away.

Tren came home on leave a few times, which meant that we could plan 'evenings out'. He was only slightly less awkward with girls than I was, but he always insisted that after three pints of rough cider he would be ready for anything. So we always began these evenings by going to the pub. Here I chafed impatiently while Tren gulped the stuff down. Every time I pecked at his sleeve and edged towards the door, he was obliged to force down another mouthful.

After a while, he put down the empty tankard, announcing that he was ready. Out in the cold air, he began to sway down the street, with me following gleefully in his wake. It is not easy to win friends and influence people in a typical wartime black-out. Apart from walking into a hedge and once being almost decapitated by a passing truck, Tren met with no adventures and led me to none. It didn't matter, because those evenings with my brother were not without a certain piquancy. We were always just about to get lucky – and though we never did, there was an element of youthful elation about each one of these sorties that I looked forward to every time.

I still entertained fond hopes of being able to keep out of the army when my time came. Someone told me they were looking for stretcher-bearers at the Exeter General Hospital, so I went there to make enquiries. Surprisingly, I was taken on there and then. No one was applying because the pay was so bad, but food and sleeping accommodation were thrown in with the job, plus a white cotton jacket several sizes too small. I suppose I had fallen for the talk about stretcher-bearers being exempt from call-up, but needless to say this was not true. The only ones who were likely to stay out of the fighting forces were the ones who were needed in the battle zones, but I was sure I had this job at Exeter General for the rest of the war.

The work was tolerably pleasant; in fact we spent a great deal of time lying in our beds in the orderlies' quarters. Each bed was equipped with a pair of earphones. We were instructed to hang about there, listening to the dance-band programmes if we liked, until a call came through the speaker system. Then two of us had to sprint upstairs at great speed. This reminded me very much of those fagging days back at college, except that now I was being paid for it.

Work was as straightforward as it could be. We lifted bodies on to stretchers, then wheeled them to one of the wards or to the operating theatre. Jerry Lewis could have done it. After each of these assignments, we sloped off and listened to some more dance music, until another call came through. This went on for several weeks, but then I lost the job through no fault of my own.

The man at the other end of my stretcher was a murderous-looking fellow who was always glancing at his watch and talking about closing-times. A pub was always on the point of closing its doors to him, so any last-minute call that came in would usually be greeted with a flood of abuse. Once he became so furious at having to work late that he cursed loudly as our stretcher became stuck half in and half out of one of the lifts. He yanked furiously at his end, depositing our patient on the floor. Blood and pieces of broken apparatus littered the floor of the lift. Luckily the patient survived, but soon after this there was a great purge of all casual labour at the hospital. I found myself back at Longbrook Street, trying hard to explain to everybody that I had lost this job through no fault of my own. Other things were now going wrong. John Watkinson had no engagements for the quartet. To make matters worse, Henry Setter had terminated his residency at Dellers, which meant that I now had nowhere I could play. As far as Exeter and the surrounding areas were concerned, the swing era seemed to have come to an abrupt close.

'Look at it this way, Benny,' said Henry, slapping the usual nickname on to me, 'the dancers aren't interested in jazz any more. Not this lot, anyway – they're all middle-aged now, the civilians. And the only thing those soldier boys want is to get pissed and sing comic songs.'

'But Henry, your swing numbers always get terrific applause.'

'Only if we ration them to about three or four in an evening. And even then the management starts to make trouble, They say I'm scaring away the regulars.'

Henry knew what he was talking about, so who was I to argue? Swing was no more than a minority craze, with very little general appeal.

One evening, I found myself discussing these things with a khaki-clad figure. He was jovial and horn-rimmed, announcing himself to me as the leader of a group called the Rapcats.

'I thought the name up myself,' explained Phil proudly. 'The initials stand for Royal Army Pay Corps, see? Which is what we're in. R-A-P-C, Rapcats – see? Clever?'

This Pay Corps band confounded Henry Setter's argument by playing jazz for at least fifty per cent of the time – or so they claimed. I asked Phil how he was able to perform this miracle.

'We put sugar on the pill,' came the reply. 'Your average listener will take anything, as long as it is loud and fast – and if the musicians are all wearing funny clothes and leaping about.'

Phil would have done well ten years later, during the trad boom.

As far as I could make out, Phil and the boys featured cheerful music with the accent on comedy, popular hits being interspersed with a lot of raucous jazz. The boys seemed to like my playing, for they asked if I would be interested in joining the band. It didn't matter that I wasn't in the Pay Corps – I would be considered as part of the show, and on some jobs I might even get paid. I said 'Count me in', and was immediately fitted out with the gaudiest of gaucho silk shirts and a pair of ill-fitting dress trousers.

When Phil put on a show he threw everything in. Curtains rose to a great fanfare and clatter of drums; lighting effects were used whenever possible and announcements took the form of comic monologues, with members of the band often capering in the background. With all this going on, an audience would at last respond to anything – even jazz. It was mass hypnosis, and it worked surprisingly well. I was given a chance to shine on several feature numbers throughout the show, including 'Sweet Georgia Brown', 'Darktown Strutters' and 'In the Mood'. Everything received riotous applause as Phil threw in every device he could think of. You didn't dare to dislike the show, for fear of being pointed out as a kill-joy.

No one expected any showmanship from me, and they didn't get any. I preferred to stand over on one side of the stage, staring at the floor. As soon as my feature number was over, I lost no time disappearing into the wings, so that I would not be involved in any of the funny stuff. For a time I fondly imagined this to be an understanding between me and the rest of the band, but it seemed I was wrong.

The Rapcats were booked to play a big variety show that was being staged at the Odeon Cinema; a full house was hoped for. Advance booking was already well under way. Phil thought it was a great chance for the band to be seen by masses of ordinary Exeter people, in contrast to the private shindigs and NAAFI concerts we'd done up to that time. I made a mental note that I would contact several girlfriends, urging them not to miss this stupendous concert which featured me as one of the stars.

'One thing we will need,' mused Phil, 'is a big spectacular opener, introducing the whole band. I want all the boys to be announced one by one as a part of our first number.'

'How about *singing* the introductions. Louis does this on "The Saints", and "I Hope Gabriel Likes My Music". Maybe if I lent you the records . . .'

'No need, Mal. That's a great idea. I'll work on it right away.'

I thought Phil had understood, but he hadn't. I had envisioned a jazz vocal that would introduce each of us in turn. 'Here comes Brother Higginbotham down the aisle with his trombone,' sings Louis on one record, and then there is a short, searing chorus from the musician named. But with the big day almost upon us, Phil presented us with his horrific brain-child.

'I've just been working on this great novelty number. The words are really good – give everyone a chance to fool about and get some laughs . . .'

'WHA-A-AT!'

'No, listen, Mal. First there's this vocal by the whole band. Then Ed comes out front and sings his bit. Then he takes a solo. Then the next man – that's you, Mal – you come forward and sing . . .'

I was already backing towards the door.

Phil had called his ghastly little composition 'Lulu'. It was all about a fun-loving woman who was always getting involved with bandsmen. First we all had to sing in unison:

Lulu, Lulu, she's everybody's best girl.
She'll go to the pictures, she'll go to a ball –
Watch the soldiers, sailors, airmen – see them all fall.

Then would come one of the solo bits. When my turn came, I would have to walk out front and sing my handful of unfunny lines. All about how I went into the lady's bedroom but was unable to perform. Chafes Lulu in the end: 'I'm tired of this my pet – come on, get out your clarinet.' This was supposed to lead into my clarinet solo, but you could be certain that it would be rendered inaudible by suggestive guffaws from the band and hoots of derision from the stalls. I blanched at the very thought of all this happening to me on a concert stage. The whole plot was too painfully reminiscent of some recent attempts of mine to have sex. No, the band would have to do this number without me.

Phil was pained. Hadn't it been my suggestion in the first place? And now I was backing out. It was time I decided whether I was in the band or only halfway in. He handed me the lyrics. Take them home, he said, and think about it.

My departure from the Rapcats thus came quite abruptly, but the mythical Lulu was not entirely to blame. My age group was now just about due for call-up, which meant that I was going to have to move very quickly if I still meant to try for a reserved occupation. In fact, there was only one faint glimmer of hope left. Munition workers were in short supply. It was announced over the radio that a short preliminary training course was being offered in certain towns. I hurried off to a local address which had been given to me, and put my name down for one of these courses, as the minutes ticked by.

The instructors were very kind and patient. It wasn't until I had ruined several pieces of expensive equipment that I was taken off the course and quietly told to go home.

Zero hour was coming up fast, but there was still one way I could avoid being sent into the army, and this time it couldn't possibly fail.

I went down to the local recruiting centre and joined the RAF.

During the next few months, in spite of my invaluable help, our country came very close to being overrun by the Nazis. My attitude during this period was not heroic. If the enemy had made landings upon our shores, I would probably have started to learn some polite phrases in German. I knew nothing about Danzig or the Polish Corridor, and in any case I had my own very important battle going on inside. The next chapter will deal almost exclusively with this inner struggle and only mention the war in passing. This may seem to put the whole thing right out of proportion but, sad to say, it helps describe exactly the way I felt at the time.

The awful skirmish for democracy and survival meant precisely nothing.

'Your country needs you,' shouted the patriotic slogans.

'I have no country,' replied a small inner voice, 'and no personal identity worth a damn.'

I had never experienced any truly worthwhile freedom – only the right to drift aimlessly and to be ignored. If we've got no freedom, Mr D'Arcy, – how can we defend it with all our might? Survival? If I'm not accepted into society, then I fight for my *own* survival, but not until I see the whites of their eyes. In the meantime, only one thing appeared meaningful and clear. Music was like a great beacon shining out of the darkness.

Listening to Django's chorus on 'Melancholy Baby', or Armstrong's on 'Knocking a Jug' was like returning to sanity from a world gibbering and reduced to self-destruction. Confused people on both sides fought one another because they had no art to turn to – no contact with real human feelings. They responded to the animal instinct for blood, because they did not have the social consciousness and tenderness towards one another that expresses itself in great art. Make music, not war – and if I wasn't able to express the view quite as succinctly as all this, it was none the less a fervently held belief.

This was how things stood when, in the last weeks of 1941, I was rounded up for military service, still abstractedly humming hot solos under my breath.

It was still possible to get all the latest information about jazz, and peruse it earnestly while others read the war news. Jazz criticism was as yet a purely private matter, not yet a question of mass indoctrination by a separate class of paid scribes. One week a writer would lay down the law about something or other, but in a later issue another chap would send in a great scorcher telling the first writer where he got off.

It was the tried and tested method, the way of the ancient Greeks. It was the arrival at truth by debate. Nobody in those days had the nerve to present their view as if it were Holy Writ.

Some of us had a good laugh at the writer who claimed Ellington was commiting artistic suicide by bringing in new sounds, instead of endlessly repeating the old. When trombonist Lawrence Brown first joined the band we were told that Ellington's music would 'never be the same again'. Later, the appearance of Rex Stewart brought forth the same dismal cry. The uncertainties of war had made some parties highly suspicious of change. All this reached the peak of absurdity when a writer described Duke's new bassist as a major catastrophe.

'Bullish Bass Bowings Endanger Duke's Reputation' ran a headline. The writer then characterized the music as 'hacked, slashed and brutally butchered' by the new bass player, who 'thumps and saws' his way through the Ellington repertoire. And the name of this newcomer to the fold? Jimmy Blanton – now generally accepted as the father of all post-war bass rhythm. It was like saying Milton didn't know how to write an epic poem.

Just before I went into uniform, I had developed a fervid interest in the music of Artie Shaw. Here again, it was no use being guided by the critics. Most of them were writing Shaw off as a deviation from the path of real jazz. To hear the talk about Shaw's music, you would think it was an illicit drug. I went on buying his records, but it was rather like asking for morphine on a fake prescription. Shaw didn't play jazz at all, but only a malignant preparation to make the senses reel.

They also told us that Louis Armstrong had 'gone commercial' in the early years of the decade. I allowed myself to be influenced by this theory at the time, and even sent a pompous letter to the *Melody Maker,* in which I ranted against Louis. I described him as being 'slightly better than Nat Gonella'. It felt good to see this letter in the correspondents' column, and to hear the angry cries of protest that I managed to stir up with my schoolboy silliness. Well, at least I had the excuse of being a novice. As long as we were all slinging our opinions around, but also using our ears, nothing but sense would finally emerge. We hadn't yet started to bow to the 'experts'. On that day, all that was best in jazz would shrivel and die.

4 The Square Peg

On a certain day in November 1941 I went into the armed forces, as a small square peg might find its way into a very large round hole. There was never any kind of firm contact between me and the Royal Air Force. I had always considered myself to be a misfit, but never more than when I first clambered into that uniform of blue. I was still looking at everything through big bewildered eyes when the recruiting sergeant began barking out his first orders. I didn't understand a word of what he was saying.

'C of Es this side – ODs over there,' was what it sounded like to me. The large room promptly divided itself off into two separate groups of airmen with me standing hesitantly in the middle. A corporal bustled up to me and asked me what I was supposed to be playing at. Speaking very slowly, as if to a small child, he explained that we were all being sorted into two groups, according to our religious denominations. Church of England on this side of the room – other religions over there. I still didn't move from where I was, but went on surveying the two groups of airmen with a puzzled frown. The sergeant, a patient man, took a deep breath and asked me to state my religion.

'Oh' I said. 'Atheist,' I said.

The man turned round to his corporal for enlightenment. Yes, the corporal had heard of atheists before. The species was not entirely unknown. He bent over the sergeant's shoulder and helped him with the spelling. Then everyone filed into another room, leaving me alone in the world.

Soon an air-force padre came into the room. He just stood there for a moment, eyeing me nervously. Then he forced a patronizing smile. 'I see you are down on this list as an atheist,' he giggled at me. 'Now then, what are we going to do with you, eh?'

For a split second a mad thought entered my head that

perhaps they didn't accept atheists in the armed forces. I could be back in Exeter by nightfall.

'Now come on, old chap,' continued the padre, 'I suspect that you aren't really an atheist at all. I think what you really mean is that you are an *agnostic*. Quite a different thing.'

Natural mistake – no harm done. They just liked to get these things straight.

I listened until he was through, and then politely broke the news. Not only was I an atheist, but I actually *knew* what the word meant. An atheist is a person who has no invisible means of support. Reluctantly the padre accepted this awful truth, and eventually I was sworn into the Royal Air Force under a separate oath of allegiance, from which the word 'God' had been duly erased. If I had known the trouble it was going to cause, I think I would have settled for C of E.

This incident seemed to underline for me, right at the start, my relationship with the RAF, which was that of a wart on the smooth features of efficiency.

As at college, the discipline came from above, and not from people organized on their own behalf. They had turned me into something called One-Four-Two-Seven-Five-Seven-Aircraftsman-Turner-stroke-second-class. I was given warm clothing and they were going to teach me a trade, while I would receive my food and living accommodation absolutely free. But, Faust-like, I had been asked to pay with my immortal soul.

My first stop was Weston-super-Mare, where I was put through the preliminary foot-slogging. Squads of us were marched up and down the seafront and cursed at by something that closely resembled a Neanderthal Man. I had the impression that, if sufficiently provoked, this fellow would tear us apart with his teeth. The best thing to do was to keep out of trouble at all costs.

This wasn't as easy as I had thought it would be. Soon I was being pointed out by all and sundry as the most troublesome man in the whole squadron. I hadn't intended it to be this way, but they tell me that one officer reached for the aspirin bottle at the very mention of my name. I seemed never to be out of trouble. The lads in my squad took me to be a very cool customer who had set himself against the Establishment. I think the trouble started when I consistently turned up on parade looking like a walking manure-heap. The inspecting officer raged and stamped, but with little effect on my personal appearance. On the next inspection I would be in trouble again.

Heads were soon craning around, to take a look at this cool blackguard who was defying authority. The truth was that I had no intention of defying anyone, but I always seemed to be caught out when there was an inspection. My time for sprucing up was always at the *end* of the day, when I would wash and shave before going out on the town. But the surprise inspection always caught me unawares.

After I had sent the inspecting officer away, sobbing and twitching, for about the fifth time, the man next to me turned to his mate and whispered, almost reverentially: 'Ee just don't care, do ee!' – to which the other man replied hoarsely: 'Ee as the narve o' the bloody Devil.'

Once again a nickname was pinned on to me. This time, I was 'Red' Turner, the airman who didn't care. Back at the recruiting centre they had put me down as a wireless operator. At home I hadn't even been able to find Luxembourg. I wasn't arguing though, as I'd just found out that the trainee wireless ops were being sent to Blackpool, for classes in morse code. Blackpool was Fun City. The dances were large-scale affairs, held every night of the week at the Winter Gardens and the Tower Ballroom. I had heard that there were three girls to every eligible male.

Blackpool gave me back some of the reassurance that Weston had taken away. The morse classes were something I had a natural aptitude for. Soon I was rattling off code messages at phenomenal speeds, while the instructor begged me to slow down and stop being a bloody show-off. I think this was the first time in my life that I found myself doing something better than anyone else in the place. One of the classes was called 'Interference'. It involved transmitting and receiving through all kinds of distortion, which meant that some of the lads became gibbering wrecks and had to be taken off the course. I managed to sail through all the final exams.

Nevil Skrimshire, my closest friend back at Dulwich, now arrived in Blackpool. He had joined the RAF at about the same time as me, and seemed to have been caught up in the same current of postings. I told him there was no jazz on the scene, so he promptly pushed me into the concert party, in front of a tolerably efficient piano and drums. I found myself playing 'Elmer's Tune' on a borrowed alto sax, before the entire squadron at its passing-out concert. Before this, Skrim had befriended a jazz fanatic called Don Chambers, who came from Sheffield. Don had a vivid imagination which he used instead of actual knowledge about jazz and its performers. He was always making up stories about a mythical jazz record collection which he had at home. He boasted the most incredible, priceless range of collectors' items. Bix in the Ellington brass section, Goodman and Johnny Dodds in the same line-up, Django behind the Mound City Blue Blowers. As soon as anyone brought up the subject of rare jazz records, this enchanting nonsense came gushing forth.

'You like Teschemacher? Yes, I have some rare Tesche-macher. His cornet solos on some of these . . .'

'But Don, Tesch is a *clarinet* player.'

'Oh, ah – yes, of course. But these days he's doubling on cornet, you know.'

'*These* days? I thought Tesch died in thirty-two.'

'Yeah? I mean, yeah, that's what I'm trying to tell you. I have his last records, made in thirty-two. You know, of course, that he died while actually taking a solo on "Basin Street Blues". If you listen closely, you can hear a thudding noise . . .'

What Don lacked in discographical accuracy he made up for in sheer imaginative flow. Once we all went to a meeting of the Blackpool Rhythm Club, having promised to give impromptu talks. My own talk on Benny Carter was a flop – after five minutes I had run out of things to say. Then Don stepped in with a talk on Chicago style, and you should have seen that audience of trusting young enthusiasts as it lapped up every word!

The second of the two W/OP courses took place on a camp called Yatesbury in Wiltshire. This time I failed miserably. The lessons were all about circuits and alternating currents – a language I have never been able to understand. At the end of the course, at the passing-out exam, I handed in a blank sheet of paper, with only my name on the top right-hand corner, and the date.

The instructor stared at this blank sheet of paper for a few moments and then strolled over to where I was sitting. 'I'm not a fool, lad,' he hissed into my ear, 'I know exactly what you are up to. Oh, it doesn't bother me – but for fuck's sake don't make it look so obvious.'

He had thought I was deliberately trying to fail the course, to avoid being sent overseas. The fact was that I knew nothing about radio then, and still do!

The rest of my class was pushed through the maintenance course and went overseas. I remained on the camp for over a year after failing the course. I had been demoted from W/OP to G/D – or General Duties. This meant that for about a year I would heave coal, clean out toilets, or else wander about making myself generally useless.

The Battle of Britain fought itself out, Pearl Harbor dragged America into the war, the Nazis advanced almost to the gates of Moscow, and my brother was transferred from a prison camp in Italy to one of the German stalags. During all this time I remained politically imbecile. If I wanted to see how the war was getting on, I took a squint at the shaded bits on those tiny maps most of the newspapers were printing, showing the extent of the German advance. There were quite a lot of shaded bits in 1943, so I was certain to be heaving a lot of coal for a very long time, either for the RAF or for Adolf and his friends.

There was a revolutionary Socialist in our hut, who thought we should be appealing to the Germans to come over on to our side. He thought that the ordinary people wanted peace, just like everybody else. This interested me.

'Do you mean to say,' I exclaimed, 'that the Germans are just like us? It could be – but what about their lack of humour? They say the best way to make a German happy in his old age is to tell him a joke when he's young.'

'I think you're falling for the usual propaganda line. People are much the same the world over, Mal.'

'But what about the terrible things they do to the British prisoners?'

'Oh? You saw something in the papers?'

'No, in that war film they showed at the Gaumont last week.'

'Christ! And they say the other side goes in for indoctrination!'

Frank, the Socialist revolutionary, was mild-mannered when discussing politics, whereas I tended to get excited and say things without pondering them first. He suggested that I attend the camp discussion circle's meetings with him. The circle met once a week, under the supervision of a large comfortable padre. This padre wanted only a nice orderly discussion group with nobody threatening the status quo. I could sense Frank becoming increasingly annoyed at the lack of open discussion on the important issues of the day.

At the end of one particularly dull meeting, the padre simpered at us and enquired: 'Right, chaps, what shall we talk about next week?'

Frank fixed him with a beatific smile, and replied: 'How

about "Why is the grass green?"' I think the padre got the point.

At Yatesbury, the inevitable Skrimshire turned up, and lost no time in organizing some live jazz. He seemed to act as a catalyst whenever I wasn't getting any music. In this instance he conjured up another guitarist and two amateur trumpet players who were surprisingly good. One of them was called Brian Danks. He was a semi-pro musician who had worked in dance bands in the Midlands. He told me I ought to be learning to read music, so that I could line up some dance-band work after the war. I said, no thanks. As long as I'm dreaming, I would much rather be an actor.

All the hard labour was by now giving me sore fingers. Sometimes I came from work with my hands covered in blisters, so that I could hardly hold the clarinet in my hands. I was also having dizzy spells. I reported sick, and told the medical officer that I thought the work was getting too much for me. He made a sarcastic remark, but after a brief examination his whole attitude changed. He told me to report immediately to sick quarters and get myself to bed. When I arrived I was swaying from side to side. I just managed to undress and get between the hospital sheets before passing out cold. They managed to rouse me about twice every twenty-four hours, for a bite to eat or a routine inspection. Then I would pass back into oblivion again. It was only after I remembered that I had a lot of leave coming to me that I forced myself to sit up and pretend to be feeling much better. If there was any recuperating to be done, I preferred doing it at home.

There was some special 'sick leave' to be added on to my ordinary leave. I had the prospect of a few weeks to spend at home, with nothing to do but lounge. Mum was trying out some addresses in Bristol at the time. I was able to have a good long rest, and to return to camp moderately refreshed.

Up until then, things had been fairly peaceful, but one day I became involved in a nerve-shattering incident. I was abruptly sent for, under escort, and marched towards the adjutant's office. There I was told that they were holding me under suspicion of being an enemy agent. The adjutant came out with it just like that, and proceeded to glare at me. I wondered if I had become light-headed as a result of my recent collapse. Was all this really happening or was I in dream-land still?

The officer handed me a small piece of notepaper. 'Is this your handwriting?' he asked me coldly, exactly the way the Rev

Dixon had done on that earlier occasion. And, just like the other time, I saw that the handwriting was indeed mine. I had been doodling on this slip of paper the day before. While chopping wood in a remote corner of the camp, I had decided to take a rest. Then, to while away a few minutes, I'd compiled a list of place names – mostly some towns in the Midlands where Brian Danks had told me I might look for dance-band work after the war. It had all been an innocent day-dream, a glimpse into an imaginary future – but how was I to explain my innermost secrets to this glowering adjutant, and expect to be understood? Naturally, this man would find it easier to believe that I had been marking down these locations for the Luftwaffe, or something of that sort.

'These are just a few towns, sir, where I plan to look for work after the war.' It all sounded so bloody improbable, put just like that.

'Towns. I see. And how do you account for these repeated references to the commanding officer?'

He handed me the paper again, while his eyes smouldered unpleasantly. Was I going insane? Repeated references to the CO? Then I understood. One of the names on the list was Kidderminster, where Brian came from. I had written it down several times, but to save time I had shortened it to 'Kidd'. And our CO's name was Group Captain Kidd. I tried my best to explain.

The adjutant withdrew for a moment, to confer with another officer. They both kept looking in my direction, scowling. Left alone, I tried to gather my thoughts. Was I about to be taken out and shot, possibly with an unfinished Mars bar dangling pathetically from my lips? Then the two men relaxed their fierce expressions, having come to a final decision about me. I was no more than a harmless lunatic after all. They smiled at me like a couple of benign uncles and the incident was closed.

But now the officers had become aware of my presence on the camp. What was I loafing about Yatesbury for, writing out stupid lists, when I could be doing something more useful? Not very long after this incident, I was sent for yet again.

This time it was a different officer, an affable man wearing something that looked like a smile. 'Ah, yes,' he said, 'Turner.' I was a marked man.

'You wanted to see me, sir?'

'Well yes, I did rather. Let me see, Turner, you've been with us now . . . rather more than a year, I believe?'

He was beaming at me, but I guessed I wasn't in line for a gold watch. He paced up and down for a few seconds, then started to talk about the world situation. He said it was time everybody started pulling their weight.

'No reason at all why you shouldn't be sent on another course. There must be *something* you can do. What were you before the war?'

'Played the clarinet for a while, sir, after I left school. Then I took up saxophone. Perhaps if I had some training . . . one of the RAF bands?'

'Not exactly what we had in mind. This war has got to be *won*. Surely, Turner, we can find you a useful job – something you have a natural aptitude for.'

I racked my brains, but nothing came readily to mind, I could do a first-rate impression of two Glaswegian drunks in a railway carriage, but there seemed no point in mentioning this. For several moments he remained silent, while I tried to recall a couple of natural aptitudes that maybe I had forgotten about. Then the officer came out of his reverie and spoke. 'Actually, Turner, I know your type. I've met it before. The Dreamer – chap with his head in the clouds. Make a damn good fighter pilot. Yes, we'll take a chance on you – and put you down for flying school.'

Now I have never been particularly fond of heights. I get dizzy wearing thick crêpe soles, so this last announcement came as something of a shock. It was fine working for the Royal Air Force, but not if they were going to start sending me up in planes. I worried about this for weeks, but then came the splendid news that they weren't putting me down for flying school after all, but for a course in codes and cyphers. This sounded a bit more like it, but what I didn't know at the time was that nobody in their right mind was volunteering for the cypher course. True, you enjoyed the benefit of rapid promotion and good pay – but on passing the course most cypher personnel were sent overseas. And this meant getting into the action, although nobody bothered to explain this to me at the time.

There were two fairly simple courses, at Cardington and Oxford respectively, and then I became a sergeant on full pay. I hadn't been exactly brilliant, but they had pushed me through the cypher classes somehow. At Oxford I went dancing almost every night, taking advantage of the very low admission prices offered to servicemen, both British and American.

This was a time when sporadic fighting had broken out between GIs and British servicemen in the dance halls. At first the punch-ups were caused by the competition for local women, who often deserted their English boyfriends in the quest for dollars and the irresistible double Scotch. Later, one felt that an element of racialism was creeping in. Some of these GIs hailed from Georgia and Alabama, and were aggrieved to find that British dance halls did not have a colour bar, so that anyone could buy a ticket and dance with the local girls. The limeys, complained a few of these white supermen, didn't know how to run their own dances.

One of these brawls had turned a bit nasty, so I backed away and stood at a safe distance, as the service police charged in to restore order. Next to me stood a tall, dignified US sergeant. He turned to me and shook his head in a dispirited sort of way. 'All this is so damned stupid,' he muttered.

'Quite crazy,' I agreed. 'What started all this, anyway?'

'Aw, some of our boys kind of forgot their manners. So damned stupid. You know what they've started to call you British? Nigger-lovers! Yeah – how about that!'

'Gosh. As if it mattered what colour a man is, just so long as he is a nice person.'

'There, you see!' snapped the American indignantly, 'you're just as bad as all the rest.' And he stalked off angrily into the crowd.

I passed my cypher tests in due course, which meant that I had now moved up from aircraftsman second-class to sergeant in one go. In the normal course of events I should have been sent straight overseas, but I was lucky to get a temporary posting to Pitreavie Castle, in Scotland. This brief respite was extended over a period of some weeks, due to the fact that someone in the admin department had mislaid my posting instructions. During this time, I worked under some WAAF officers in the cypher wing, which was a devastating experience. A sergeant had to address his officer as 'mum' – something I found it very hard to do without breaking into a giggle. Some of these girls were not much older than me, and oozed sex appeal. I enjoyed myself at this RAF station very much. Perhaps too much, for by the time someone spotted the posting error, I had somehow managed to forget about all but the immediate present. I was also playing regularly with a NAAFI band, sensing a rapid improvement in my tone and technique on the clarinet. The three stripes on my tunic also helped to convince me that I was not a total failure after all. It was foolish, however, to imagine that this could possibly last.

When my overseas posting arrived, I was not psychologically prepared for it. Now I was curtly informed that a troop-ship was waiting to hoist anchor at Blackpool, and that I had better get there in time – or else!

The next few hours were just about the most unpleasant ones I have ever spent, and I remember wishing I was dead at one stage. Some nit-wit had spilled tea over my posting date, and now I was getting all the blame for it. At Blackpool I was cursed at and made to do everything at the double. I was called a rogue and malingerer, then made to fill in forms, get fitted up with tropical kit and run puffing and choking to a place where they gave me the required number of heavy injections. An officer took me to the quayside at a very brisk pace. I was in full kit and staggering under the large kit bag. My arm had begun to throb painfully and the officer was shouting obscenities into my right ear. If I had been a masochist, I would have been having the time of my life.

I made it as far as the quayside and then fell sprawling. I was barely conscious when the officer bent over me to inform me that the administrative error had been spotted and that everyone was sorry about the mistake.

'You are quite entitled to make out a complaint, if you want to,' he told me. 'I'll show you how to make out the form, if you like. Least I can do.'

'No thanks,' I croaked at him, 'all I want to do is lie down and go to sleep.'

Two airmen helped me on board. They took me to a small cabin, where I was able to spend the entire trip, instead of having to sleep in a hammock along with the other postings. My cabin did have one other occupant, though, a stocky little Australian sergeant called Starky-Jones. I looked across blearily at my fellow-traveller.

'Welcome aboard,' said Starky, 'you look as though you've just been on a commando course.'

'Where are we heading for?' was all I could find to say. 'Nobody tells me a damned thing. All they do is call me names.'

'Somewhere in West Africa,' said my companion. 'Other than that I couldn't say. Cigarette?'

Starky was rather taken aback when he found out that I didn't smoke or drink, and that I was crammed full of Socialist nonsense. But he was a big-hearted man, and decided to overlook these little things. We were on a Dutch vessel, with a crew that was mainly Indonesian. For most of the voyage, we argued with one another about the Race Question. Starky implored me not to be sentimental about the natives. All they ever understood was the whip.

Starky-Jones was a kindly soul, deep down. At meal-times he passed me his helping of semolina pudding as a matter of routine. So, in the end, did just about everybody else at our table. This pudding was always incredibly salty, though I usually managed to force it all down.

Halfway through the journey, someone suggested that we ought to complain about the salt, as it was getting so that no one except me was able to face up to the semolina. This we did, but the kitchen promptly denied that any salt at all was used in the puddings. Starky and I, and a couple of others, went down to investigate. The first thing we saw was this huge cauldron of semolina pudding on the boil. Leaning over it, and stirring it with a large wooden implement, stood the little Indonesian chef – stripped to the waist. We watched in fascinated silence as the sweat poured off him in a steady stream, plopping down into the grey mixture.

'Uncouth, that's what they are,' insisted Starky as we returned to our cabin. 'Don't tell me that hasn't put you off darkies once and for all.' 'It's certainly put me off the pudding,' was all I could say. 'I don't think I could face any more semolina after this.'

We finally arrived at the port of Lagos, from where we travelled inland to Maiduguri. It was the last I ever saw of the little Australian. Maiduguri, a mud-hut community situated hundreds of miles from any town and thousands of miles from the nearest jazz-record shop, was to be my home for the next eighteen months. At least I wasn't going to die from an enemy bullet in this God-forsaken hole – more likely it would be from malaria or typhoid.

Or perhaps from the sheer, unrelieved boredom of this unattractive place. The old lags in the mess had a saying. After six months at Maiduguri, you started talking to the lizards on your window-sill; after another six months they started talking back to you. It was Christmas Day soon after my arrival, celebrated with a giant sing-song in the main building.

'I'm dreaming of a white mistress,' was sung in fervent tones. Nobody paid too much attention when I claimed I was a jazz musician, and by that time I scarcely believed it myself. I had stuffed a very cheap clarinet into my kit bag before leaving the UK, but now the wood had warped in the intense heat and I couldn't get even a squeak out of it. It didn't matter much anyway, for no one would have listened. All the boys wanted was to sing at the tops of their voices, when they were not discussing their home towns with one another. Reminiscing about home was the only way to pass the interminable hours. Being a non-boozer, there wasn't even this way to help the time go by. To make matters worse, the water tasted strongly of chlorine, even when mixed with the cheap orange concentrate they sold at the bar.

On the first day at Maiduguri, I introduced myself as Bruce Turner, for it seemed a good idea to drop my first name once and for all. 'Malcolm' wasn't a bad name if you happened to be a Highland chieftain, or perhaps a middle-class country squire, but it wouldn't help me to feel like 'one of the lads'.

It was, however, a custom in the sergeants' mess for newcomers to be given affectionate pet-names, and the one I was saddled with right from the start was 'Trot'. I suppose this was on account of my tendency to quote Trotsky any time I felt like running the system down – which was often. I had never been able to get through two consecutive pages of Trotsky's writings without falling into a coma, but the man's sheer boring intellectualism appealed to me. One sure way of winning a political argument, or at least bringing it to a close, was to quote from Trotsky and watch the hunted look that would come into your adversary's face. *He* hadn't read any Trotsky, so how could he possibly follow the discussion to its next logical phase!

Then the boys thought they would play a trick on me. A new sergeant was to be posted to our camp, and this man was known to be a devout Marxist of the orthodox school. It was no secret that the newcomer admired Stalin and thought of Trotsky only as a rather unpleasant pain in the arse. When this new man arrived, he was nicknamed 'Timmo' after one of the Russian generals. He was then sent to occupy the spare bed in my room, with the assurance that the two of us would have 'a great deal in common'. Thereupon the boys sat back and waited for the sparks to fly. It didn't work out at all as they had planned. 'Timmo' and 'Trot' soon became the closest of friends.

Politically, the two of us couldn't agree about a thing, but it didn't matter. It was so much more stimulating to argue about Socialism than to walk across to the mess and watch people throwing up over the furniture.

I believe I would have found Maiduguri much harder to bear if it hadn't been for those philosophical set-tos with the redoubtable Timmo. Time passed very much more quickly than it would have otherwise, until suddenly the war with Germany was over. The Red Army had taken Berlin, with my vociferous room-mate egging them on for every inch of the way. Now the fighting had stopped. A letter came for me. Tren was not only alive and well, but back at home and going hammer and tongs at the Bruckner symphonies.

The news that my brother was safe at home affected me in a curious way. I think I must have subconsciously written him off in my mind. At any rate, I felt great surprise as well as relief – as if someone long dead had been miraculously brought back into the world. Now all I could think about was getting home, going back to the old pleasures I had had before. There would be jazz records and hall cricket, swiss tarts for tea and the occasional Laurel and Hardy film. And then there was symphonic music, which I'd never taken much interest in up to that moment. Now I began to wonder about the symphony. Had I perhaps been missing out on something all this time?

I wandered over to the sergeants' mess, feeling strangely elated. There was a wireless set in the bar, and a symphonic work was just starting up. Any moment now, I thought, someone is going to walk over to it and change the station. Nobody did. Everyone was too excited about the war coming to an end. Through all the crackle I heard the work to its conclusion. At the end, someone announced the name of the work – the Pastoral Symphony of Vaughan Williams. I had come over to an appreciation of composed music at last.

On the way home, I had to sleep in a hammock just like everyone else. All I could think of was London, with its attractive place names. I had managed to get hold of a street map, which I studied intently during the entire voyage.

'Marble Arch!' I repeated over and over again, savouring every syllable. 'Kensington! Golders Green by moonlight!'

I hardly knew London at all, but already I was thinking of it as the most exciting place in the world. Soon I would be joining my brother in this veritable Shangri-La.

The voyage home appeared to be taking longer than an all-Yorkshire opening stand. Then I found a book in the small ship's library, a simple introduction to the great composers. Every day, after that, I amused myself by planning the course of my future musical listening. Debussy sounded like the sort of composer I could get along with, and Delius's tone poems would have to come into it somewhere. Before we had arrived at Morecambe, I was a rabid fan of the impressionists, although I hadn't heard a note of their music.

It was great to be back in England again. They now sent me to a RAF camp in a remote corner of Hampshire, but I didn't mind. I joined a music circle, then quickly became engrossed in Brahms, Sibelius and Ravel. This took my mind off the depressing fact that I had no jazz-record collection any more. All my wonderful records had been left behind, on the camp at Yatesbury, when I had been sent overseas. I often wonder if they were able to find good homes. Now I didn't have these to listen to, and my clarinet was out of action. Consequently, my return to the jazz scene was delayed for another three or four months.

Listening to the romantic First Symphony of Sibelius was not the same as listening to a tenor chorus by Lester Young. A symphony is like a great novel, with its carefully delineated plots, but jazz is more like an urgent conversation. It invites an active response. The listener finds himself personally involved. He identifies with the musician he is listening to, has the urge to dance or, better still, to go out and buy an instrument of his own – anything but just sit there. Panassie described jazz as performers' music – and he was right first time. What a pity he changed his mind later! Jazz is the performer making his own music in his own way and, after a while, even Sibelius was not going to pacify me for long.

Labour won a landslide victory at the polls; Japanese civilians were used as guinea-pigs to test the new A-Bomb, and rumour had it that certain age groups would not be demobilized as speedily as was at first thought. The fighting was over, but I would be in uniform for some time to come.

'Never mind,' said my brother, 'time will pass more quickly, now that you are listening to serious music at last.'

He meant symphonies, as opposed to jazz. In those days, the recording companies were listing their composed works under the heading serious music, and their jazz under light entertainment. This was pretty funny, when one considered the last tortured years of Bix, Billie, Lester and others. Tren, however, was being flippant, so I didn't let it worry me. He sometimes enjoyed putting me on.

Tren bought me a recording of the 'Prélude à l'Après Midi d'une Faune' by way of a belated homecoming gift. I almost wore it out with repeated playing, but time continued to drag. I kept thinking my watch had stopped. RAF Stoney Cross was about twelve miles from Southampton, and there were dances at the Civic Hall almost every evening. Debussy was all very fine, but he wasn't able to take my mind off girls. There was plenty of RAF transport into town, and every day I had to be on one of these crowded little trucks that made off towards the Southampton bus station. If there hadn't been any transport, I am quite sure I would have tried to make the journey on foot.

Things were happening in the towns which could have happened only in the aftermath of a great military victory. People were dancing and singing in the streets, and you don't find the staid Englishman doing these things unless he has become light-headed. But we had come through the war together and there was much celebrating to be done. Everywhere one encountered this feverish, scarcely articulate bonhomie.

Once I missed the last transport back to camp. As I arrived at the bus station, there was the little RAF vehicle disappearing round a corner. The driver of a huge double-decker bus was just coming off duty.

'Hop in, mate,' he shouted at me, 'we'll catch up with them at the next turning.'

He had to shout at me again before I realized that he was serious. Soon we were speeding through the countryside, just one skinny, frightened airman and a driver who now had the set facial expression of a contestant at Brands Hatch. We never did catch up with that air-force truck, but it wasn't for want of trying. This monstrous double-decker took me all the way to camp, after a nightmare journey that I will never easily forget. I jumped down, my face an ashen grey colour.

'Very many thanks,' I mumbled, 'you shouldn't have gone to all that trouble.'

'What? Oh, that's all right, mate,' said the friendly bus driver absently. 'What beats me is how the other bloke got away from me. He must have been doing at least fifty – and on these country lanes! I tell you, some of these young drivers – they just don't care.'

The corporal at the guard-room looked surprised. Airmen had been known to hire taxis, if this was the only way they could get back to camp, but never a public transport bus! It must have been quite a sight, but somehow this was the way things often happened that mad, hilarious summer of 1945.

5   Brave New World

Returning from the wars, it wasn't long before I discovered that rhythm clubs were a thing of the past. They had been replaced by jazz clubs, and these worked on a different principle altogether. The old pre-war rhythm clubs had mainly featured good recorded jazz. They had been run by record collectors who waxed lyrical on such matters as the Iambic Concept in Early Negro Folk Song. The post-war jazz clubs were run by a similar type of enthusiast at first, but very soon they began to do quite well, and were then taken over by enterprising business promoters. These sat in little back rooms, away from the incomprehensible din, adding up figures and thinking of the Iambic Concept only rarely.

Personally I didn't mind who ran the club sessions. What worried me was that the friendly old free-for-all jam session was now on the way out. In the past it had been a regular practice to invite musicians up for a blow at the end of a club meeting. These sessions appeared to illustrate that jazz was very much a musical Esperanto; musicians who had never even met one another before could sit together and hold forth in this common language, but with the demise of the rhythm club had come the simultaneous demise of the jam session.

The jazz clubs now revolved around fixed regular combos, who kept to their own set repertoire and frowned upon sitters-in. Another curious fact was that this music of a thousand styles had now been whittled down to only two – traditional New Orleans and modern progressive. If you didn't happen to conform to either of these stereotypes, you just didn't have anywhere you could go and play. As far as the traditionalist type of club was concerned, the sound of jazz had become restricted to the extent that one band sounded very much like another. Whichever club you happened to be in you would hear the same tunes played in very much the same manner. Everywhere, kids in corduroy trousers and duffel-coats came into smoky little underground cellars to play and dance in this extraordinarily predictable way. This was the new indoctrination. The musician was no longer at the helm – only the pundits, expounding their well-publicized theories and calling the tune.

For a while I wasn't even aware of these changes, having become far more absorbed in the classics. I hadn't played the clarinet or bought a jazz record for almost two years, but I was getting a lot of pleasure out of listening to the Sibelius symphonies. Then the pendulum swung the other way. I became restless, identifying this change of mood as a desire to get back to the clarinet and to music-making again. I was now fidgeting in my seat during a recording of the great Seventh Symphony.

'Perhaps you're not quite ready for Sibelius,' suggested Tren. 'Why not try something with more of a tune to it? Here is a work for violin and piano . . .'

'Got any more of those hazel-nut bars? Why don't we buy some before the shops close?'

'Later. Come on, now. I want to know what you think about Franck's sonata.'

'A good singer, but I still think Bing was the greatest of them all.'

'Oh all right, let's go and get the chocolate.'

There was no mistaking the symptoms. I liked listening to highbrow music but now I was feeling the old urge to get back on the clarinet again. I wanted to blow some jazz, but there was nowhere to go. Post-war dance music had gone all professional and streamlined, where it hadn't gone into the trad clubs. Young musicians of the modern school now sat in big, sleek commercial bands and waited for their chance to shine. Under the batons of Roy Fox, Oscar Rabin and Geraldo modern jazz sizzled away and waited to explode. At odd, unexpected moments, modernism burst through the rigid confines of orchestrated schmaltz, resulting in arguments, and even in sackings. The man who was now rather left out in the cold was the self-taught player with a 'thirties' style and a home-made technique. Musicians who were unable to read the dots didn't stand a chance. The 'natural' musician had about as much social prestige as the natural child.

Looking around post-war London for somewhere to play, I felt rather like Rip Van Winkle rising from the long sleep and searching around for some familiar landmarks.

One weekend, I applied for a leave pass and then decided to spend it in London, instead of heading for my mother's address in Bristol. I had found a cheap Buscher alto in one of the second-hand shops, and was anxious to try it out. All I knew about saxophones was that the gold-plated ones cost more than the silver-plated ones. Mine was a sort of dull grey, with a spot of green tarnish here and there. I wondered if it would last through a jam session without some of the keys clattering on to the floor.

My plan was a simple one. I would get to London by train, then buy a *Melody Maker* at the station bookstall. There had to be something in the 'clubs' column, I thought. Somewhere there had to be a place where guests were cordially invited to sit in. Then, provided George Shearing was not around, I would be all set for a good time.

To my chagrin, all I could find was an address in Oxford Street calling itself the Feldman Club. You wrote off to a place in Edgware for membership forms. Acting on an impulse, I travelled to Edgware by tube.

Papa Feldman was intrigued by my unexpected and completely senseless visit. 'You could have signed forms at the club. What is it about Edgware? You wanted to see some of our fine old buildings?' He had never met such an enthusiastic jazz fan. 'Stay for something to eat,' he chuckled. 'I'll tell you about my son, Victor.'

Victor Feldman was still only a kid in short pants when I paid this visit to London. I had already seen him in a short musical film, beating it out on the drums like any veteran. He was currently being billed as the Kid Krupa, which just about summed up his astonishing talents. The Feldman Club was built around Vic's show drumming, but I found out there was also a time at the end of the evening when guests would be invited up.

'Bring that sax of yours,' said Papa Feldman as I took my leave. 'We'll fit you in during the last two numbers. You're a member now – you can do anything you want.'

That evening I arrived at the Feldman Club just as things had started up. There were two tenor-sax players in full cry, one of them a tall good-looking girl. They played with a forcefulness and confidence that stopped me in my tracks. I had brought my own alto along, but now saw that there was no way I could go up there and compete with players like Jimmy Skidmore and Kathy Stobart. A noisy Dutchman, gaunt and wild-eyed, sat next to me during the performance. All through the evening, he heckled the musicians in hoarse, peevish undertones. He used an insulting word which at the time was only vaguely familiar to me – he called the music 'bebop'.

At the end of the evening I went up with my alto for the two final numbers. Alongside Jim and Kathy I felt as if I was playing on a paper and comb. I went back to where I had been sitting. The Dutchman's face was now wreathed in smiles.

'That was what it needed,' he said effusively. 'You showed them what it was all about. You didn't play a note of bebop.'

I had a faint idea he had just handed me a very special kind of bouquet.

After Stoney Cross I was sent to Bourne, near Cambridge, where I had a few more months to wait until my demob number came up. At Bourne, I met a very small, bespectacled airman who owned a set of drums. The remarkable thing about Billy Kaye was that he had everyone on the camp leaping about at his bidding, regardless of rank. He had become what can only be described as a self-appointed entertainments manager for the whole area. If Billy wanted a camp concert, then there would be a camp concert, and who do you think would be the star of the show?

When Billy wanted to form a jazz quartet, with me on alto, I simply sat back and let it happen.

We played concerts, NAAFI dances and cabarets at the officers' mess. At all of these functions, Billy ordered everyone about with a cool disregard for their status. All I knew was that I was getting into action again, with a chance to play regular jazz solos about twice a week. This kept me happy for a time.

But now the machinery of demobilization seemed to be grinding to a halt. I would be lucky if I was out of the RAF by next spring. The situation required some thought.

'Billy,' I confided in him one morning, 'I can't stand much more of this. I am seriously thinking of trying to work my ticket. There must be a way I can get myself fired.'

'Impossible. How would you go about it? By pretending to go round the bend? But everyone knows you are a complete nut. They wouldn't think anything had changed.'

One of the nice things about Billy was his engaging candour.

'Wait and see,' I retorted. I had always fancied myself as an actor. Now I would put on a display that would rock the thespian world.

I had never got on very well with my WAAF officer. She was a lean, hatchet-faced woman who could never seem to get it into her head that I was merely slow at my work, and not a complete imbecile. One morning, after I had been given several verbal trouncings by this woman, I decided that the time had come. I took a deep breath, and started to moan horribly. I clutched at my forehead, emitted one or two mirthless laughs, and staggered about the room. Then I went on with my work as if nothing had happened. The woman's face had gone as white as a sheet. It wasn't until some days later that I found that the ruse had worked. I was to be sent to an address in Brighton for psychiatric analysis. With luck, I would be out of uniform by the end of the month.

The nerve specialist in Brighton was full of concern for my state of mental health, which he found to be in need of a thoroughly good overhaul.

'You worry too much,' he concluded, after making the usual tests. 'You're a bundle of nerves. Try to relax. But there's nothing seriously wrong. Why on earth did they bother to send you all the way down here?'

I felt my chances of escaping from the air force slowly slipping away.

'Two or three times,' I explained to him, in a quiet apologetic voice, 'I've had this urge to bite my WAAF officer. Of course, it passes very quickly – but all the same . . .'

'Odd. Why on earth should you want to do that?'

'I get terribly hungry at times. Maybe I lack vitamins.'

'Any other problems?'

'Hate crowds. Can't stand crowds. I feel people are hemming me in on all sides. If I could just get away . . .'

The man shone lights into my eyes and then walked around me several times, tapping things.

'A simple nervous condition,' he concluded. 'Try and relax more. Eat as much as you can – chew each mouthful seventeen times. Good day.'

The trip down to Brighton had not been an entirely wasted effort. On my return to RAF Bourne I was transferred from the cypher office to a lonely part of the camp, where I was placed in sole charge of a food store. This opened up some wonderful possibilities for day-dreaming, sometimes for hours on end with nobody to interrupt. But the months dragged on until at last my number came up. The clothing issued to me at the demob centre in Uxbridge was unspeakable – everything seemed to be in faded dark blue and of sombre, funereal design. To celebrate my freedom I took my little book of clothing coupons down to

Cecil Gee's in Charing Cross Road, and splashed out on some garish American styles. I had some savings stashed away, but sooner or later I would certainly have to think about finding a job. It was either that or go on a rigid diet of breadcrumbs.

Tren and I shared cheap digs near Hammersmith for a while. Mother had moved to London by this time, and was good for a few bob whenever I needed anything. It was more or less taken for granted that I would be sponging off the two of them until a job came up – but what sort of job? I couldn't read music, so the musical profession was out. Maybe I would have a go at being an actor or something. But first there had to be a few weeks of pleasurable relaxation. I took myself to the Hammersmith Palais, dressed like a skinny transatlantic hep-cat, painfully conscious of the fact that at twenty-three I had still not made love to a girl. This was serious, and had to be put right before I could set my mind to other things.

Sex wasn't at all pleasant the first time around. I felt that I had been cheated, and was quite rude to the poor girl afterwards, a fairly standard reaction with the immature and befuddled. At the end, all I could feel was: 'That's got *that* over and done with. Now it's back to my *real* thrill – music.' But playing jazz records, interspersed with some classical works, gets to be a bore if you keep it up for several hours every day. I was driven by sheer, inexpressible boredom to look for work. Someone told me about an office in Leicester Square where one queued up for crowd parts in British films. What was not explained to me was that queueing lasted for hours and you were lucky if you got as far as the desk. I had two unsuccessful attempts, but then gave it up as a waste of time.

The second time I tried, a long stringy youth stood behind me and chattered, pointing out that I stood not a chance in hell of obtaining work, even if I did manage to see anyone. I didn't have the necessary qualifications.

'You probably aren't in Equity,' he said. 'No? I thought as much. To find stage or screen parts, you have to be in Equity, you know.'

I promised to go and join immediately, but there were more problems.

'Not so fast. Ever done any acting before?'

'No, how could I, I'm not even in Equity.'

'Just as I thought. Now, to get on their books, you have to show them that you are actually in the profession, and not just an outsider trying to take the bread from their mouths.

You have to have done some stage work.'

'Yes, but in order to *get* stage work . . .'

'Exactly. Coming for coffee?'

The stringy youth plied me with coffee and further advice. Had I come straight from college into the armed forces, when the war started? Ah, he thought so. Well, then, there was the problem solved. I could apply for a government grant. All I had to do was to claim Interrupted Education. They would push me into RADA as a subsidized pupil. He suggested that I meet him on the following day, when he would be happy to provide more details.

It wasn't until I'd had two more meetings with this bloke that I sensed something not being quite right. He would say peculiar things, such as that I would look even *more* attractive if I wore bright-yellow socks with the dark-brown ensemble, and that my hair would look twice as devastating with the application of a little Brylcreem. At last I understood, and wafted my enticing presence out of the poor man's life. It was a case of having to be cruel to be kind.

At the Royal Academy they were most helpful, but not exactly encouraging. If I decided to attend the auditions, which were not for some time, I would need to prepare two set speeches, one from Shakespeare and one from a contemporary playwright, but it would be a shame if I built my hopes up too high.

Here was the old vicious circle again. I had to be a good actor in order to go and learn to be a good actor, otherwise I would not be able to pass the entrance test. I hastily made arrangements to see an ageing ex-actress who took classes in speech-training and deportment. My interview with her didn't do a lot for my self-esteem.

'An actor? Whatever makes you think you could become an actor?'

'Don't know really. I always felt I had some talent for it.'

'And who has led you to believe this?'

'Gosh, I dunno. My family – one or two friends.'

'I see. And upon what have they based this belief? Have they seen you perform upon a stage?'

'Nope. That is, not really. What I mean is, I do impressions sometimes. Different accents – stuff like that . . .'

'Hardly a basis for the dramatic stage. Now I must inform you that the waiting-list for the Royal Academy is rather long. Do you not feel that we would be wasting our time, preparing you for an audition which might never take place?'

'Well, I heard that these government grants . . .'

'You would indeed be lucky. With no stage experience at all, I can just see the academy rushing to subsidize someone like you. Forgive me, it is necessary to be brutally frank!'

Having successfully dampened my spirits, this tired Desdemona took me on as a pupil. I paid for a short course of sporadic insults and at the end of it all I turned my back upon the acting profession. The woman was right. Who in their right mind would want to bother with *me*! My self-confidence was now at its lowest ebb. I turned back to music because there wasn't anything else I could do. Blowing into a saxophone, at least I felt like somebody important – usually the jazz giant whose phrases I was copying at the time. One major problem was that every time I started to play, irate neighbours pounded upon the walls. The only thing was to find myself an amateur band, however dire, who would not mind me augmenting their line-up from time to time. This would be better than blowing into a rolled-up towel two or three times a week.

Soon I was getting myself booked for crummy little makeshift dances in the seedier halls and back rooms of outer London. These dates didn't turn up very often, so when they did I was grateful for the chance to play some jazz without anyone pleading with me to stop. On one of these gigs I even got paid. I was offered 'something towards expenses' plus, in the interval, 'all the bread and butter you can eat'. It was better than playing in the digs for nothing at all, so who was I to complain?

The evening started quietly, with two couples on the floor. At the ticket desk, a stout middle-aged gent waited for more customers to arrive. He waited in vain.

The band consisted of two altos, one pianist and one drummer. The latter was not being very kind to his bass drum. I began to wish I had stayed at home and blown some jazz phrases into the wardrobe. The woman upstairs would have rapped on my ceiling, but no doubt this would have swung more than the drummer. Then three stubbly-chinned figures pushed their way past the ticket desk.

These men wore shabby, nondescript suits and open-necked shirts, and for a few moments they stood glaring about them at the almost empty room. The man at the ticket desk was tactless enough to ask them for some admission money. They pushed him so hard that his head smacked up against the wall. Then, with every evidence of enjoyment, they started to beat up the male dancers, while their partners let out falsetto shrieks of protest.

I turned to the other altoist, to ask him whether he knew the chords of 'Perdido'. I had remembered what happens in the movies, when a fight breaks out in a saloon. The band keeps on playing, and is largely ignored. Now and then a musician might have to duck his head to avoid a flying chair, but that is all. But the other altoist had blood streaming down his face, and so was in no position to think about the chords of 'Perdido'. I realized that one of the three hooligans had found his way up on to the bandstand, and was not granting immunity to anyone. Things were really going a bit too far.

As far as I could see, the time had come for someone to take decisive action, so I laid my saxophone under the piano and decisively stepped behind a potted fern. If God had meant saxophone players to be heroic, he would have given us muscles.

It was no use. One of them spotted me lurking there in the shadows. His first blow landed on my chest, and the second one smashed into my face, very hard. It was the first time I had experienced physical violence, and I was very surprised. The hooligan was drawing back his fist and taking careful aim. At this juncture, I did the only thing that seemed to make any sense. I turned my back on him and sat down to mop up the blood with my handkerchief.

'I don't get it,' I said indignantly, over my shoulder, 'what did you go and do that for?'

The man just stood there, his mouth hanging open. I could see that he was very taken aback. He grinned at me, almost apologetically, and shuffled away. I suppose a pacifist would have said that I had scored a great victory.

I wasn't feeling exactly victorious. I arrived home with an upper lip that was three times its normal size but, miraculously, with no teeth missing. All I had lost was my desire to play the sax in public – ever again.

My mother was most sympathetic, but reminded me that I had come to this pass on account of having no work to keep me occupied. Work! Hold on, I said. This was no time to be throwing that kind of language around. Mother had moved to Kensington, where she was doing a brief residency. I had the small spare bedroom, but now she told me it was high time I made a small contribution towards the rent. The idea of me going out to work had obviously become an obsession with her.

She made repeated references to it during the next few days, which saddened me because she had always been such a brilliant conversationalist before. In the end I made up my mind that I would humour her by finding something – but what? To buy time, and in order to reflect on this problem undisturbed, I went to the Hammersmith Palais and sat looking down from the balcony upon Lou Preager's balding pate. I wanted to think very seriously about this business of actually going to work. It was not a decision that ought to be taken lightly.

My reflections were cut short by someone calling my name. The someone was a jazz guitarist called Stan. He said he had been searching for me high and low. 'I've come to warn you,' said Stan. 'Billy Kaye is in town and he wants you to join his band. Perhaps you could go somewhere and hide . . .'

'*Me*! Billy wants *Me* in his band! But listen, I don't read music.'

I never used the word 'can't', preferring to make it sound as if I abstained on principle. Stan explained that there wouldn't be much reading involved. The Billy Kaye band was only a five-piece, but after they had completed their winter season in Chelmsford they would be ready to take on another front-line instrument.

'Seriously,' continued Stan, 'after we're through at Chelmsford, the job is yours if you want it.'

'Can't wait,' I burbled. 'Why don't I come down to Chelmsford and get used to the arrangements? The money isn't important – I could just sit there and get the feel of the music. I could pay my own expenses, maybe help with the heavy equipment . . .'

'You must be joking! I mean, we could find you some cheap digs, and get you a few bob towards your food, but that's about all.'

'Marvellous! I'll just go home and pack a few things.'

And that was how I came into the band business. At Chelmsford Town Hall, Billy used trumpet and four rhythm, but with a sax added to the front line we had to use a few written parts. The reading was easy – the title of the tune was written in big bold letters at the top of the page, and then the melody line was written out. All I had to do was follow the trumpet in unison if I already knew the tune. We played a number of familiar things like 'Kiss Goodnight', 'How High the Moon' and 'Apple Honey'. Halfway down the alto part, I would come to the instruction: Solo Ad Lib, my cue for improvisation.

These free solo passages were usually referred to by Billy and his musicians as 'The Jazz'. When these were under way, nobody paid much attention to the paying customer. On the dance floor, middle-aged couples and callow youngsters groped for a point of contact with the queer sound, wondering where the melody had got to. Now and then, but not very often, the boys would condescend to throw in a waltz medley, but with that out of the way it was back once again to 'The Jazz'.

Chelmsford was in the grip of a record-breaking cold spell. Snow lay around for the entire winter, causing havoc everywhere. The town hall just didn't have a heating system that could cope with this intense cold. The band played in thick woolly sweaters with the initials B.K. on the front, while early arrivals clustered around the radiators or sat with their overcoats on for the first hour or so.

Every week I took a sum of money out of my savings account so that I could pay for my bed and board. Billy and the boys made a small contribution out of their own pay packets, but it didn't amount to a great deal. The Musicians' Union would have been fascinated at the spectacle of a saxophone player begging to be allowed to play for almost nothing.

'Wait until we get to Cambridge,' Billy consoled me. 'Everyone knows me there. That is where I live, and you can stay at my place for free and still be on the same money as the rest of the boys.'

Cambridge was the band's next stopping place. We hadn't booked any work there but Billy was confident that he would be able to take charge once we arrived, as he was a most respected figure in this town. As we drew closer to the end of our Chelmsford season, Billy became increasingly lyrical about the opportunities that lay in store. He now accepted me as a regular member of his band. I wasn't so hot on the saxophone but it was discovered that I could take a mean vocal. One night I had stood up and warbled on 'Be Careful, It's My Heart', just the way Bing Crosby had sung it in the movie. I'd meant it only in fun, but ever afterwards Billy insisted on featuring me in two vocals a night. The crowd liked it too, since it made a change after all the jazz. It was rotten singing, but quite good mimicry, so I managed to win more applause than the other numbers received.

At last we were in Cambridge, ready to take the place by storm. By this time some work had been lined up for the band, but once these commitments were behind us it all became very quiet in the town. Apparently the Cambridge promoters could be separated into two categories: the ones who had never heard of Billy and the ones who knew him only too well. But the diminutive drummer would not give up – he worked ceaselessly to set the band before the public gaze. He was certainly not short on grit, but it was a losing battle. Soon the trumpet player, Derry Gascoyne, and I were having to queue up outside the British Restaurant every day for a special cheap lunch. It was the only meal we could afford, but in the evening there would be sandwiches in the digs and enormous quantities of strong tea.

During these few months I made a great hole in my wartime savings. In a very real sense I was actually *paying* to be a professional musician, and yet I might never have become a full-time saxist at all but for this invaluable stint with Billy Kaye. I do not regret the experience for one moment and in any case, for a bumblingly inadequate player like me this was probably the only way in.

It was only Billy's sunny optimism that kept us all going. Fame and fortune were always just around the corner.

'Fellers,' said Billy one day, 'our luck seems to have changed at last. We have been picked for a big variety concert at the Civic Hall. Star billing! Some fabulous names on the bill, too. I told you it was just a question of time.'

'Wait a minute. Who's putting on this mammoth show, Billy?'

'I am. Hey, what's up? Why are you looking at me like that?'

Billy had staked everything on this last desperate throw. He had even persuaded a couple of jazz drummers, Flash Winstone and Murray Faber, to appear on the show as comedians. True, these two guys really *were* funny, but they hadn't had much experience on the boards. Murray, whose real name was Mario Fabrizi, later joined the Goons as an extremely talented comic, but all this raw talent wasn't yet ready to knock Cambridge audiences for six. At rehearsals we shaped up reasonably well, but there was no professionalism. We were just a bunch of jazz musicians having a bit of a giggle. Billy added a good cabaret singer, Leila Rowlands, which added a touch of class to the proceedings. He also gave us the encouraging news that advance bookings were well under way. Nevertheless there was a general feeling that we were now financing our own inevitable downfall.

We opened the concert in a state of nerves. The crowd was very quiet in the first half. When anybody started to applaud, other people craned their necks round to have a look at them. There was a feeling of hushed expectancy, as if the earlier part of the show was only a build-up for some great climax that was to follow. Murray and Flash did well, and so did Leila, but all that was left in the second half was the Billy Kaye band with a few jazz standards.

During the interval, Billy said: 'We will just have to pep things up a bit. What we need now is some audience participation.'

I turned a little pale when he said this. A slumbering audience was bad enough – an audience stirred into action could be nasty.

Said Billy: 'I have just the thing. We'll try them with one of Bruce's vocals. What about giving them "The Things We Did Last Summer"? That should do it.'

'Never! I'm no singer, but at least let's not spread it around.'

'Rubbish. That number will stop the show – I promise you.'

He was wearing a faintly satanic expression as he said this. Then the curtain came up and we went into an opening number. There was some polite clapping at the end, but after our second number you could feel the audience becoming restless. What was coming up now? Not another *jazz* piece!

The band went into my vocal feature, confronted by a sea of glum faces. Out to the microphone I went, and began to sing. I seemed to be ploughing my way through this song for an eternity, like a participant in some huge Wagnerian opera. At length I came to the final lines: 'The things we did last summer,' I croaked sadly, 'I'll remember all winter long.'

There was a full-throated roar from the crowd, followed by loud applause. It was the kind of warm rapturous acceptance every performer dreams about and I turned round towards the band. What I saw was Leila Rowlands tripping briskly across the stage behind me, wheeling a large pram. With this deft touch, Billy had at last managed to break the ice. Thereafter, the audience was in a more receptive mood, and the concert had been snatched from the jaws of death. Isn't it strange how one simple little routine can save a show? I am afraid it didn't save the Kaye band, just the same. We had more lean times during the spring, and by early summer the morale of the band was in decline.

We had split ourselves into two rival musical camps. Stan and

Author's father as a major in the Indian Army

Author's mother, Hastings, 1930

Author (*right*) with Ruby and Tren,
Hastings, 1930

Author as a teenager

Blew House cricket team, 1939. Pat
Street is fourth left, back row; author
third right, back row. S.C. Griffith is
second left, centre

Rapcats, 1940. Author on clarinet;
leader Phil on guitar

Billy Kaye Sextet: Michael Grant,
piano; Ron Furness, trumpet; author;
Stan Watson, guitar; Thelma, vocals;
Lennie Bush, bass; Billy Kaye, drums

Author aged thirty

Author in the RAF

Queen Mary quartet: author; Cyril Collins, piano; Kenny Harris, drums; Peter Ind, bass

Author and Humphrey Lyttelton playing with Sidney Bechet (_left_)

Jump Band front line: John Mumford, John Chilton, author (*left to right*)

Jump Band: John Chilton, John Mumford, author, Jim Bray, Collin Bates, John Armatage (*left to right*), Oslo, 1960

**Author with Stan Levey (*centre*) and
Lee Konitz (*right*)**

Lennie had become disciples of bebop and progressive jazz; Mike, the pianist, shared my enthusiasm for Ellington, Shaw and Benny Carter. Billy veered towards the modernists, while our trumpet man, Derry, tried to keep an open mind. It was clear that Mike and I were considered to be closing our ears to the new sounds. Mike was goaded by this into some rather heavy sarcasm, but I'm afraid I took it all as a personal attack upon my own playing.

'You play that modern stuff if you want to,' I said, 'but I just don't happen to think along those lines.'

'But how can you close your ears to what's going on in music today? Oh, we've got nothing against the old swing players – played that way myself once. Then I gave it up, when I started listening to Charlie Parker.'

'Charlie *who*?' I enquired. After that, things were never quite the same.

I tried to get hold of some Parker records, but there wasn't much in the catalogues. Stan and Lennie told me to listen to some things by Kenton and Dizzy Gillespie. I did as I was told, and then asked Billy Kaye if one week's notice would be sufficient. Soon after that I was on a coach and heading for London, with two large carrier bags containing all my worldly possessions. As soon as I arrived in London, I sold my alto and went out to look for a day-job. The one I found was at the Ministry of Food.

This was straightforward work, even for me. It consisted in popping messages into the appropriate pigeon-holes and occasionally helping to pour the tea. You had to be a filing-clerk, I reflected bitterly, if you wanted to sort out all the slick classifications that were fast becoming the stock-in-trade of jazz criticism. And if you didn't have a neat little compartment they could slot you into, it was just too bad. Bebop and New Orleans were the two slots that directly confronted me, and I couldn't see any way I could fit into either of them. Better to leave the jazz scene and take up a sensible everyday job instead.

The ministry was predictably sane and uneventful, which suited me just fine. If somebody accidentally dropped a tea-cup, we talked about it all the next day. The office was close to Oxford Street, at the rear of Selfridges. On a fine day, I set off nice and early from Shepherd's Bush, so that I could make the journey on foot. That would mean I could afford sandwiches in the lunch-hour, but if I came to work by tube there wouldn't be any sandwiches and I would be staggering by the time I arrived home. Things improved greatly when the Civil Service spotted my dilemma and sent me to an address in Gloucester Place, where there was a low-rent bedsitter available on the ground floor.

The housekeeper was a wonderful little Irish lady called Mrs Lanahan. This Lanahan collected show people like some folk collect stamps. As soon as she found that I was a clarinettist of sorts, she ushered me aboard. I now had a comfortable pad only five minutes' walk from the West End. She even wanted to know if I needed to practise occasionally. Would it disturb anyone, I asked hesitantly.

'Distorrb, was it? Not at arl, sorr. We arl cad do wid a bit o' cheerin' op.'

As soon as Skrimshire learned that I had found myself the ideal bedsit, he moved in. So did several other aspiring jazz musicians, especially after it had become clear that late-night orgies and things left in a permanent state of disarray didn't seem to be upsetting Mrs Lanahan in the least. She had come to the conclusion that show people were like that, and that it was all a part of their charm. For a long time, Skrim and I shared a double room on the ground floor, with the Christie Brothers (Keith and Ian) next door to us and agent Jim Godbolt taking charge of the remaining single. In addition, random corpses were to be seen at night, sprawled about after many a social evening. One night I stubbed my toe on Mick Mulligan on my way to the toilet, which gave me rather a start and almost ruined the prospects of that prostrate figure.

According to Skrim, there was a lot of raw talent shaping itself around the revival. Bands were springing up everywhere, to follow in the footsteps of early New Orleans jazz.

'Why New Orleans in particular?' I wanted to know. 'Why not Chicago or St Louis – or Harlem?'

'I suppose they feel that they have to get right back to the roots – back to essentials. Like collective play, and the blues.'

'I can see that. But some fine things happened after New Orleans. What about Duke, Hawkins, the Basie band with Lester Young . . .?'

'Well, you know, these are my favourites too. But the revival is like taking a refresher course – a reminder of how it all started out, before the swing era confused a lot of people with some unpleasant noises that only superficially resembled jazz.'

I said: 'Wow. Didn't realize that listening to music could be so complicated. In any case, is it really possible to bring back the past?'

'Go and listen to the George Webb band. You may get a surprise or two.'

I promised to go and hear George, who was at that time championing the revival from a club in Barnehurst. People who had heard the band were coming away with dazed expressions on their faces, so evidently something was afoot.

I hasten to point out that the above conversation with Skrimshire has not been recorded verbatim, on account of my memory not being all it could be. As a matter of fact, we had worked out a kind of code language at school – something that might be described as a conversational shorthand. It was rather like wording a telegram. Certain words, such as the definite and indefinite articles, were left out altogether. It took up less time and energy that way.

'Man!' I blurted out, on my return from the Webb session, 'have just been to Barnehurst. Heard Webb band. Unable to believe ears. Thought was listening to negro band of early twenties. Surprise of life, must admit.'

The Webb band didn't feature the usual string of solos, but adhered to a disciplined collective sound. As a result of my visit to the Red Barn, Barnehurst, I came to know some of the boys slightly. Humphrey Lyttelton was to become a leading light in the revival for as long as it seemed to be a vital force. Then, when the tendency seemed to be for it to move backwards instead of forwards, Humph doffed his cap to it and went his own way. Wally Fawkes, by far the best clarinettist of the genre, also took off in a direction of his own choosing after a while. Eddie Harvey moved forward rapidly to a fluid trombone style, ending up in the Dankworth Seven. There doesn't seem much doubt that the revival was often used, and quite rightly in my view, as a stepping-stone to greater things. Or to a far more individual kind of expression at any rate.

I am grateful to Skrimshire for prodding me out of my apathy at this time. All I wanted to do was start a jazz-record collection again. Sprawled before my record player, I could fend off the necessity to go out and meet people. I wasn't keen on talking to anyone I didn't already know. It was hard enough trying to be understood by people I *did* know.

Nevil then talked me into visiting the Leicester Square Jazz Club. Lyttelton had recently broken away from George Webb to form a band of his own, with Wally Fawkes on clarinet.

Almost immediately the band caused great interest. It was more than the New Orleans collective sound – both Humph and Wally had powerful individualistic styles, although firmly based on Armstrong and Bechet respectively. The club was on a floor directly above the offices of the RSPCA in Leicester Square. Oozing with complacency, I went along with my clarinet and got ready to blow Wally Fawkes off the stand.

If I'd had any humility at all, I would have been daunted by the size of the crowd, and also by the fact that it contained several well-known experts who were taking everything down in shorthand and subjecting everything to the most exacting scrutiny. There were also some members of the Australian Jazz Band, resting after a successful European tour.

I had not come to listen, but to show those traditionalist musicians what I could do. It never occurred to me that the last thing many of these puritans wanted to listen to was some young upstart trying to sound like Benny Goodman, Frank Teschemacher and Artie Shaw.

So I sat there in between Humph and Wally, and proceeded to give my all. Wally Fawkes was in excellent form, dishing out those big majestic phrases, with a purposeful sound that made my own contributions seem like a cross between Disney's Chipmunk and somebody walking past the microphone with squeaky shoes. The thing wasn't working out at all as I had planned. After the first number I said thanks very much and was ready to call it a day.

'Why not stay for one more,' said Humph politely, 'I like that unusual sound.'

I wasn't sure which way to take the remark, but I remained for the next number and played some more unusual clarinet. Then I blurted out my thanks and ran. At the end of the evening, as I was at the back of the bandstand putting my clarinet back in its case, one of the Australian musicians came to have a word with Humph.

'Who the hell was that joker?' said the Aussie, excitedly. 'I never thought I would hear that sort of noise coming out of a clarinet. Not what you or I would call music, but Christ it was *different*! That boy has got on to something *new*.'

Sarcasm? Or inarticulate praise? I didn't wait to find out, but made my way to the exit and unobtrusively crept away. About a week later I found that I had indeed made an impact with my playing. Two amateur jazz bands wanted me to join them, with a view to building up a following and eventually turning pro.

One of these groups was the Roy Vaughan Chicagoans, the other was the Tony Finnis Jazz Band. It seems that what I had been playing was Chicago style, in which both of these groups specialized. Even at this early stage, jazz bands were refusing to follow servilely behind the unbending advocates of 'back to New Orleans'.

This Chicago jazz had been summarily dismissed by the critics as a failed copy of New Orleans music, so that at first it did not receive anything like the attention it deserved. Chicago groups often used a tenor sax in place of the customary trombone, and guitar instead of banjo. Bix was the Chicagoans' God, and Eddie Condon their ringleader and most tireless propagandist. Condon's own music did not follow the revivalist pattern. It was based on a repertoire of simple tunes rather than upon such material as 'High Society' and 'Ory's Creole Trombone', with their subdivisions and occasional changes of key. In Condon jazz, the theme is stated fairly unadventurously, the clarinet often following the trumpet in close harmony or wailing away on a sustained 'blue' note. There are few complex contrapuntal passages. Everyone is impatient to get away from this opening statement and into the solo choruses. Thus we hear only a cursory opening theme, after which these sparse show tunes are totally transformed into the tense paraphrasing of the soloists.

After the tightly knit collective approach of the New Orleans bands, Condon and his associates sounded almost blatantly individualistic. In Britain there was one band which managed to play in this loose, uninhibited manner. This was the Freddy Randall band.

During the revival I was sharing a large bedsitter with Nevil Skrimshire. Living so close to my place of work, I could be home a good half-hour before Skrim. This meant that I could hastily prepare salad before he arrived, and would be halfway through my own meal before the room started to smell of such carnivorous concoctions as he was likely to place over the gas ring. One evening I had managed to get through a large salad and some nut roast before he finally showed up. I was standing at the wash-basin, brushing my teeth, when Nevil came through the door. He surveyed me for a moment, then said briskly: 'How would you like to join Freddy Randall's band?'

I went on brushing my teeth. After I had rinsed and spat, he tried me again.

'Randall's band. Do you want to join, or don't you?'

'Love to,' I said. 'Hey, you're not going to fry bacon, are you? That stuff really pongs the place out.'

Nevil placed three rashers in the pan: 'Never mind all that nonsense. Listen, Fred is at the Cooks Ferry Inn this Sunday and he wants . . . are you listening, man? . . . he wants you to do the session on clarinet. If he likes you, you're in the band for good. Shouldn't be any problem – just play your usual stuff.'

Even then it took time to sink in. What Humphrey Lyttelton was to the connoisseurs, Fred was becoming to the more adventurous club promoters and to a section of the working-class youth confronted with dixieland for the first time. I had heard the band on a broadcast, and knew the way they played. That was why I hadn't dared to take Nevil seriously at first – but now, it seemed, I was in with a chance.

'I told Freddy you'll be there at twelve sharp. You can discuss tunes before the crowds get there.'

'Jazz on a Sunday! Won't everyone be at church?'

'In East London, Fred is the only true God.'

Only we didn't discuss it in exactly those words. I was so preoccupied after this news, that I watched in a trance as Skrimshire devoured his greasy fried bacon with an air of self-satisfaction. The lad had done it again. He had sent the ball whistling back into my court – just as I had felt I was losing interest in the game.

6 Fred

Here's a fable Aesop never got around to. It is pertinent, nevertheless.

It concerns a moth and a caterpillar, confronting one another on a cabbage leaf. Said the caterpillar: 'I couldn't help noticing those wings of yours. Terrific! One day I hope to get me a pair, and when I do . . . just watch me go.'

The moth only smiled condescendingly. 'Listen' he exclaimed. 'You don't know when you're well off. I tell you these things give me nothing but trouble. I keep flying into candle flames and singeing them. No, take my advice and stay just the way you are. You're so simple and unspoiled – so close to the solid earth. I envy you.'

'Nice of you to say so,' sighed the other, 'but – if only I had your *freedom*. I'm fed up sitting around on cabbage leaves all my life.'

'Nonsense,' came the reply. 'A moth is a flimsy thing. You are in every way more *natural* than me. Anyway, the Big Book says so – so it must be true.'

'Sounds interesting,' admitted the caterpillar. 'Who wrote this Big Book anyway?'

'I did,' replied the moth, and flew off into the resplendent night.

Since writing *Le Jazz Hot*, Panassie had changed his mind. He now told us that jazz was the music of southern negroes, and that whites could play it only by adhering to the 'natural' music of New Orleans. Those negro musicians who wanted to depart from the prototype, having things of their own to say, were quickly dismissed as 'bogus' or 'derivative'.

Le Jazz Hot had defined jazz as performers' music – an oversimplification perhaps, but the germ of an essential truth. In *Le Vrai Jazz* we are told that the only 'real' jazzman is a black musician – or a white one pretending very hard to be black. Self-expression? Not a bit of it. If a white musician wanted to express some European influences in his playing he would soon run into trouble from the scribes.

On the day I took a bus to Edmonton to have my audition with the Randall band, I wasn't aware of any fine distinctions between black and white music. I had thought we were all through with racial categories now that Hitler had been defeated in the great ideological war.

Cooks Ferry Inn turned out to be a four-square, contemporary-style pub on the fringe of a very busy main road. It was brashly unpicturesque, with a stream of heavy traffic clattering past its front entrance. On Sundays, it was quieter, so that I could hear Freddy warming up as I made my way to it from the bus stop. Some fragmentary outpourings of a man who had heard the best of Muggsy Spanier and other players of the Chicago school, but who was carrying it on from there.

Randall was chubby and baby-faced, greeting my arrival with a sigh of relief. He was suddenly without a clarinettist, and hadn't been able to locate anyone who could play in the required style. 'We could do a few of those Bix Beiderbecke things,' he said, as though I had known him all my life. 'I'm sure you know "Jazz Me Blues" and "Virginia". Skrimshire tells me you eat a lot of cake. Is that some kind of joke? Cake! He says it helps you to play better.'

Freddy was chuckling to himself at the very thought of a jazz musician riding into a solo while under the influence of chocolate gateau and cream meringue.

'Milk chocolate will do just as well,' I assured him. 'I noticed some behind the bar. If you ask for cake in a pub, they think you are a bit odd.'

Freddy stared at me intently for a minute, still not quite sure if I was to be taken seriously. Then he laughed and said it was quite incredible.

We were seated during the Cooks Ferry session, bobbing up occasionally for our respective solos. I played the first couple of numbers with my eyes screwed shut, nervous as hell. When I opened them at the end of the second number, it was to discover that Freddy was enjoying my playing which, due to some nervous muscular constrictions around the throat, had begun to sound rather like a strangulated Pee Wee Russell. At the end of the session I was welcomed into the band, and continued to play like Pee Wee for the next five years.

This band was not every jazz critic's cup of tea, not by a long way. The truth was that a rift existed between the itinerant dixielanders and the New Orleans bands doing it all for 'love' . Hugues Panassie had managed to publicize jazz, so that in France and Britain it was gaining acceptance everywhere. Unfortunately this French critic had seen fit to magnify the importance of one small corner of the jazz scene, at the expense of everything else. Rudi Blesh soon went even further than Panassie, in a book called *Shining Trumpets*, which encouraged young white musicians to imitate negroes rather than express their true selves. In Britain, Rex Harris brought out a paperback *Jazz* which sold an alarming number of copies.

Yet even in spite of all this opposition, the Randall band became enormously popular. At some concerts, the audiences simply went wild. Faced with the increasing popularity of a white dixieland music, the purist writers twisted and turned. A strange jargon came to be invented, to describe music of this kind. Our music was 'courageous', 'well-intentioned' or even a 'plucky attempt' to sound like the real jazz of black New Orleans. Eddie Condon, on the other side of the Atlantic, also received his share of patronizing criticism from the great French pundit. In the end he was goaded into making a classic reply: 'Do I tell him how to jump on a grape?'

The simple truth was that Chicago-style jazz never was an attempt to be like New Orleans jazz. The best of the white musicians – Bix, Pee Wee, Bud Freeman and the youthful Benny Goodman – took their influences from very many sources as well as New Orleans jazz. They then emerged as individual voices in their own right.

'Bruce,' one purist writer whispered in my ear, 'you are playing very well with Freddy, but I feel you would both improve by listening to King Oliver and Johnny Dodds. You don't mind me saying this, do you?'

'Not at all. But it's hard to see what you're getting at. The way I feel *now* is not the way Dodds felt in 1922.'

'Yes, yes. All I meant was that the real negro music ought to be studied first. Then you would have a proper basis for your own style.'

'But *is* it a real negro music? I always thought it belonged to all of us.'

'Well in New Orleans, most of the jazz musicians were negro.'

'So were most shoe-shiners, cotton-pickers and railway porters.'

'Bruce, you can't ignore a historic fact. Jazz was invented by negroes – it is *their* music, whether you like it or not.'

'So in that case, you would say that the symphony is "Austrians' music" – I mean, in deference to Papa Haydn and his school?'

'Oh, now you're just being difficult . . .'

But it was by no means easy to persuade the purists that Goodman, Tesch and Eddie Condon were the Tchaikovskys, Dvoraks and Sibeliuses of jazz.

With Freddy's band I felt the critics were getting to know me. My name started to appear not infrequently in the record and broadcast reviews. Either I was 'sacrificing all attempts at correct tone and technique', or else I was praised as a good white imitation, or something along those lines.

Skrim admitted that some of his best friends had become strongly biased against white musicians on account of all the propaganda for New Orleans jazz. He brought some of these friends back occasionally and we played records of Louis's Hot Five and the Ellington band. As soon as we put on anything by the white orchestras, these guys started looking at their watches and remarking that it was getting late. I will never forget the time we played a record which had the white cornettist, Ruby Braff, featured alongside a lot of very fine negro musicians. Hardly anyone had heard of Ruby at that time.

'What do you think of the cornet solo?' asked Skrim, giving me a sly wink.

'Just wonderful. Who is it? Edison, Buck Clayton?'

'Fellow called Braff – a white boy.'

It was interesting to watch our companion's jaw, as it dropped nearly all the way down to the hearth-rug. We listened to some more Braff, but now this man was no longer grinning and snapping his fingers as he'd been doing before we dropped our bombshell. After a while, he smiled a condescending smile and remarked: 'Yes, quite a pleasant sound. But you know, I'm beginning to find him rather tiresome.' Just who was being tiresome I will leave for the reader to decide.

It wasn't long before Randall's band received the break it had been hoping for. An agent called Harry Dawson saw the band's possibilities and set us up with some regular concert tours. Fred hired a bandwaggon and we went 'on the road'. At first these tours were more or less restricted to the south of England. For a while, the furthest north we played was Birmingham. It was at Birmingham Town Hall that it all started happening for Freddy.

They didn't like the band much, but Fred's forceful playing ensured that we would be back time and time again.

I soon became accustomed to the stony silence that would follow each of my clarinet choruses before the Birmingham crowd. What made matters worse was that we often played opposite the Yorkshire Jazz Band, whose own clarinettist was a big favourite there. Whatever Alan Cooper did was greeted with rapturous acclaim. Then it would be the Randall band's turn, and my clarinet solos had this curious effect of silencing the vociferous crowd. It was as if I had barged in on a private party and been coldly requested to leave. This was hard to take, considering the wild reception my rival, Alan Cooper, was always guaranteed to receive. I turned to Fred for advice.

'I can't think what this guy is doing that's so special,' he replied. 'I suppose you could try bobbing up and down the way he does. All I know is, he's stealing all the applause.'

After that, whenever we had a concert opposite the Yorkshire Jazz Band, Fred stood behind me and whispered: 'Give it the Cooper sound – if he can do it, you can.' But neither of us ever found out what the Cooper sound was, or how it could be achieved. And from that day to this, I have always found Birmingham audiences to be less receptive to my own playing than almost any other. It is just one of those things that can never really be explained.

Soon the band received its first important assignment. We were asked to tour West Germany with a variety show, as part of a policy of entertaining our occupation force. The show was called 'Revelry in Rebop', in spite of the fact that we were the only band on the bill and played nothing even faintly resembling bop. The other acts included a stand-up comic, a man who did impressions and a troupe of dancing girls – none of whom had even heard of Dizzy Gillespie. Still, what's in a name? The important thing was that 'Revelry in Rebop' launched Fred into prominence as never before. It also turned out to be quite a fascinating experience.

Germany in 1947 was a pathetic shambles. In the rubble, children and old women rummaged for cigarette-ends and anything else they could sell for a few coins. The British and American servicemen crowded in, laughing and cursing and perhaps wondering what the hell they were supposed to do to Germany, now they'd conquered it. Everywhere there was a sense of anti-climax and deep frustration, with thousands of war-weary soldiers now feeling a need for some kind of imported fun. That's where we came in.

Concerts were often tense affairs, the performers sensing that no one was in the mood to sit back and be passively entertained. If anyone didn't like a particular act, he said so at the top of his voice. Poor Jimmy Bruce, the comedian, came in for some rough treatment at the hands of one very loud Scottish heckler during a noisier-than-usual concert. Jimmy, a true professional, handed out blow for verbal blow in this rapier-like exchange:

Heckler (*for about the fifth time*): 'Get yer hair cut.'

Jimmy: 'Come on mate, pipe down. Give us a chance . . .'

Heckler: 'Get yer hair cut.'

Jimmy: 'Oh . . . get your throat cut!' (*some applause*)

Heckler: 'Get yer suit cut.'

Jimmy: 'Oh, very good. Now, as I was . . .'

Heckler: 'Where did you get that f— suit?'

Jimmy: 'A darn sight better place than you got yours.' (*loud cheers*)

The punchline wasn't lost on all those khaki-clad characters, who cheered the comedian until they were hoarse. Our boys had spent six years trying to get into Germany, and now they wanted nothing but to get right out again, and back home. Large areas of Hamburg and Düsseldorf had been strafed into a fine powder by our own planes. There wasn't anywhere to go in the evenings, unless you liked such places as the notorious Winkelstrasse, which provided a bizarre mixture of desolation and hard porn.

The Germans had no awareness of jazz at that particular time. They were not even able to pronounce the word correctly. At our hotel, the barman pronounced the strange four-letter word in phonetic German. 'Yachts!' he murmured, glowing with enthusiasm, 'I hope one day to make yachts – yast like you boys.'

Nobody knew what to make of this, until our interpreter bustled forward. No, the barman was not under the misapprehension that we were all members of a boating club. The interpreter said, 'He say he want to play chess, like you guys. He very fond of chess – only he don't speak English so good.'

We met some nice people during the tour, both English and German, but it was a great relief to arrive back home. The band was now more proficient in many ways, some of us having learned a thing or two about stagecraft. I now saw that music should not simply be enjoyed, it should be *seen* to be enjoyed. I had never been one for florid or violent musical displays, but now I understood why Freddy always received more applause for his solos than I did. He bounced around that stage like a rubber ball, exuding charm. Fred didn't merely attack a thirty-two-bar chorus – he positively violated it. I knew that I would have to produce something along the same lines if I was going to become popular with the fans.

Not many people can possibly understand what it must have been like to play in a band like this one, at the very start of the revival. There were the smooth professional dance bands who specialized in dixieland arrangements (Sid Phillips and Harry Gold were the supreme examples of this type), and there were the eager young amateurs bobbing up in the wake of Lyttelton's first band. Somewhere in between stood this unique figure, Freddy Randall, the self-made player who had more improvised technique and brash self-confidence than all the others put together. It wasn't easy to pinpoint this remarkable talent. Somehow he had this amazing flair for off-the-cuff invention, plus a trumpet tone as big as a house.

Not many people realized, either, just how spontaneous Fred's music was. It was ninety per cent extempore, based on virtually no musical training at all.

We began to make quite a number of records. First we recorded for Fred's own Cleveland label, later we went to Parlophone. Ed Harvey played a lazy kind of trombone, in the Teagarden manner. The rhythm team was better than the one Humphrey Lyttelton had at that stage. Al Mead was a good swinging pianist, and Bobby Coram a very solid rhythm guitar. Coram was also a very funny man – a raconteur and spontaneous comic who wouldn't allow the band to stay in low spirits for very long. At the start of a recording session, I needed words of encouragement from Fred and Bobby, otherwise I would land myself in a terrible state of jitters. The worst time was when we had to do just two sides with the singer, Billy Banks. I suppose I kept recalling those classic sides he made with Henry Allen and Pee Wee Russell in the remote past, which alone would entitle him to a place in the Hall of Fame. I think I must have got it into my head that we were supposed to be 're-creating' those historic sides.

'He sings just like on those old records,' I marvelled, after the first take, 'I can't believe all this is happening.'

'You don't look at all well,' said Randall, 'your face has gone sort of green.'

I tried to pull myself together after that, but it was the first time I had been asked to record alongside an American negro of some repute. He was a nice friendly little man, but I just couldn't get those fabulous early recordings out of my head. Then Banks wanted to do another take on 'Walking the Dog'. We had tried one, but he wasn't happy with it.

'How about some clarinet after the vocal this time,' he called out. It was now or never, as far as my reputation was concerned. If Banks liked me, I was good – if not, well, there was always the Foreign Legion.

'I think,' whispered Fred, as we waited for the red light to come on, 'he will be expecting you to do a Pee Wee.'

'I think I've already done it,' I replied, but the take went quite well and afterwards Billy said my solo had reminded him of someone, but he couldn't remember just who.

The band's first important broadcast was a nerve-racking occasion for everyone concerned. None of us knew how to sight-read, and there were gasps of dismay as parts were peremptorily handed round. Paul Fenhoulet, the musical director of the programme, had naturally assumed that, being professional musicians, we were equipped for this sort of thing. There were four bands facing one another in the studio. The parts were for an introductory number in which each band would be spotlighted in turn. A tense situation, as you can imagine. There was Fenhoulet solemnly raising his baton, and there sat the Randall band, staring at the sheet music in horror. All around us sat the other bands' sidemen – every one a skilled reader of parts. This was only a preliminary runthrough, but it didn't alter the fact that in a moment we would become the laughing stock of the profession.

Fenhoulet beat us all in, and the opening theme was under way. Next, one of the other bands – I think it was Tito Burns's – played its section of the written arrangement, then another band took over, and then a third. At last it was our turn. Fenhoulet pointed dramatically towards Freddy with his baton, the music swelled to a loud sustained chord, and then . . .

Total silence. We just sat there goggling at the sheet music, unable even to find the way in. Someone over on another bandstand giggled. Fenhoulet stood scratching his head and looking down at the score, searching for an explanation. At last the awful silence was broken – by the sound engineer. He rapped upon the glass partition, waved his hands about, then came into the studio, looking worried.

'I'm so sorry,' he began, 'our fault entirely. We seem to be having a technical problem. Something has gone wrong with the Randall band's microphones. I'm not getting a sound out of them.'

In spite of this unpromising start, the band was soon lining up plenty of broadcasts. We were now accepted as the band which had an unusual gimmick – seven professional musicians who couldn't read! Singer Pearl Carr was delighted when we shoved aside the musical accompaniments she had written out for us, and jammed away behind her singing; Diana Coupland asked for the Randall band to accompany her on several broadcasts and concerts, after she had discovered that our smooth dixieland style made for a crisper vocal backing than any written score. Fred was in demand everywhere, not only for jazz performances but also for these instant backings in which the band was beginning to specialize.

It must be remembered that in these early days of the New Orleans revival only three bands could be described as major influences, each in its own way. The George Webb band had started the whole thing, so its importance can hardly be ignored. After this, there were the two great rival bands led by Humph and Fred respectively. Each had its own devout followers, each inhabited a quite separate world from the other – the ersatz, the suspect form. Randall's adherents thought of Lyttelton's music as quaintly archaic and even amateurish, while the Lyttelton disciples often dismissed Fred as a vulgar exhibitionist and his music as a debased pseudo-jazz. Most of the pundits took sides against Freddy, following the fashionable view that to be a pro musician somehow smacked of insincerity and 'commercialism'.

Until the early fifties, I am not aware that there were any other important traditionalist bands on the regular circuit – they came along later. One had glimpses of the other contending groups a bit later, once the dust had settled. The Yorkshire band had its own strong local following, as did the Mick Mulligan contingent. In Scotland, Alex Welsh was busy forming a group that would later rival even Freddy's. By that time, we would have started to hear from Ken Colyer, and the 'revival within a revival'.

Apart from this savoury top layer, the revivalist pudding didn't have much of a kick in it. In its early stages, the revival used the same old recipe over and over. Every time you entered the portals of a typical post-war jazz club, you were hit by this changeless sound. A cornet or trumpet played the lead, while ornamentation was provided by a clarinettist whose very life seemed to depend on his sounding exactly like Johnny Dodds. The third wind instrument, the trombone, never actually joined the front line at all, confining itself to rhythmical figures in the lower register, or lavatorial sound effects. The important man in the band was unquestionably the banjo player. Without a banjo, no band was acceptable or credible. I asked George Lewis and Albert Nicholas about all this banjo-mania in British trad. They both thought the guitar had a far warmer and richer sound, and swung more. In the early days, banjos seem to have been used in situations where a louder and more percussive rhythm was needed, so that they would be heard in the general clamour.

These small-time 'trad' bands, whether marching under the banner of dixieland or New Orleans, too often had a self-conscious, parochial air about them. They could copy their betters, but that was all. Only the two arch-rivals, Humph and Freddy, managed to inspire the revival and bring it forward to better things.

The New Orleans revival had always worked on the assumption that you could force your own young people to identify with another race's folklore and another period in time. All they really succeeded in creating was a passing phase. Trad jazz had never had its deep roots in this country's own culture, and so the kids would desert it as soon as a more indigenous kind of expression came their way.

New Orleans music lasted for a few years, as an amusing craze. Then came the mass exodus from the jazz clubs, with everyone turning to cockney and Liverpudlian rock music. This was about as predictable as anything could be. The revival was strangled by its own mystique. Instead of nurturing the concept of an *international* music pouring from a cultural melting-pot, the pundits produced their race theory. Jazz was the music of the Black South.

Freddy's boys didn't talk much about music, except to make jokes about some of the things that were written concerning our broadcasts. Fred was himself a very far-out humorist. Some of the things he did were absurd, but reduced the rest of us to helpless laughter. At one stage, he claimed that he could turn anyone, whether male or female, into the singer Dick Haymes. All he had to do was stand behind you and press your nose and cheeks in a certain way with the tips of his fingers. The extraordinary thing was that it worked. The slant-eyed, pug-nosed American crooner soon appeared before us, even if Fred's latest 'victim' was an unsuspecting autograph-hunter, or even the promoter himself.

Fred was just about the opposite of a jazz purist. He would try his hand at anything, if it amused him to do so. Our shows usually included at least one elaborate comedy number, somewhat in the manner of Spike Jones. He didn't hold to the view that jazz was something that had to be kept pure and unsullied. In fact, he sullied it quite a lot, and deliberately. This led some people to describe him as a vulgar player, but in fact he was no more a vulgar musician than, say, Dizzy Gillespie or Jonah Jones. He was simply a mischievous child – a veritable Peter Pan in jazz.

I was always a little more serious in my musical approach. I was acquiring a taste for modern sounds. Up until this time, I had been a clarinettist who occasionally doubled on alto sax. Now I felt the urge to play more saxophone than hitherto. Why not? was Fred's response, and he even tried his hand at writing some bebop compositions for the band to play on dance dates. I won't say that these tunes were Fred at his best, but they certainly showed him to be a man of considerable tolerance where music was concerned.

John Dankworth and Ronnie Scott were the two most important saxists on the modern scene – as far as this country was concerned. I became fascinated by what these two players were doing. The two master craftsmen played at a place called Club Eleven, in Soho. When I started going to Club Eleven on my free evenings, it was not with the object of sitting in on alto, and showing off my own skills. That would have been a pretty stupid thing to do, with a consummate musician like Dankworth around. Instead I sat quietly and kept my ears open. Bop was a foreign language, but I thought I might be able to learn some of the easier phrases. After a while, I sensed that I was coming along quite well. On some of Randall's numbers, I was able to sneak in a few nice modern ideas, and nobody seemed to mind. Billy Kaye was running a small bop club, which he called the Contemporary Jazz Club. It was doing so badly that musicians were calling it the Temporary Jazz Club and taking bets as to when Billy would have to fold. I played a few times at Billy's club, and was grateful to the little drummer for this much-needed experience.

Meanwhile, the Randall bandwaggon rattled up and down the country with a pile of sleeping-bags on the back seat.

Sometimes we kipped in the waggon but in cold weather we piled into one of those scruffy guest-houses that took in jazz musicians and lorry drivers at a reduced rate. By sleeping in these austere premises, four or five in a room, we could bring money home from a tour.

Britain was still licking its wounds after the war. The economy was by no means back on its feet. Rationing was still on, wages were still at subsistence level, and I was obtaining bootleg caramels from a barrow-boy in Charing Cross Road.

The critics were closing in on me by this time. Well, only the die-hards, but I didn't like some of the implications that were being made about me and some of the other dixielanders. I think I liked it better when I was being completely ignored. These critics had little time for any music that wasn't strictly in the New Orleans mould. Even the big important players like Basie, Adrian Rollini and John Kirby were being treated as if they didn't exist.

I want to make it clear that when I use the word 'critic', what I really mean is 'pundit'. Critics are fine with me, especially when they report with honesty what is actually going on in jazz. I study their discographies and enjoy their fair-minded reviews. It is when a critic tries to tell me how to play that he becomes a pundit, and confuses the whole issue. The pundit is well-intentioned, and tries to understand this strange, alien world of jazz – but he is peering in from the outside. He sees, therefore, through the distorting lens of his own imagination. He is the perennial armchair critic, the back-seat driver, the gatecrasher who tries to claim that he is the host's best friend. All he knows is how to work a typewriter, and how to dish out great handfuls of private opinion posing as fact. If he also has a willing publisher, then you can be sure a theory of jazz will be on people's shelves in no time.

The way such theories make instant headway is something like this: a man has a lot of jazz records, he suddenly notices that some of the music hits him more forcefully than the rest, so he concludes that this must be the *real* jazz. He then sees in a kind of revelation that jazz is authentic only when played by left-handed non-smokers with red hair – or something of that sort. He rushes into print, and is soon contacted by other individuals who share his opinion. These start up jazz clubs or promote concerts, making quite sure that only musicians who fit the above description are hired to play. Pretty soon the only available work for jazz musicians is that which is carefully supervised by a few theorists who don't themselves play.

This is the darker side of the picture. There will always be music which is played for sheer pleasure and which defies categorization, along with the regimented music of pundit jazz.

Early New Orleans music was a link in a chain of development. Oliver and Morton were sophisticated modernists in their time – forward-looking and flexible – but the pundits were tied to their static concept. They wanted to wrap the music in a protective cocoon, and keep it in a warm safe place. From time to time they could take it out and examine it, reassuring themselves that nothing had changed, and that at least one form of music would remain in a state of nature for all time. But change is in the very nature of things.

My stay with the Randall band covers two distinct periods of about two years each. In between, I left the band for one year, but this brief period will be dealt with in the next chapter. On my return to the band I found Freddy to be just the same as ever, but the band had changed quite a lot by this time. Norman Cave was on trombone in place of Eddie Harvey, who had at last found his true niche by joining the Dankworth Seven. The drummer was now Lennie Hastings, and for a short time we had Lennie Felix on piano. The two Lennies are both gone now, British jazz having lost two of the greatest characters and most remarkable stylists of their kind.

At the time of Lennie Hastings's stay with the band, both Freddy and I had become involved with diet reform in a big way. We found that fresh citrus fruit, wholewheat bread and pressure-cooked vegetables helped to keep us clear-eyed and light of step during the more strenuous band tours. This finally made a deep impression on Lennie Hastings, who said he would like to join. Fred at once suggested that a short, sharp fast would do Lennie a world of good. The drummer willingly agreed, but after only one day we heard him groaning in a corner.

'Bugger this!' came the plaintive cry, 'I feel worse now than when I started. I thought you said fasting was *good* for you.'

'Now, Len, you're quite sure you had nothing to eat all day?'

'Only a few of those pickled eggs while I was in the pub.'

'But what were you doing in a pub, anyway?'

'I was filling up on booze, wasn't I? Well, blow me. I mean, fast or no fast – you've got to get *something* inside you.'

Lennie Felix was, in my opinion, a wayward genius who never managed to fit in with whatever music was going on around him. He had all the grandeur and panache of the great jazz pianists, but not their innate sense of discipline, with the result that he remained a 'loner' right to the very end. In conversation, Lennie carefully presented the more superficial side of his nature. He became a mixture of Edward G. Robinson and George Sanders, often peppering his sentences with clichés from the Hollywood films.

'Hit me with one more!' I once heard him call out behind a chorus of mine, and then, 'Now you're getting to me!'

I would have felt irritated to hear this sort of gross hip-talk from almost anyone else, but coming from Lennie Felix it was sincere. I think I knew the real Lennie better than most, and felt very close to him; I still can't believe he is no longer around.

I was growing skinny in those days, if not downright emaciated, which may be accounted for by the fact that I was living on raw salads and cream buns. The salads were supposed to make me healthy again after my orgies of cake. For a man who had just chosen the path of vegetarianism and diet reform, I wasn't too well informed about these things. By the time my father flew in for his second post-war visit, Red Norvo could have taken xylophone solos on me. Dad took one look at me and reached for his chequebook.

'You need help,' was his verdict. 'I might have known you would come to this – playing jazz on the trumpet is a fool's game.'

He liked to appear as though he couldn't tell one musical instrument from another. It was his way of putting the profession down.

'Things aren't as bad as they seem,' I assured him. 'There's money coming in all the time.'

'In that case, you might try spending it on food.'

'I do, I do. You should have seen the size of the salad I had for lunch.'

All I really needed was a small handout from the old man, but predictably he was not about to start throwing money around. What he had in mind was a small business venture. He was thinking of buying a newsagent's shop or a restaurant in one of the quieter market towns. Under his supervision I would learn how to run the place and get to grips with things. Life would be hard for six days in the week, but on Sundays there would be trout fishing and long walks in the country. I think it was the trout that really turned the scale.

'The Randall band is doing quite well,' I said meekly. 'No,

seriously, there isn't anything to worry about.'

But there *was* something to worry about – Freddy had booked the band into the West End Restaurant, Edinburgh, for one week. This was the town where my father was staying, and I knew that he was planning to visit the restaurant on one of the evenings that we were there. Somehow I could not even begin to imagine Dad in the same room with a crowd of uninhibited jazz fans. I informed Freddy that my father was about to come to one of the jazz evenings. Unlike me he was able to see the joke.

'We must get him a good seat up front. It's odd, I never thought of you as having a father – I always assumed you . . . just happened.'

All through the first things we played, Fred kept peering about the room for a sign of my dad. At last the stern figure put in an appearance, seating himself ponderously like a High Court judge. Fred gasped at the resemblance between father and son. Dad was doing a little gasping too, as the waves of loud dixieland very nearly swept him off his perch. In the interval he was commendably polite to Freddy, saying that he had suddenly recalled a previous appointment. I could tell that he had been deeply impressed by his first taste of live jazz.

Scotland wasn't any longer the romantic place Dad had retained in his mind's eye. You had to look far and wide for the sight of wild clansmen and picturesque villages in the Lothian of 1951. Even the semi-rural Scotland of Dad's early years, let alone the land Walter Scott describes, wasn't more than a faint memory. Jazz and factory chimneys had come with the altered times, bringing with them the sounds and smells of a new industrial age. He stayed on for a while in Edinburgh, writing a great deal and spending a lot of time at the Conservative Club. Then he went back to India, probably to dream about the Scotland that had disappeared from his life. According to the doctors, he would have lasted only a year or two in the severe Scottish climate, but once back in the warmer climes he managed another twenty years. When I last visited him, he was living in Bangalore and when we went on some early-morning jaunts together I was scarcely able to keep up with him.

I never did inherit this man's powerful physique and iron determination, but only some of the pig-headedness that went along with it. I had made up my mind to stay in jazz, and even he hadn't been able to talk me out of it. Fred's date sheet was beginning to look good, and I was even putting on a little weight. We made cheese-and-onion flans to bring on coach journeys, sometimes even preparing tasty vegetarian meals in pressure-cookers at the back of the waggon. The primus stove overturned once, and we had to douse the flames with onion soup.

Rex Stewart came to this country as a solo variety act. The only way Americans were able to play in Britain was to call themselves variety entertainers as distinct from musicians. Somehow or other, the celebrated Ellington trumpeter was teamed with the Randall band for a special show. How this was arranged I could never ascertain, but it was certainly a big occasion. Later on, Rex came to one of the Cooks Ferry sessions, supposedly to 'sit in'. It was a unique experience, and a big treat for the fans. In the finale, Fred and Rex blew four-bar phrases at each other for about ten minutes non-stop. The crowd simply went mad. My old dad would most certainly have cleared the court, and put both trumpeters under restraint for breaking the peace.

Fred was brazen enough to challenge a man like Rex Stewart to a musical duel, but in other respects he was a rather shy sort of fellow. When it came to firing a member of his band, for whatever reason, he became embarrassed and did things in a very roundabout way. Once he sent a telegram to one of the boys, to tell him he was fired. He timed this telegram so that it would reach the man just after the band had returned from a tour. Unfortunately for Fred, the thing arrived far sooner than expected. We dropped the man off at his home, and there was the man's wife with the unopened telegram in her hand. The waggon was still pulling slowly away from the kerb as the sideman opened Fred's message and read it. All of us were choking with mirth, except Fred. He had ducked under the seat.

When my own time came to leave, nothing like this happened, and Fred and I parted the best of friends. It had been a wonderful experience for me, but now other things were on the agenda, and I was moving on. The important role played by this band in the revival was never clearly understood at the time. Perhaps the historians will set the matter right one day. What we played was close to what Eddie Condon and his boys were doing at about the same time but we were certainly not copying Condon. Freddie was amazed when some critics told him he sounded just like Wild Bill Davidson. He had scarcely even *heard* of Wild Bill, and in any case he didn't listen to recorded jazz a great deal. It just seemed natural to make music in a certain way, reflecting in our own sounds an environment not unlike theirs. The Condon boys had lived through the era of Al Capone and prohibition; ten years later we had experienced war jitters and the black market. What I found harder to understand was the revivalist who sought to escape from his own time, to a picture-postcard New Orleans and an indigenous culture not even remotely like his own.

New Orleans jazz is of enormous historical significance, but you can't duplicate it in present-day Britain and expect to be taken seriously. The revival justified itself for as long as it claimed to be taking a 'refresher course', but after that it was absolutely vital to move forward. I have a special fondness for Bix, Teschemacher, Eddie Lang, Miff Mole, Adrian Rollini, Goodman, Pee Wee, Django, Bud Freeman and Jack Teagarden, who were influenced by New Orleans but then went on to make their *own* music. Purist writers described this as a 'falling short' of the one true sound – Panassie's real jazz. It was a long time before it was realized that these were great individual players and not clever fakes. They are now the acknowledged masters of pre-war jazz, along with the best negro musicians of the same period.

The middle period, from about 1927 to the war years, gave us some of the finest music in the jazz idiom. It may be a bitter pill for the purists to swallow, but all the old racial barriers were breaking down. After Louis, it was almost impossible to talk about a narrow, regional music belonging to some areas in the Deep South. Jazz belonged to the world. Cross-fertilization, the coming together of Africa and Europe for the first time, resulted in a new music that had to be judged by new standards. And this new music was being made by a new kind of human being, a sophisticated world citizen who simply did not fit into the old racial categories.

The traditionalists not only failed to understand this pattern, but they connived to change it. They preached an inverted racialism which has survived to this day. Negroes were 'different' from the rest of us, and black art was something to be protected from the corrupting influence of whites.

This habit of thinking doesn't help the critic to point the right paths for jazz to take. He refuses to see in Morton, Oliver and Yancey the burgeoning modernism that owed so much to European forms. Instead he tries to fit the phenomena of jazz into his existing world view. Civilization has made slaves of us all and we must now break the shackles and get back to nature. The jazzman is seen as Rousseau's noble savage.

The traditionalist is conditioned by his own class instincts to regard jazz as elemental and childlike. This is the way he would like things to be. He is the doting parent figure who shuns the thought that his little angel is going to grow up one day. It is really too bad of those jazz musicians who are not prepared to play the pundit's game – who are not willing to remain always in the fond parental gaze. Chicago style, swing music, the queer nonconformism of Django and Charlie Parker – all this is disturbing to the traditionalist mind.

But it is as inevitable as the fact that a chrysalis will one day acquire a pair of wings and take to the sky.

7 The Art of Improvisation

A bass player called Danny Haggerty had just departed from the Randall fold. I don't remember what the reasons were, but in the end Danny received a letter, probably forwarded from Hong Kong and typed out by an under-secretary, to the effect that his services were no longer required. A few weeks later, Danny telephoned me to ask if I was interested in working on the *Queen Mary* for a year. The pay was £6 a week and all found. Danny gave me the phone numbers of the other two musicians in the quartet – Cyril Collins and Kenny Harris. Neither of them had absolutely made up their minds to go, on account of the money being so incredible.

'Six pounds a week!' I expostulated. 'That is slightly more than I made when I was a filing-clerk. I don't know what you chaps feel about it but . . . I'll take it.'

All the London musicians were at that time falling over one another to get any kind of a job 'on the boats'. The pay quite obviously wasn't the attraction. Everyone wanted the chance to go over to America and listen to the great jazz musicians, maybe even meet them and discuss various aspects of the jazz scene. Due to the Musicians' Union ban on all US stars, this was the only way we could hear the live music of some revered players – so this was an offer I couldn't very well turn down. Cyril, Kenny and Danny were of the same mind. I immediately sent a letter to Fred, timing it so that it would get to him on the morning after our next job together. I explained that I absolutely had to leave, in view of the great musical opportunities that were involved. Some of the boys then working on the *Mary* had already contacted their favourite US players for special tuition, so it looked as though British jazz was at last being given a much-needed shot in the arm.

Cyril Collins was leader of the quartet at first. Like so many other pianists he had fallen under the spell of George Shearing. Every one of our arrangements would start with clarinet and piano phrasing together in the jerky, syncopated manner George was popularizing with his own group.

This first trip to the States was very much a trial run, Cyril explained, for the Geraldo office wanted to be absolutely sure that we were the right men for the job. The first wave of *Queen Mary* musicians had included more than one emancipated bopper who had refused to play what the passengers wanted. The story was going around that one bunch of musicians had placed their chairs so that they were playing face to face with one another, with their backs to the audience. Then they had become deeply involved in some Miles Davis arrangements. A small, timid man and his dancing partner had approached the players, tapping one of them on the shoulder.

'Excuse me for mentioning it,' said the man, 'but we can't dance to this. Do you think we could possibly have a waltz?'

The bopper had snapped back, without even looking up: 'Do you mind, George – this is a rehearsal.'

Then, with the two dancers still within earshot: 'Hey, fellers, did you hear *that*? This bloke only came up and asked me for a sodding *waltz*!'

The whole band then stood and pointed at the unfortunate couple, roaring with laughter and holding their sides.

Allowing for some exaggeration, this story was probably not too far wide of the mark. Geraldo had afterwards made it quite clear that he wasn't going to tolerate any more discourtesy to the passengers. If the customers wanted schmaltz, then they must have it. Also, dark glasses, berets and goatees were mentioned as unsuitable items of evening wear.

The emphasis was now upon tuxedos and suave announcements, but it was noticed that the musicians were still playing jazz for most of the time. In the rough weather, nobody was listening anyway. The passengers either remained in their cabins or staggered about holding on to the solid fixtures for dear life, while the band bopped away undisturbed. I didn't find my sea legs until the second trip to New York. During the first crossing I threw up several times, but after that I had no more trouble. This was just as well, for there was no sweet rationing once you were on board. A man could stupefy himself with chocolate if that were where his pleasures lay. Once I had overcome my seasickness, I was able to delight in these things.

Cyril's quartet performed in the tourist class, where most of the passengers were emigrant workers, departing GI brides, or small businessmen who had saved up enough to splash out on their first post-war cruise. The next one up was cabin class, which had a rather larger and more sophisticated band. Their chaps could even read music. The pianist, Ronnie Ball, was a good modern musician who had already started to take lessons in New York from the remarkable Lennie Tristano.

The first time the *Queen Mary* docked in New York, all of us were impatient to hear as much jazz as time would allow. Usually we had two days, sometimes three, in which to fill our ears with the precious sound. That morning, a small party of serious-faced Britishers might have been seen trudging away from Pier Ninety in the direction of Birdland.

'Parker is likely to be playing there tonight,' said Ronnie, 'but we'd better make sure. Lately, they've been putting on dixieland bands to get the customers in. This doesn't happen often, but when it does – don't worry. There's always Bop City.'

There was deep concern over the commercial decline of Birdland. At last we were at the famous little home of modern jazz, and noting with relief that the great altoist would indeed be appearing. He would be alternating with a dixieland outfit starring Bobby Hackett and Vic Dickenson, but then one couldn't have everything. It took all sorts, and besides, one might even have a chance of talking to Parker during the Hackett set.

'I suppose all this modern jazz will be new to you,' grinned Ronnie in a friendly way, 'it isn't likely you played much alto with Randall.'

'Only the occasional quick-step. But I like Bird. I have two of his records at home – "Stupendous" and "Cool Blues".'

'It's going to be some session. The trumpet will be either Miles or Red Rodney. Bud Powell is sure to be on piano.'

I had heard of Miles Davis, but the other two were just names to me.

'You boys seem to like bebop to the exclusion of all else,' I commented. I hadn't meant it to sound like an accusation, but Ronnie came back with: 'Hey, look, I just like jazz. But there's a special importance in the stuff that came out of Minton's. You might say it's altering the whole course of modern music.'

Minton's was the place where Dizzy and Monk and the other modernists went to try out their new ideas. Some writers claimed that these sessions were 'revolutionizing the jazz idiom'. We were walking slowly through the freezing cold streets, towards Times Square. Every few minutes we all had to crowd into one of the big department stores and pretend to be buying something. Then, when we were nice and warmed up, we would proceed on our way. All the shopwalkers looked like Franklin Pangborn and all the sales girls looked like Veronica Lake. We had stepped off the huge steam ship into Movieland, but all I could think of was Parker, and whether he would turn out to be as electrifying as the reports had made out.

Six or seven musicians standing in a small room and 'altering the whole course of jazz'. But not too much, I thought to myself. For I dearly loved what had gone before. You can't stop things from changing, no matter how hard you may try. A leopard will grow to maturity, but there is no magic detergent that will get rid of the spots. Jazz must grow, and jazz must change – but in the process its wonderful Promethean essence is not to be destroyed.

And the essence of jazz is improvised style.

To define jazz simply as improvised music doesn't get us very far. What is so new about improvised music? It held sway for almost a couple of centuries, and culminated in the prodigious figure of Bach. You could write down a Bach improvisation, get a competent musician to play it on the organ, and it would be beautiful music. Try doing that with the Coleman Hawkins solo on 'Body and Soul'. The variations are pleasant, but spring to life only when they are played by Hawkins himself. Improvisation can be written down, but jazz can't. It is the intimate, personal style of the performer that matters in jazz.

Charlie Parker, on that first evening, played jazz of the highest order, with style and originality – but he was not at his best. He seemed like a deranged man, often wandering off the stage for long periods after his own solos. It wasn't until our second visit that we would hear him in surer control, looking much fitter and playing superbly.

Afterwards, a few of the British contingent were introduced to him at the bar. The first thing he said was: 'So – you guys are interested in bebop?'

It was such a mundane opening remark. but Bird was uneasy in front of us and fishing around for a point of contact. When he understood that we were not the enemy, he opened up considerably, becoming very interested in the *Queen Mary* and what it was like on board. We had all come thousands of miles to meet this legendary musician, and now here he was cross-examining us about an ocean liner. Then the subject turned to private tuition: 'Lessons? No, I don't give lessons – how could I? I don't know what the hell I do.'

Parker was in effervescent mood, and would not take seriously the idea that he might actually explain his music in words. I had the impression of a man unable to cope with simple everyday problems. The world was not a place in which he could feel at ease. He could satirize it in his music but, though he was an articulate man, I think he had only one serious form of communication, and it wasn't human speech.

For the second trip, Peter Ind replaced Danny on bass, and stayed on for a year. Peter and Ronnie were both devout modernists who practised several hours each day. Kenny Harris also tapped away on a practice pad, so you can imagine how it felt to be the only lazy musician around. When this practising was going on, I was nearly always strolling on deck with my mind focused upon an entirely different kind of 'bird'. I wasn't yet having any luck with girls. At Southampton the GI brides came on, with their phoney American accents and eyes like dollar signs. Then we stopped at Cherbourg, where we took on some of the loveliest French girls you ever saw. This seemed to be the pattern on each trip outward. After Cherbourg, I wouldn't have been able to concentrate on music even if I *had* been a Tristano pupil. Ronnie became quite derisive about my glassy-eyed expression every time the French came on board.

Ronnie Ball had always doubted that Bird would ever take pupils, and so he had enrolled with Lennie Tristano. Lennie had something of the charisma of Bird, but was more willing to explain himself. He was always ready and able to account for the various patterns in his music, so it was to him that Ronnie and Pete and some others were directing their attention.

Lennie was the coolest of the cool. He greeted his visitors in a Noël Coward-type silk dressing-gown, and a pair of impenetrable dark glasses to shield his blindness from the inquisitive stare. His voice seldom rose above a careful undertone. When amazed, or deeply concerned, he pronounced the single monosyllable: 'Wow'.

As a matter of fact, this was the first thing I ever heard him say. He could not, of course, see any of us, but he could at once sense the nervous attitudes and awed reverence with which his British fans always seemed to approach him for the first time. It was bad enough that most of us could hardly think of a thing to say, and simply sat terror-stricken before this fount of modernism – each man waiting for someone else to break the ice. But then one of our number, a jittery kind of person at the best of times, suddenly started chattering about his own feelings. What a great honour it was, prattled this effusive man, at last to encounter the music's 'giants' and acknowledged masters in the flesh. The speaker then gushed on for a while longer. The gist of his excited appraisal was that we had all learned our jazz by studying the great players on record. Miles had always been 'the coolest', Dizzy and Bud Powell were just 'out of this world', and now at last we had made our pilgrimage to meet this assortment of super-beings face to face. As for finding oneself in the presence of Lennie Tristano himself . . . and here our speaker's voice became incoherent under the strain of suppressed emotion.

'Wow', murmured the man in the silk dressing-gown, who then began to talk gently and persuasively about relaxation. As soon as you learned to relax, and to give yourself to music, you would find it possible to swing – and then the ideas would come. Relaxation and swing were important. Many fine musicians had found themselves caught up in what Lennie called the star system. Because of the star system, players attracted attention to *themselves* instead of to the music, by posturing and striving after effects. The result – hero-worship and a cult of the individual in modern art. Some of the finest modern jazz is thus stifled at its birth, degenerating into the cliché forms. Conclusion: music is not there to serve the performer – he is there to serve music.

Lennie wanted none of the extravagant publicity and adulation so lavishly bestowed upon jazz's leading figures. Far from attempting to set a trend, he seemed to be withdrawing from the public gaze, needing only to be left alone with his music.

Relaxation was all very well in theory, but I was on the threshold of so much that was new and staggering, it wasn't always easy to remain composed. The older musicians on board had seen everything, and were by now pretty well shock-proof. They remained exasperatingly calm whenever the Statue of Liberty hove into view, even protesting that they had seen through 'the American façade'. These were mostly the veterans of straight dance music, and violinists who played salon music in the first-class lounge. They can have had no idea what it must have meant to a young jazz musician to visit the home of jazz for the first time.

Ronnie sometimes played different times from ours, so that he was able to listen during the end of our set. He told me he was looking for a sax player for a sextet he was forming, something along the lines of the Lennie Tristano sextet. He wondered if I would get Cyril to feature me on alto in one number, so that he could hear me play some modern jazz. At the end of my alto feature, Ronnie came up shaking his head and looking disappointed. 'You seem to be well and truly into that Parker phrasing. I love it, but it's not the sort of thing that I have in mind.'

Me, a Parker graduate! It was the nicest thing anyone had said about my playing for a long time.

We were approaching New York for the second time. Ronnie handed me a screwed-up slip of paper and said: 'Lee Konitz's phone number. When we get to New York you could give him a call. He takes pupils and I'm certain he'll be in town.'

Ronnie's polite way of telling me I could use some help. I stuffed the slip of paper into an inside pocket and forgot all about it. I couldn't even use an English telephone without getting into difficulties, so I wasn't going to start learning this strange new system. In any case, I was terrified of Konitz. He would see through my phoney pretences immediately and bring me face to face with my own shortcomings. I wasn't having any of that. Later, after a few more trips, I might get through to him and pay for some advice about chords.

The day before we docked, the quartet was called out to play for a children's tea-party in the afternoon. Tunes like 'Teddy Bears' Picnic' and 'Good Ship Lollipop' just didn't sound right with the George Shearing sound. In the evening we had to go and accompany some acts during a ship's concert, so that by the time we dropped anchor there was a great need for the stimulus of some good jazz.

At Birdland, the tiny compère Pee Wee Marquette was just announcing Parker on to the stand as we arrived. Bud Powell was at the piano, looking very forlorn because he had been banned from using the club's bar facilities for a while. Drinks were ordered for him by one of the ship's musicians, and slyly passed to him during the night. Both Powell and Parker played divinely, almost at the apex of their powers. Then the other band came on, fronted by the incredible Fats Navarro.

'Why do they call him Fats?' I wanted to know. 'He looks as if he could use a square meal.'

'Navarro is a sick man,' sighed Ronnie. 'He's just a shadow these days. If you had seen him a couple of years ago – well, he was quite a big guy – but now . . .'

Ronnie's voice tailed off as the music started up. Navarro was a fat man grown sparse and wrinkly, like a deflated balloon, but the trumpet still sounded with enormous power and authority. We all stayed very late at Birdland and slept until noon the next day.

It was while I was mooching around in Macy's department store that my hand knocked up against the ball of paper with Lee Konitz's number on it. I was feeling as though the city had revealed most of its secrets to me, having just partaken of two Hershey Bars and a Babe Ruth, washed down with a large chocolate malted. My pocket was full of nickels and dimes, and there was this phone booth only a few feet away. I went in, dialled the number, and a voice answered right away.

'Lee Konitz speaking. Hello? You sound an awful long way off.'

I tried bringing the receiver up to my face, like they tell you in the instruction leaflet. I owned up to the fact that my name was Turner, and that I badly needed a few lessons on the alto sax.

Konitz said he still wasn't hearing me too well.

'Say, isn't that an English accent?' said he. 'You must be ringing long-distance.'

I hastily explained that I was right there in New York, but that I wasn't too good with telephones. Or with saxophones, for that matter. How soon could I have a lesson? I would be leaving for England in the morning, but would be back in two weeks' time, if that was OK with him.

'What are you doing right now? Nothing special? Well, come right over. We might as well get started right away.'

Konitz wasn't living in the best part of town. For a while he was turning down an enormous amount of session work because it would interfere with his studies. He and tenorist Warne Marsh were rooming together in fairly spartan accommodation, while they worked with Tristano and occasionally appeared with his sextet. It was not clear where the critics had acquired their verdict on Tristano's music, which they often dismissed as cold, clinical and closer to classical music than to jazz. Lennie, Lee and Warne were all deeply concerned that jazz ought to be played with feeling and not simply as a technical exercise. When Lennie's sextet played at Birdland, all agreed it was the warmest and most potent of jazz sounds.

As usual, the misunderstanding had been over a simple

four-letter word. To the hostile critics, 'cool' implied something that was low-temperature, heartless, intellectualized; to Tristano and Konitz it meant subtle musical feeling and sensitivity ranging over a widened area of sound. There was more real down-to-earth feeling in Lee Konitz's music than in a host of Parker copy-cats reducing modern jazz to a string of parrot-phrases.

Ronnie and Peter were impressed when I told them that I had started lessons with Lee. On the way back to Southampton, Ronnie came along to find out whether my playing had improved. He listened intently, while I took some solos on the alto.

'You still phrase like Parker,' he reproached me, 'but it can't be helped. You're sure to snap out of it, after a few more lessons. Meanwhile, how about coming in on clarinet, when I form my sextet?'

The Ronnie Ball Sextet was openly and frankly a Tristano-style outfit, an extension of Lennie's own study group in New York. It was a way Ronnie could try out practical applications of what he was learning from Lennie.

'What I don't quite follow,' I ventured, 'is all this aversion to sounding like Charlie Parker. The last time I played in a modern group, they complained I didn't sound enough like Bird. I'm all mixed up.'

'Well, what Lennie teaches is improvisation. You don't improvise by copying another man. Parker is a giant, but all these imitations that are going on now – it just adds up to a load of . . .'

'Plagiarism?'

'I was going to use a rather stronger word.'

During my first months on the *Queen Mary* I had moved out of the bedsitter in Gloucester Place. I now had an arrangement with a girl singer, who had a small room in Mornington Crescent. We shared the same narrow bed for the occasional nights that I spent in London, in between trips. For the rest of the time it was her own pad, and my personal belongings were packed away in a cupboard pending my return. It worked out fine at first, but later there were problems when the boat happened to make the return journey ahead of schedule. Then I was likely to arrive home in the middle of the night to find the bed already overflowing with people I knew.

The girl was fond of modern jazz, and even fonder of the people who played it, so every now and then we liked to visit the Club Eleven for an evening of relaxed listening. These modernists knew me slightly, as a Randall alumnus who had lately come into the news as a Konitz pupil. They also knew my girlfriend and heads snapped round as soon as the two of us entered the place.

On one of these Club Eleven evenings the atmosphere seemed particularly foggy, especially around the bandstand. I was seated close to the music, trying to sort it all out in my mind. It looked like being just one more night like the rest, when slowly I became aware that the place was filling up with men in blue uniforms. I was right in the middle of a police raid.

Now this may sound naïve, but for a long time I couldn't imagine what the police were doing in a bebop club, unless Ken Colyer had recently been appointed Chief Custodian for the Arts. Two plain-clothes men searched me from head to toe, but I hadn't the faintest idea what they were looking for. Then we were all sent outside while the police ransacked the premises. The girl had already been searched by a couple of police-women.

'Drugs, you chump,' she explained, in answer to my baffled look. 'Half the band has been taken away in a van – and just as I was enjoying my night out.'

'Wonder why they picked on the musicians.'

'That's what seems so unfair. The boys were up there in full view, while everybody else was flushing theirs down the toilet, or kicking it under the tables. It makes me so mad.'

We all went back into the club, some to collect hats and coats from the cloakrooms, others to stand around discussing the recent events. The place now bore a ravaged look. A good trumpet player called Leon Calvert was standing disconsolately by the piano, where a pianist and a bass player had started to show each other some chord changes as if nothing had happened.

Leon Calvert looked like a Latin American general, but played the trumpet like Miles Davis. He was a big favourite with the fans at Club Eleven, and now that the evening had ended so disastrously he went to the microphone and said a few words: 'Perhaps this has taught us all a sharp lesson,' he said. 'We don't want to see this fine club being closed down by the police. So in future, folks, let's make sure we are clean when we come here to listen to our favourite music.'

I still hadn't a clue what had been going on, and what the word 'clean' meant in this context. I had paid to hear some modern jazz, and now there was a distinct shortage of musicians up there on the stand. People were already heading towards the exit, having had enough excitement for one day.

'Will there be any more jazz?' someone asked, but Leon wasn't able to say.

'Bruce,' he called out to me, 'how about helping out for the rest of the time?'

He was pointing to a tenor sax which had been left on top of the piano in the course of events. I've no idea who the owner was, but he had made a very hurried retreat from the scene.

'Gosh, I don't believe I can play a tenor.'

'How do you know – if you've never tried?'

And that was how I came to play at the Club Eleven, for the one and only time in my life.

The newspapers were not kind to jazz or its practitioners on that occasion. It looked as though journalism had made up its mind to connect the jazz idiom with everything lurid and underhand. Players who occasionally took a few puffs of the weed now found themselves described as debauched villains who were not fit to mix with decent folk. Some of the headlines smacked of an unscrupulous attempt to make jazz seem a very sinister business indeed. As much cheap publicity as possible was being squeezed out of the fact that a few musicians had become addicted. The word 'jazz' was quickly taken up as a vaguely insulting four-letter adjective by certain news-hounds. One read of the 'jazz girl' who had become a fallen woman, or of the shady practices that went on at 'jazz parties'. This cheap sensationalism was no credit at all to the newspaper business, but in spite of it all the Club Eleven affair was soon forgotten. The club continued to operate as this country's Mecca of modern jazz.

Back on the *Queen Mary*, I found that Cyril was thinking of leaving us, which would mean that the quartet would be without a leader and that we would have to find a piano replacement as well. I agreed to renew my contract for another six months, as leader – but only if we could get Dill Jones on piano. Dill and Lennie Felix were my two favourite pianists in this country. I thought Dill might agree to join us, for he was anxious to visit the US. In this way our quartet inherited a brilliant piano man, as well as a change of leadership.

We now had a formidable line-up with which to foist even more jazz upon the passengers in tourist class. Pete Ind was starting to show great promise as a Tristano pupil and Kenny

Harris was drumming very well. My own playing was coming along slowly.

Lee Konitz had agreed to give me lessons only if he could be sure that I was serious, and prepared to work hard. From bitter experience he had found that some pupils came to him so that they could copy a few of his phrases, and then go away to advertise themselves as star pupils. For a while, all I seemed able to do was copy Lee, which was not what he wanted at all. Every lesson became a renewed struggle to get me away from these musical impersonations and towards a free improvisatory style. One of our biggest problems was that I usually arrived late for my lessons, and in a state of near exhaustion. When I wasn't getting on to the wrong street-car, I was on the right one but going in the opposite direction.

Lee didn't make matters easier by changing his address a couple of times. I must have learned plenty about the geography of New York City during those first journeys to Lee's home.

Once I nearly had to forgo my lesson completely. I had the instructions all carefully written down, so nothing seemed likely to go wrong. Then, as I was making for the exit at Pier Ninety, a uniformed figure blocked my path.

'OK, open up,' said the figure, pointing to the sax case.

'It's all right – it's a saxophone,' I assured him. 'It's mine. I'm a professional musician. I work on the *Queen Mary* . . .'

'I ain't saying it isn't yours. But it goes right back on board, get me? I've told you guys before – you don't work in this country without a special permit.'

'No, you don't understand. I'm not going to play for money. I'm on my way to a saxophone lesson.'

'Listen, buddy, you must think I'm dumb or something. If you claim you are a professional musician – OK, *how come you need a lesson?*'

The logic was inescapable. I took the sax back to my cabin, and then contacted Lee by telephone. The following day, he came on board and gave me a lesson in my cabin, but only after he had made me show him round the ship several times. Here was another great alto sax player full of questions about life on this famous ocean liner.

I now felt convinced that Lennie and Lee were the most important voices in modern jazz, leaving aside the unique talent of Charlie Parker. In Lennie's music, the patterns of improvisation had been set free from certain fixed ways of thinking.

Earlier attempts to be 'progressive' had consisted either in young musicians marking time behind Parker, or in a strict adherence to some classical book of rules. Instead of improvising, the younger players were making Bird noises, or else running up and down the chord changes at dizzying speeds.

After Tristano, the idiom became adventurous once again. Jazz performance now started to have real organic growth, an architectural logic which one finds in the best symphonic writing, but which is rare in jazz. Then, almost as an afterthought, Lennie produced some works in free form, about ten years before it became a self-conscious 'school'.

Ronnie Ball's Sextet was really intended as a student group, an extension of what Lennie was teaching in New York, but it made a few brief appearances at the modern clubs around London. I played clarinet and Gray Allard played tenor. Ronnie wrote some lines, based on the extended chord principle, and we kicked them around. Later I moved over to the alto sax, but I was always the backward boy who never quite got the hang of these progressive changes. Ronnie was patience itself. As we came near to the end of our contract with 'Geraldo's Navy', he told me about a pad in Goodge Street. Some of the boys were now rooming there so that they could work together on some chordal things, and I was invited to move in too. The landlord had put up a lot of hardboard partitions so that we each had our own private den, just big enough to hold a bed, with a communal living-room at the end of the hall. Trumpeter Jimmy Deuchar and drummer Tony Kinsey were in there, and Dennis Rose came to some of the practice sessions.

Dennis alternated between trumpet, piano and drums. He was a creative musician but the sort of man who could never make up his mind which instrument to focus on. He liked to get his fingers on anything that was around.

John Dankworth also came to one of these private sessions.

'He looks sort of emaciated,' I whispered to Ronnie. 'Don't you modernists ever eat anything?' Ron and Tony Kinsey both looked as though they had been assembled out of matchsticks, and Pete Ind wasn't exactly robust.

'Fine words,' retaliated Ronnie, 'especially coming from a tall thin vegetarian. By the way, how *are* you going to eat from now on? The contract expires next month.'

I hadn't even given it any thought. All I knew was that I wouldn't be renewing my contract at the end of the six-month period, as I'd done last time. The situation on board had become more than a little strained. Musicians on some of the big liners had never had their status clearly defined. Technically, they were 'crew'. This meant that in their free time they had no right to be anywhere but in their own cabins – everywhere else was out of bounds. And there were four musicians to each small cabin, so to have obeyed the letter of this absurd law would have made life a bit hard. Lately the pursers had been coming down heavily on the ship's musicians, if they were discovered in any of the lounges after working hours in anything like a recumbent position. I felt that they were being grossly unfair. If a female passenger wanted to be entertained, then I was willing to give of my best – even if it meant working overtime.

Time was ebbing away, and I was trying to take in as much music as I could. To keep up with everything that was going on, it would have been necessary to grow an extra pair of ears. There were occasional disappointments. Bird wasn't always the featured attraction, or Tristano's boys, or Lester Young floating on his own private cloud. Sometimes we heard the inferior Parker copy-cats or, worse still, the contrived excitement and fake emotionalism of rhythm and blues. Birdland, like any other club, had to keep one eye on the box-office receipts.

Once, when Parker wasn't at Birdland, we travelled down to Greenwich Village to hear him. The place where he was playing was about the size of somebody's through lounge. There was no problem about getting in, but in order to stay in it was necessary to keep buying drinks at the bar. The prices were astronomical. After we had bought the first round, hardly any of us had anything left but loose change. All we could do was sit there trying desperately to avoid the barman's eye. Parker came out and played with only a rhythm section. He stood almost motionless, staring straight ahead, his expression trancelike. We were so close that we could hear the breath coming out with the notes. There was an air of unreality about it all – music like this being frittered away in a small sparsely attended drinking saloon.

What made it all the more incredible was that Art Tatum was due to come on after the Parker set – one fabulous jazz star alternating with the other.

It wasn't until Parker's last number that the barman finally gave voice: 'OK, you guys. What's it to be?'

That took care of the Tatum set. We all got to our feet and prepared to leave, but now the man had diagnosed that we were 'Britishers'. The scowl died away and was replaced by one of those looks policemen have when they are helping old women across the road.

'You can stay a while longer, but stand over there behind the piano. The seats are for my drinking customers. OK?'

We said we didn't mind standing over by the piano. When Tatum started to play, we were almost breathing down his neck, and by the time he had finished Ronnie was shaking slightly. There were no words, we just stood and stared at each other.

Then we thought of offering our profuse thanks to the barman, who had made it all possible. When he saw us coming, this man let out a throaty chuckle and turned to where the great pianist was standing at the other end of the bar.

'Hey, Art! Come over here, will you – I want you to meet some nice guys from the *Queen Mary*.' The bulky figure wended his way forward.

'Say, what's it like, working on the *Queen Mary*?' said Art Tatum interestedly.

At that juncture – although I know it is only supposed to happen in books – I believe I pinched myself to make sure all this wasn't just another of my dreams. Tatum was not the suave, rather princely sort of fellow I had somehow imagined he would be. His conversation was terse, proletarian and disarmingly casual. Here stood one of the unique figures in modern music, yet all he wanted to talk about was the kind of pay and working conditions that went with our present contract. The rate of pay horrified him, and he laughed uproariously when we told him that we had to wear evening dress for most of the time.

'You're kidding!' chuckled Art Tatum, and demanded to hear more. During the whole of our encounter, he carefully manoeuvred the conversation away from his own music. Like Parker, he seemed to feel that music wasn't something you talked about. When pressed, he admitted to a great liking for Duke Ellington's way of playing the piano, which had been an influence on his own playing. Tristano? An exciting player, but maybe a little strait-laced. A brilliant teacher, Lennie. Say, on a big luxury ship, I guess the pianos must be really something!

I don't think I contributed much to this memorable tête-à-tête. I just stood there in a daze, trying to figure out how this big man with the ravaged face of an ex-pugilist managed to express a beauty and natural dignity which was not in his words. 'A station like the herald Mercury, new-lighted on a heaven-kissing hill' would just about sum up my first impression of the great pianist, viewed at close quarters.

That night we stayed in the ship's kitchen until five, chattering away over cornflakes and fresh cream. Sleep, of course, was out of the question.

In that same month I heard the Ellington band live on stage at one of the big movie palaces off Broadway, the Basie band with Buddy De Franco at Radio City and a group led by Ernie Caceres in a small bar downtown. I also had an impromptu private session with guitarist Irving Ashby and percussionist Jack Constanza, who were crossing over with Nat Cole on the way back from a European tour. Nothing like this was happening in Britain because of the MU ban, so the only reason I decided to leave the *Queen Mary* at the end of the year was that my money had run out. I needed to start making some more, and had started to think about joining one of the regular touring bands in this country. But there wasn't a band in all the world that was likely to take on a musician like me, now hopelessly stranded in between my dixieland past and some recently acquired modernism – except one. I contacted Freddy Randall again, and went back into the vacant clarinet chair. Now Freddy wanted me to double on sax for certain swing numbers so I was happy to be back once again.

I had studied alto with Lee Konitz for almost a year, but was now back where I had started, plaguing the purists with my Chicago-style clarinet and swing-era saxophone.

For British jazz criticism was now all about labels. Nobody spoke about music any more, but only of dixieland, bebop and the roundly chastised and discredited cool school. Later the term traditional jazz would come into play, identifying the kind of music approved by Panassie, Harris and Blesh. It was all very confusing, if you simply wanted to go somewhere and blow jazz.

When somebody asked Dizzy Gillespie to define 'bebop', he told them it was 'just the way jazz sounds when it's played by me and some of my friends'.

You can't argue with that. Here were a bunch of young post-war musicians with attitudes determined by the altered times. There was no chance at all that they would play in the same way as the older men. The world was different now. At the same time, bebop was not out to supersede other forms of jazz, but only to refresh these other forms and to be refreshed by them in turn. Dizzy knew that he could play faster than Louis, with a wider harmonic range, but he always held the master in reverent awe. Dizzy and Bird were aware of music as a personal form of expression – yet all the pundits could see was its technical expertise.

In a book entitled *Bird Lives*, there are constant admiring references to Charlie Parker's sheer speed and dexterity, and it is almost as though the great altoist were seen simply as a musical version of the Sundance Kid. But the essence of Parker was in his ability to throw off subtle and witty self-portraits which were also fascinating studies of the world in which he lived. This man knew all about the blues, and how to update and make them relevant to his own time. He also originated a wistful ballad style. I know of no one in all jazz, after Lester Young, who could charge a ballad with such copious warmth.

I was one of the lucky ones. I heard Parker and Tatum in their heyday, stood in the presence of Navarro and Lester before their passing, and received guidance from Lee Konitz for almost a year.

'I understand you've been studying with Konitz,' said a young altoist by the name of Harry Klein. 'How is it that you studied modern jazz for a year, and then came back and joined a dixieland band? What was it all for?'

'Well, for a start, Lee didn't teach me to be a modernist. He helped me to find my own way of playing. The idea was to get me to sound like a fellow called Bruce Turner.'

'And this Turner – does he turn out to be a trad musician after all?'

'I don't understand all these labels. I try and play with my *own* sound. If a lot of critics want to slap a label on it, that's their affair.'

The search for Turner was still going on. Konitz had only pushed me in the right direction and shown me what route to take. I don't know if I started to play *better* after my stint with Konitz, or if I sounded more '*modern*' afterwards, or just as old-fashioned as before. These are just words that the critics use in their strange vocabulary.

What I do know is that the cool school, as it became known, gave me confidence in myself and altered some deeply ingrained attitudes to music and life. I now understood the importance of relaxation. I had watched Lennie Tristano very closely at Birdland. Sometimes, while people in the audience chafed and fretted, he had sat motionless at the keys, breathing in deeply, exhaling, waiting for the moment to come. After a minute or two, one could sense a change in the whole atmosphere. The drone of conversation would cease, as heads were craned forward and enquiring eyes were directed at the waiting musicians. What were we all waiting for? Why hadn't the music started? Then the wonderful cascading sounds would begin, quietly at first but building up in intensity. If any section of the audience became noisy again, down would come the music, to a restrained whisper. Almost at once, the noise of conversation came down too. In this way, Lennie always commanded respect for his music. He not only managed to relax his own tensions, but the audience's as well.

This ambience at Tristano's live sessions was something I came to admire greatly. Jazz had always placed a strong emphasis on pounding rhythms and on emotions being laid bare. With cool jazz you had to read between the lines. The warm feeling was always there, though not immediately on display.

For a few weeks, after I had left the *Queen Mary*, I continued to blow with Ronnie Ball's quintet, before returning to the Randall fold. Ronnie soon found that it wasn't possible to make a living by playing cool music in the London clubs. Soon afterwards he and Peter Ind went to live in the States, taking further lessons from Tristano and slowly building up reputations – two of the most creative musicians this country ever produced. I almost went along too, but decided at the last moment to remain in this country, where I was beginning to enjoy things more keenly than in the past. Simply being more relaxed was making a world of difference, and not only in the sphere of music.

And this, I suppose, is what it's all about.

8   On Stalling Between Two Fools

In January 1953 I accepted an offer from Humphrey Lyttelton, who wanted an alto sax in his band. It was rather like being invited to blaspheme in church. The first time I brandished that saxophone before the crowd at 100 Oxford Street I could almost hear the sound of teeth being gritted together. Gasps of outraged horror could be discerned above the drone of existentialist chatter and the slurping of lemonade. For every good traditionalist knew that the saxophone was not a jazz instrument at all, but part of a seditious plot to overthrow New Orleans music.

These purists were only a small minority, but for a while they just wouldn't leave me alone. I am sure they only came, and kept on coming, in order to exude horror and incredulous disdain. They would even huddle close to the band in order to back away from the saxophone solos. This period was short-lived, and in no time at all the new line-up was accepted by all. The bigots became tired of their sport and made way for a more appreciative type of listener.

I rather gathered that Humphrey had once said, or written, something about New Orleans jazz being a 'refresher course'. The implication was that it was a sharp reminder of some of the basic elements in jazz, which had lately gone out of fashion – such as tonal expression and collective interplay. Humphrey had no intention of remaining in this comfortable niche, like a retired pensioner, fenced off from the necessities of development and change. He would move forward from this, trying out various things and more or less playing for pleasure. One or two of the pundits thought this was mischievous talk, coming from Britain's most illustrious revivalist. To many of the hard-line traditionalist writers, jazz did not only start in New Orleans but finished there as well.

The 100 Club in Oxford Street was the very same place where I had once gone to hear Victor Feldman, the kid drummer, and where I had played my timid and vacuous solos in the presence of superior musicians. Maybe I had become intimidated by the place, but at any rate I wasn't blowing with much confidence on those first Lyttelton dates.

'Try not to be so polite,' suggested Wally Fawkes, 'you have all those nice phrases, but they're not getting past the edge of the stage. Throw the music at them. Project!'

Wally had this big rich sound on clarinet, and I knew he was handing me some sound advice. My playing up to that time had been rather ornate, almost decorative, but now I was learning how to project. The fans were now almost ready to accept a saxophone in the band, in place of the conventional tailgate trombone. It was up to me now – I had to justify my selection and start playing for the team.

Then we played at a big concert in Birmingham. When we arrived, I realized that the Birmingham Town Hall held unpleasant memories. When I'd played there with Freddy Randall, nobody had wanted to know. There had been an icy silence after every one of my solos. It wasn't easy to see what I had done to make this Midlands crowd so consistently unfriendly, but there it was.

We filed on to the platform to the accompaniment of warm applause. Humph was a big favourite up here, there was no doubt about that. When we started playing, all seemed to be going well, and even when I stepped forward to solo there was some kind of audience reaction. It sounded as if the people out there had been stirred to some lively response.

Then Humphrey whispered: 'Look over there!' and nodded his head incredulously in the direction of a row of seats some distance back. We all craned our heads round. At the start of my solo, the occupants of this row of seats had raised a long white banner on which had been inscribed the words 'GO HOME DIRTY BOPPER'. Every time I took a solo, through-out the entire concert, this banner was raised aloft, and the strange slogan displayed there for all to see. By the time we had played our closing tune, I was wearing a hunted look and blowing with my eyes closed, but Humph and Wally had never seen anything so funny for a long time.

Even today, I give an involuntary shudder when I'm told that I have to play in Birmingham. Whether I am appearing as guest star at a small jazz club there, or getting myself hopelessly lost in the city's notorious one-way system, I am overtaken by a feeling of panic and wish desperately that I were home in bed. I suppose to the boppers of Birmingham, if such exist, I am that 'dirty traditionalist' and likely to be packed off home. The place has given me a complex, and that's the way it's been for a long time.

Soon after my first appearances with Humph's regular band, I found myself in a subsidiary group directed by him, but consisting mostly of West Indian musicians. This was the Paseo Band, with which Humphrey liked to experiment from time to time. The so-called 'Spanish tinge' was a facet of early New Orleans music which the revival had rather tended to neglect. I hadn't paid much heed to it myself, I have to admit, but now I became absorbed in at least some of it. It was always a thrill for me when I sat down to blow with the Paseo boys. Mike McKenzie was the Paseo Band's deputy leader, and played a very authoritative piano. Mike came originally from Guyana, and had been walking on crutches for a very long time. Once Johnny Parker, Humph's pianist, was pushing Mikey in a wheelchair through one of the main-line stations. I was walking behind, carrying the cases. We were looking around for the rest of the boys, the Lyttelton band and the Paseo Band, but they were nowhere to be seen.

'Blast it!' said John, or words to that effect, 'we've gone and arrived here too early – the very thing I always try to avoid.'

While we were standing around by the wheelchair, two large characters came up to us and stood one on each side of the chair.

'How come,' said one of them, 'you are pushing a bleck boy? Whites don't wait on bleck boys, where we come from.'

John had turned rather pale. He explained quietly that we were *not* where these two gentlemen had come from, but were right here in England – a country that did not recognize apartheid. The two South Africans did not like this at all. Right there in broad daylight they started to push John and me back against the wall. Then the two bands showed up, in full force. Wally and Humphrey tended to dress like Canadian lumber-jacks in those days, and Micky Ashman, our bass player, looked rather like an underworld thug in his teddy-boy top coat. Behind them swarmed the Paseo gang in flash American suits and sinister dark glasses. The two South Africans took one look and made off at high speed.

Jazz musicians, as a rule, shun violence like the plague. It is just that their mode of dress, and the fact that they sometimes make rather a lot of noise when crowds of them get together, can often give a false impression. At times like these they can appear rather like a host of invaders from outer space.

In the early days, the Lyttelton band made most of its longer journeys by train, since none of us could afford a car. We made so many return journeys in the sleeper that one of the senior officials came to recognize us as soon as we hove into view, referring to us collectively, if somewhat sharply, as 'you Lytteltons'. He evidently thought of us as an unruly mob, sent by Providence to try him. I wouldn't say we were disciplined, yet we did manage to arrive at most places on time. I was usually on hand, with my instruments. As a rule, I arrived at railway stations ahead of Johnny Parker. Our regular pianist had it deeply ingrained in him that to arrive on a railway platform before the exact departure time was to be guilty of conduct unbecoming a jazzman. If by accident he did arrive a few minutes early, off he would go on some pretext, to be conspicuously absent when the train was about to move off. We would listen for the guard's whistle, and then the man nearest the window would lean out and glance back over the line of carriages, as a matter of routine. Sure enough, the dapper form of J. Parker would be espied leaping on to one of the rear carriages as it slid by, eyes alight with the excitement of the chase.

Meanwhile, I was receiving twice as much publicity as anyone else in the band. Every time anyone wrote to the musical journals about the evil influence I was causing with my saxophone, somebody else would rush to my defence. One of the consequences of all this was that I became a man with a rather busy sex life. What I had fantasized about for years was now coming true. Girls were flocking around, not because I possessed any magic sex appeal but to take a closer look at the controversial fellow who had started to upset the pundits everywhere. I also had the advantage of being the only member of the band with no marital ties. Soon it became necessary to purchase a little black book, so that I could keep track of all the addresses and phone numbers that came my way.

Within the year, trumpeter Mick Mulligan was referring to me as the most engaging sex maniac on the jazz scene – a graceful compliment, coming from the master himself. I now had delusions of grandeur and moved into a vast apartment in Maida Vale. The place had three bedrooms and a sizeable lounge. Just what I thought I could hope to accomplish with all these bedrooms I can't imagine, but in any case just before I moved in someone drew my attention to the small print. Subletting was definitely out, and the landlady was ensconced on the floor directly below mine, so now I had to find a way of paying the rather steep rent every month. Then I met this extremely attractive blonde woman. She had two girlfriends. All three of them were desperate for somewhere to stay, and then they found out about my apartment with all the vacant space.

'You could tell your landlady that you just got married. Then I'd move in and start paying half the rent, and I'd cook some meals for you as well. Think of the money you'd save!'

I stepped smiling into the web. Later, the other two girls moved in, as close friends or sisters or something like that. My 'squaw' promised more contributions.

'And they will put something towards the rent, too. You'll be living here almost free.'

It was hard to resist this offer. Needless to say, the thing didn't work out. After a short while, we all went our separate ways.

I was lucky to find a room again at Gloucester Place, so that my life of confirmed bachelordom could continue where it had left off.

Humphrey was far and away the best thing that came out of the revival. His early playing reminded one of Louis Armstrong's work with the Hot Five, but in some uncanny way he had stamped his own personality upon the music. When I was in this early band, he had discovered a great liking for Buck Clayton and the middle-period trumpeters, but refused to be trapped into becoming a mere copy. I don't believe I quite understood about Buck's unique position in post-war jazz until Humphrey proceeded to bend my ear on the subject. After a while, I had to agree that Clayton had emerged from being a very good player before the war, to becoming a great one after it. Buck's sensitive use of vibrato and all the subtle tonal inflections were carried on in Humphrey's own playing, which made it a pleasure for me to be in this band.

I also enjoyed reading the occasional references to Humph in certain jazz mags. A critic's choice of words was conditioned by the extent to which he agreed or disagreed with the Lyttelton creed. One writer would wax lyrical over Humphrey's 'single-mindedness' in continuing to go his own way. Another would complain that Humph was being 'bloody-minded' and that he was incapable of listening to the voice of reason. There was certainly no lack of controversy whenever he was around.

One day, just as things were swinging along nicely, my disc slipped as I was climbing on to a train. I had to be taken home in an ambulance and helped into bed. The next day I had to do a concert with the Lyttelton band, somewhere on the Sussex coast, I believe. It wasn't too painful as long as I was bent almost double, doing the whole concert like a Quasimodo without the bells. The applause for my solos was quite deafening. Afterwards, in the band-room, I tried to straighten up, but was locked in a crouching position.

'Why is it,' enquired Humphrey, 'that every time you meet a vegetarian he is either covered in boils or writhing in agony on the carpet?'

'Don't be fooled by all this,' diagnosed Ashman, 'Bruce is as fit as you are. He finally discovered a way of hogging the entire show.'

Thanks, fellers, for your gracious sympathy! The National Health doctor put me in a plaster cast which stretched from just below my neck to just below my navel. I was able to go straight to work that same evening. After the show a girlfriend came back with me to my room in Gloucester Place. It was agreed that if she spent the night, it would be on the understanding that I would only make love if I could do so without discomfort. We lay there side by side, and about halfway through the night I couldn't stand it any longer. I crawled out of bed and got rid of the plaster by sawing through it with a bread-knife.

Somebody had the idea of teaming us with a couple of folk singers. The two singers were Ewan McColl and A.L.Lloyd, and they were the real thing – folklorists of repute, as distinct from the type of folky 'pop' singer who crashed into the top twenty every now and then. We did a whole series with these two, for radio, improvising behind sea shanties, country ballads and some craggy Highland songs. At the end of the series, Ewan offered me a fortnight in Bucharest, as part of a team of folk musicians who were going there. I accepted, after checking with Humph that he would be able to spare me for a while.

One thing then led to another. Alan Lomax heard me with McColl and thought I would be just the man for a radio series *he* was planning. He worked with prison songs, field 'hollers' and even songs about factory pickets. I was ready for anything by this time. It looked as though improvised jazz was something you could fit into almost any musical context, and nobody would mind. Elstree Film Studios wanted me to provide music for a film soundtrack, along with the singer Lonnie Donegan. Lonnie was not yet a big star, but was still popularizing skiffle in the smoky London cellars.

'This film, see,' explained Lonnie when I arrived, 'is all about a truck driver. Diane Cilento works in one of these transport caffs, and her lover – that's Lee Patterson – is in some kind of trouble. There are these close-ups of wheels going round, and Diane staring out of the window with those big tragic eyes.'

'How about a medium-tempo blues – with maybe a shuffle rhythm?'

'No, it's all been sorted out. I will be singing this ballad about the South – and all you have to do is play an obbligato.'

It seemed incongruous somehow, but I went along with it. My next assignment was even more hilarious, for I had to *appear* in a film during a nightclub scene. Other musicians in this scene were Don Lusher, Benny Green and Dill Jones. Was I going to be given a chance to act at last? The director quickly put us all straight. Not only would there be no acting for us to do, but no playing either.

'Just play any notes that come into your heads – or none at all,' we were told. 'The music will be dubbed in later.'

During each take, the boys simply went mad. They played long sustained notes, honked, squealed and went deliberately off pitch, while continuing to hold serious expressions for the camera. As soon as the man said 'Cut!' everyone exploded into fits of insane laughter, now that it didn't have to be held in any more. It came out later that the sound that was to be dubbed on to our scene would be that of a twelve-piece band – five more people than we had on the bandstand. I hope I get a chance to see this film some day, on the box, and enjoy a good laugh. We appear in brief, split-second shots in close-up, but for most of the time we operate in a fuzzy background somewhere behind Dane Clark's left ear. After all those years, I had at last made my appearance on the silver screen.

I can't say I enjoy standing with a sax in my hand and not being allowed to play music on it. This happens a lot during television and film work. Sound balance and camera positions seem to take an eternity, yet even a couple of furtive warm-up notes will be likely to draw fire from the man in charge.

'Silence in the studio, *please!*' he snarls at you. You put your instrument down somewhere and wander off to the side, hoping to sit down for a moment. The voice takes on an even more irate tone: '*Will* you keep to your positions!'

it says, and another millennium ticks by.

There was plenty of work available for a young hopeful like myself, who had slowly managed to make a name for himself in the profession. It wasn't always pleasurable work, but it was certainly nice to feel that one's services were in demand. It was also a good feeling when one received a phone call from somebody on the staff of a musical journal, asking for a quote on some aspect of the jazz scene. Good heavens! Do they really care what we think after all? For a heck of a long time, nobody *had* seemed to care. Theories and definitions had always seemed to come from outside, from a handful of literary men who couldn't possibly know what was in the jazz musician's mind.

Humphrey Lyttelton had completed *I Play as I Please* and was working on his next book. I thought *I Play as I Please* put the case for jazz succinctly, in simple language, coming closer to the truth than the intellectualized jargon used by some writers of that period. In order to illustrate the cerebral nature of most books on jazz after the war, it would do no harm to quote a passage from *Heart of Jazz*, by William Grossman and Jack Farrell. Try this for size: 'The feeling of unity-in-diversity, with its religious connotations, has little significance for mass man. It implies a cosmic quest that is meaningless to him, for his orientation is egocentric and therefore, although utterly fallacious is simple and, so to speak, homophonic.'

So to speak! But what jazz musician speaks like this, or would be likely to explain his own music in these terms? But it doesn't matter anyway. The books are not aimed at the likes of you and me, are they? Pundit speaks to pundit, turning musical discussion into a refined indoor sport practised by the few. In fact, there is a lot of sound common sense in the book I have just quoted from, hidden behind all the verbiage. The trouble is, that unless you have just completed a course in advanced philosophy, you may not understand a word of it.

A great, yawning, intellectual gap had appeared between the pundit, clever in the use of words, and the sweaty, grunting, inarticulate jazzman. It was like something out of a Wellsian fantasy, where silent Morlocks smart under the dominance of the Beautiful People.

The performers wrote only about themselves and their lives in jazz. I suppose those autobiographies by Billie Holiday and Bechet came closer to explaining jazz than all the clinical arguments about evolution and essence. The last time a jazz musician tried setting down his opinions about right and wrong music, it didn't work out very well. Mezz Mezzrow's *Really the Blues* has the sickly odour of decadent romanticism on every page. I believe it sold a lot of copies in this country and helped promote the absurd notion that brown-skinned people are fundamentally different from white-skinned.

Another book that sets a great chasm between light and dark people is Roland Gant's novel, *World in a Jug*. Here we read of the 'real low down-to-earth natural genius that seems to have been given to negroes', and learn that they 'only have to open their mouths or lay their fingers on strings or piano keys for feeling to flow with the ease of water from an open faucet'. Here is the romanticizer again, with his mystical force which makes one race of people superior to another. Without meaning to, it drives yet another rift between groups of people who are essentially alike.

How could you answer the professional writers? They had the gift of words and a mere sax player could cross swords with them only at his peril. I wrote a few short articles for the jazz mags, but only after I had been goaded by one of these people almost beyond endurance.

Such an occasion was the appearance of an article by Benny Green in the *New Musical Express*. It was entitled 'On Falling Between Two Stools', and was all about mainstream jazz in Britain. Apparently some of us were dithering about between the rival camps of trad and modern, ending up by being neither one thing nor the other. Benny had given up trying to play the tenor sax by this time, and was emerging as an amusing writer and raconteur. In his 'Two Stools' article, he cited the three British musicians he considered to be most typical of this nondescript mainstream. They were Keith Christie, Dill Jones and myself.

Now honest criticism is one thing, but I was fairly sure that Benny had taken only a very cursory glimpse at what he now sought to condemn. He had once heard me imitate some other players for a joke, and promptly labelled me 'the Florence Desmond of the alto sax'. It's true, I do come up with these comic impressions from time to time, but I must say that I resented Benny's implication that I had nothing of my own to express. Later, when challenged, Benny denied that he had meant to deprecate my playing.

'We all go in for copying,' he wrote, 'Bruce is just better at it than most.'

So that was all right then – or was it? Maybe I was becoming paranoid about the hit-and-run tactics of some writers. It was at this point that Benny embarked on his one-man crusade against mainstream. Dill, Keith and I were sternly reproved for wandering between the fixed categories.

I replied to Benny under the heading 'On Stalling Between Two Fools'. I like a good spoonerism, and this one seemed to say it all. The two 'fools' were, of course, the devotees of hidebound 'trad' and 'progressive' jazz respectively. The article took me such a long time that by the time it appeared in print the whole thing had been forgotten anyway. I pointed out the danger of working with all these exclusive labels, and suggested that no two individual styles are going to sound exactly the same. We play the way we do because we are what we are, and no amount of criticism is going to change that.

At least, this is what I *intended* to say, but I lacked journalistic skill. Well, they say all publicity is good publicity, and perhaps I should have left it at that. I was getting to be fairly well-known by now, so it was inevitable that things both good and bad would be said about me in the press. In those days it was still rather diverting to see one's name in print. Sometimes the mags would want to interview me, either at some appointed meeting-place or by someone calling at my home. When the interviewer arrived, there would follow a casual conversation about jazz, until it gradually dawned on me that the interview had officially begun. The other person was always trying to keep the talk as offhand as possible. It didn't do for me to get too serious or use any long words. Jazzmen were supposed to be easy-going hedonists who expressed themselves, if at all, in quaint epigrams or violent expletives. Answers were expected to be amusing rather than informative, and in words of not more than three syllables. The interviewer would provide the literary 'style' – that was what he was there for.

Anyone could see that this wasn't going to work out to my advantage. Your average journalist is no seeker after the higher truths, but simply an ardent young news-hound trying to find a market for his imagination. He just wants copy and in the end he will present the other person as he sees him. In my case I was to be presented as the fluffy-minded eccentric with nothing much upstairs. Nobody is as interested in carefully weighed judgement, as in oracular sayings meant rather to startle than to inform.

'What,' enquires the interviewer, 'is your opinion about

Sonny Stitt and his influence on music today?'

I am flattered to be asked, and try to give a cautiously worded account of my feelings about Stitt. Full marks for technique, perhaps two out of ten for originality – he's no great favourite of mine, but I don't suppose that will keep him or anyone else awake nights.

Weeks later I remember that the issue containing my interview is out in the bookstalls. I invest in a copy, wondering how the thing will appear in print. Soon I have found the page I am looking for, and find myself staring in horror at things I am supposed to have said.

' "What, Stitt! But Dad, he just can't *play*!" mumbled Turner, in between mouthfuls of strawberry cheesecake.'

The rest of the article is presented along similar lines. Soon thousands of readers will have it impressed upon their susceptible minds that I am an inarticulate moron with his mouth full of cake. I vow never to give another interview unless there is a team of lawyers standing by.

But it isn't long before I am again caught out in an unguarded moment. I am with some other musicians in a bar in the north. We're having an interval, and I am being my usual scintillating self. I am whiling away the time by making bad jokes.

'Have you heard that they are bringing out a new short-play cassette – a C-One? It is called *The Best of Sonny Rollins*.'

Not exactly side-splitting, but it helps me to pass the time. A few feet away there is a jazz critic talking to Humph. He overhears my remark and quickly jots it down in a notebook. Later I find out that I am about to be quoted in print as having scathingly ridiculed Rollins. It becomes necessary to make frantic phone calls in order to disclaim the remark and restore sanity.

Maybe Rollins *isn't* my favourite tenor player, but it would be a dull sort of world if we all had the same musical tastes. Maybe I *do* prefer the underrated Warne Marsh – but what has this to do with anybody but me?

The point I am trying to make is that it is relatively easy to attract the attention of jazz magazines if you say something idiotic enough, in an unguarded moment. But just try getting a thoughtfully worded article into print! Serious musical discussion? That is the pundit's private domain.

At least, this was the case many years ago. Perhaps the situation has improved now. Today, with the decline of general interest in British jazz, the papers are more likely to leave us alone. Throughout the 1950s, British jazz performers were receiving publicity, but there was a prevailing ignorance about the whole subject. Jazz was something you imported from the USA. Good jazz was what you read about in books and listened to on some scratchy old records, and then tried to duplicate over here.

Then, all of a sudden, the union ban on visiting Americans was lifted. The big names began to come over to this country, first at an almost imperceptible trickle, then in a steady flow. This was good for British jazz, for almost all the great players that came over were clearly not going to have our labels pinned on to them. There were no 'traddies' or 'progressives', but only musicians who had their own very personal things to say. As soon as the first US stars came over, it was clear that the old labels were not going to have much validity any more.

When the Louis Armstrong All Stars played their first British concerts, it was as though a veil had been lifted and we were able to face up to what jazz really was all about. Louis exploded all the popular theories one after the other, as he played his timeless music. Some of us complained that he no longer improvised in the classic sense, but had settled on a more or less fixed routine each night. The amazing thing was that it all *sounded* so fresh and improvisatory, on account of the accents and cadences he invariably used. This was always the essence of Louis's style, and of jazz itself. One of my very favourite performances in all jazz is that plain ordinary show tune, 'Thanks a Million', as played by Louis on an early recording. In the first chorus he sticks close to the melody, simply adding a grace note here and there, or altering the rhythmic stress, using tonal expressiveness to transform the melody and make it his own. It is sheer magic. The melody is nothing until Louis plays it, and then it is transformed. It becomes a beautiful and memorable tune. And now here was Louis doing it all for us in person! It was a glorious time for jazz in Britain.

The Louis concerts took place at the Empress Hall, on a revolving stage. The Lyttelton band alternated with the All Stars, and Humphrey acquitted himself well. He really rose to the occasion, but it was almost impossible to take one's attention away from Louis. Even when not on stage, he dominated the proceedings, bestriding Empress Hall like a colossus, filling the long silence that had gone before.

At the end of the Louis tour, there was a big banquet in the great man's honour. All the eminent critics were there, and a jam session was arranged so that certain young players would have the opportunity of blowing with Louis. It was awe-inspiring. I was pushed into the arena along with some other young hopefuls. Then Louis beat us in, and I realized that here was the one man I didn't want to blow next to on any account. Mere mortals, yes, but not Louis.

I started to take the first solo, and became aware that Keith Christie was launching into his. Neither of us was inclined to give ground, and I knew I was playing very badly indeed. Someone had to back down, but by this time I was in a state of shock. Suddenly a hand fell on my shoulder, and a voice like Al Capone's intoned in my ear: 'Louis says for you to hold it'.

Louis had evidently signalled for Keith to carry on and for me to drop out. I opened my eyes to find that the voice was that of Mezz Mezzrow, as usual acting as Louis's doorman and personal adviser on tour.

Then another voice, a hoarse whisky-sodden one, sounded in my other ear. It belonged to Spike Macintosh, trumpeter, veteran of the impromptu jam session and my own personal fan. In a stage whisper that could be heard all around the room, he urged: 'Carry on, Bruce. Don't pay any attention to that c— Mezzrow!'

That was the end as far as I was concerned and, as soon as I possibly could, I crawled away into the shadows.

The experience of talking to, and sometimes even working with, the greatest jazz musicians of all time was immensely valuable to young players like myself. The very first concert by Count Basie's band was a shattering experience and has to go down in the records as a milestone in jazz listening. People were still twitching as they left the theatre. So this was what jazz *really* sounded like! It wasn't at all how the romantic writers had been describing it for years. Even Bechet, whom many had pictured as a surviving New Orleans-type player, came here and made music you couldn't conceivably cram into the trad category. He just let loose, with an uncanny sort of authoritative beauty, on a wide assortment of things – ballads, 'jump' numbers, early show tunes and French Creole songs.

We had shared the Empress Hall billing with Armstrong, and now we went on tour with Bechet, so that Humphrey was able to renew a friendship which had started between him and Bech many years earlier. Sitting next to the mighty Bechet in a band coach, sometimes for hours on end, it was inevitable that we would talk shop. At first I couldn't think of a thing to say. I asked Sidney how well he knew Johnny Hodges.

'Hodges,' grinned Sidney, 'I taught him everything he knows.'

In conversation, the great players often seem to be saving up their energies, unwilling to get into detailed discussions because they don't really start communicating until the music starts up. Bechet was a hardened professional musician. He travelled with a group of accompanying French musicians, and it was noticed that he kept them always on a fairly tight rein. They were expected to retire to bed at a reasonable hour, and not to drink too much. At every concert Bechet gave everything he had, and he expected others to do the same.

The only visiting American whom I personally found disappointing was Lionel Hampton, who came over with a rather hairy 'rock' band which made a lot of noise. The leader himself treated us to the usual torrid, swinging vibraphone jazz. After one of his concerts we went backstage to look for Hamp. A female attendant, bearing a tray of tea-cups, pointed us towards Hamp's dressing-room.

'Such a nice man,' she enthused, 'and ever so kind to his musicians. I went in just now, and he only had this one cigarette. But do you know, he passed it round to everyone in the band, so they could all have a puff. Wasn't that nice of him?'

For me the greatest experience of all was the tour we did with Eddie Condon and his band. The two bands, Humph's and Eddie's, travelled in an enormous luxury coach with a toilet at the back. During the longer journeys, some of the Americans liked to sit and ruminate there while enjoying a quiet smoke undisturbed.

It was usually foggy around the back of the coach when these therapeutic sessions were in progress. Eddie Condon, reputed to be a man who liked his stimulations in liquid form, never seemed to me to be less than sharp. He always kept up a lively, pungent flow of conversation, never appearing to be at a loss for the right word. My constant craving for cream buns and con-fectionery, and the fact that I never drank anything stronger than Pepsi-Cola, amused him greatly. He couldn't take it seriously. As far as he was concerned, I had discovered a delightful new gimmick which none of his acquaintances had ever thought of. It was a huge joke, and whenever I came into the coach bearing before me my little box of assorted pastries, Eddie held his sides and laughed until the tears came.

In Leicester, clarinettist Bob Wilber fell asleep in his hotel room and failed to appear for the show. I was pushed on to the stage, to do the entire set with Eddie Condon's band. Playing clarinet in front of that rhythm section was like walking on clouds. George Wettling, take it from me, is one of the great drummers. He didn't have to hit anything particularly hard – he had this very beautiful sound which was able to carry to all corners of the de Montfort Hall. If British drummers played with this kind of finesse, more British sax players would be able to get off the ground.

After one of the very last concerts in the London area, I had a late supper with Eddie Condon at a place called Olivelli's in Soho. We talked about things connected with music, from drummers to the kind of pills I needed for my insomnia. Every few minutes the waiter would bring drinks to the table, and Eddie would offer me some. Each time that I politely refused, the Condon features registered amazement and some good-humoured impatience. It was a good joke, but wasn't I carrying it just a bit too far? 'I mean,' this facial expression seemed to be saying, '*nobody* actually prefers cream cakes to booze.'

By this time I had been with Humphrey long enough to have picked up a sound musical education, but not of the kind they supply you with at Juilliard. Humph was doing important pioneer work, when you come to think of it, since nobody else was attracting large numbers of enthusiastic listeners to this main area of non-aligned jazz. Everyone now admits that the trad–mod polarization was pointless and obtuse. To stay outside the two rival 'schools' was the only sensible way, and after the Americans came over, it was only a question of time before a broader and more eclectic musical approach would be adopted here. A critic called Stanley Dance made up a name for this unclassifiable sound. He described it as 'the main stream of jazz', as distinct from the various backwaters and rivulets that had sprung up since the war. It wasn't Dance's fault when somebody shortened this into one word. 'Mainstream', like it or not, was here to stay.

I was now passing through my promiscuous phase. The girls at the Lyttelton Club were making a big fuss of me by this time, and I wasn't exactly fighting them off. It was now 1954, I was coming up for thirty-two and I was feeling a need to have sex regularly, like any normal red-blooded male. In the past, there had been times when this sense of inadequacy had been almost too much to bear. Now I had grown to be very adequate indeed. It felt good. It was rather like coming out of prison, after being in solitary confinement for a number of years. I wanted to leap about and perform cartwheels.

A big, voluptuous girl made her appearance at the Lyttelton Club. In the intermission, I went straight up to her and made chatty conversation. I could never have done this a few years earlier. The big girl confided to me that she was desperate to lose weight. She considered herself to be much too fat.

'Utter nonsense!' I croaked, scarcely able to take my eyes off her. 'You are my idea of the perfectly shaped woman.'

'If you really fancy me so much,' she replied archly, 'I want you to do me a big favour. Get Humph to play a number especially for me.'

'Certainly. Which number would you like?'

'Oh, I'm not fussy. Choose one yourself – but be sure and dedicate it to me.'

It sounded a bit pointless, but I promised to get Humphrey to play a tune of my own choosing, immediately after the interval. But Humph has a mind of his own. He ignored my request, took hold of the microphone, and announced: 'We are going to open this second half with a number that's just been requested by Bruce Turner – Fats Waller's "All that Meat and No Potatoes".'

I never saw the woman again.

My friends were at first rather incredulous when I became engaged to marry a shy, well-behaved young girl from out of town. She had moved to London from a sleepy little village in Sussex, and evidently thought jazz clubs were the last word in debauched nightlife.

'Bruce!' protested one of the boys in the band, 'what are you up to now? That poor child ought to be warned about people like you.'

The rest of the band evidently felt the same way. In one of our regular numbers, an old jazz standard called 'Sister Kate', Humph, Wally and I sang a vocal chorus in harmony. Every time we came to the classic four-bar break, Humphrey abandoned the written lyrics and substituted the lines: 'Who let the *learner* go out with Bruce *Turner*!'

Pat and I later became married, in spite of the advice of nearly all our friends. We moved into a small terraced house. Apart from carpets and fittings, we had only two items of furniture – a bed and a ping-pong table. Chairs and second-hand wardrobes came along later, during that first year of our precarious union.

We were on stage at a place in Liverpool when Humphrey announced over the microphone that I had just become a father. He had received the phone call during the interval, but hadn't been able to find me. Three or four hundred Liverpudlians, therefore, heard the news about five seconds before I did. For the rest of the concert I wandered off into dreamland, wondering what my daughter would look like, the sax operating by remote control. Mother and daughter were both doing well when I came to see them, but the proud father wasn't in very good shape. This new responsibility of fatherhood really terrified me. No doubt about it, I was a retarded manic-depressive and hadn't even been able to cope with life's simpler problems. I had always wanted children, but now I was scared to hell.

Was it Adler who invented the inferiority complex? I had already convinced myself that I was one of life's inglorious failures, even when the going had been relatively simple. Now I was many things I had never thought I would be – professional musician, husband, parent, proud owner of a mortgage repayment book. Caroline was a terrific baby, but every time I looked at her I felt like Norman Wisdom carrying a Ming vase across a long, slippery floor. I needed advice, some kind of pep-talk, but Adler was long gone and Tristano was a thousand miles away. All those years of being carefully shut up inside myself hadn't prepared me for this. My wife Pat was pretty stoical about me shifting all the responsibilities of marriage on to her shoulders. She took it for as long as she could, but within a couple of years more it was clear that the marriage was in trouble.

Humphrey must have been a very patient man in those last months that I was with the band. Every time the curtain went up, he must have glanced round to make sure I was on stage, and not lying on some restaurant floor, stupefied with sherry trifle. My trouble in those days was not so much tardiness, as being punctual at the wrong theatre in the wrong town. This hardly ever happened, but when it did it must have been hard on everybody's nerves. On one occasion, I set out for a recording session but never arrived. Humph and the boys waited for as long as they could, but at last had to do the whole thing without me. As to what really happened, my mind is a blank. All I can remember is that I was in Antwerp when I rang

147

home and was told that everyone had been searching for me for three days.

One of the tunes the band recorded on that session was 'Looking for Turner', a slow blues hastily composed by Humph while someone else was out telephoning my home. It is a nice little tune. About three years later, my own band was playing at the Bath Festival, and I thought it would be amusing to feature this number on the programme, deliberately making myself absent until halfway through the aforementioned item. I stayed away longer than I had meant to, and came back having missed an entire number. It hadn't even been the right one – just a little opus which had needed my services on lead clarinet. Nobody was amused,

In the jazz clubs, one detected the first signs of diminishing interest in the revival. Attendances were falling off slightly, as the kids discovered the music called rock 'n' roll. Some of the trad bands hoped to counter the trend by appearing in funny hats, or by just having funny heads, but Humphrey continued to bring the crowds in with a policy of playing for pleasure at all times. It was no use avoiding the fact, however, that jazz was in for an uphill struggle from now on.

At the start of the rock phenomenon, the Lyttelton band was involved in a television spectacular which also starred Tommy Steele and the singer Dennis Lotis. At the end, as we were preparing to leave the studio, a herd of excited teenagers rushed towards us with autograph books. Politely, we started to fumble for our ball-point pens, but that's when we realized our mistake. Humph's jazz and Dennis's songs were not what this faction had come to hear.

'Do you think you could get us Tommy's autograph, please?' came the shrill cries from all sides. We did so, and then heaved our way through the crowds outside Tommy Steele's dressing-room.

At the time, I was foolish enough to let it get me down. Jazz musicians give their lives to the sounds they believe in, and then an adolescent rock singer moves in, and becomes a big star overnight. It seemed outrageous, but there was absolutely no point in taking it out on Steele. Tommy had what the kids wanted, and although no musician he was a good light entertainer with a friendly personality – a young man of considerable charm. When they made *The Tommy Steele Story*, Tommy asked for Humph's band to appear in the film, in the final sequence. Anyone going to see this movie must have wondered what was wrong with the saxophone player, in this final episode. He played throughout with a ferocious expression on his face, like a man nursing a bit of a grievance.

I suppose I felt at the time that jazz and rock couldn't possibly go on living together in the same world.

9 Jumping for Joy

I would be a liar if I claimed that the idea of leading my own band had ever appealed to me. Let's face it, I was no leader of men, whatever else nature had cut me out to be. The only reason I wanted to become a bandleader what that I hoped in this way to develop a purely personal style on the alto. In other words – I wanted to be *me*.

Needless to say, the notion that fronting my own band would increase my chances of being left alone with my music was fatuous nonsense. Under the protective umbrella of someone else's leadership I could always count on some artistic leeway, but now I found myself at the mercy of forces I hadn't even dreamed existed.

Promoters threatened, agents and managers cajoled, critics sniped with an even deadlier accuracy than before, and now I had to contend with five obstreperous sidemen, each with his own firm conviction that his concept of music was the right one.

Two months before leaving Humphrey, I went to his agent Lyn Dutton to see if he would be willing to handle the new combo.

'It won't be anything esoteric,' I explained to him. 'I'm calling it the Jump Band and we will aim to provide plenty of swinging music for dancing – so maybe the clubs will be interested.'

'Leave it to me,' replied Dutton. 'If your band is any good at all, we'll find something for you. That's what agents are for.'

Six weeks later, with only a handful of Lyttelton engagements still to go, I thought I had better go in and see how things were shaping with my engagement sheet. Maybe we had only been booked into a few of the smaller clubs, but it would do for a start.

Lyn Dutton looked up from a pile of paperwork, faintly bewildered.

'Work for your band? I don't think I follow you – what band

are you talking about? Show me the band, and we'll see about finding it some work. But now, if you don't mind, Bruce, I *am* rather busy.'

As an aspiring bandleader, I had just been handed my first lesson on how *not* to launch a new jazz band upon the world. I now hurriedly attended to all those things that anyone in his right mind would have seen to at the start. I contacted the *Melody Maker*, providing the details of my new venture and explaining that jump music was what the small Harlem groups had been playing just before the incursion of modern jazz. My plan was to try and revive interest in this neglected period and, inspired by this music, move forward to a more personal style. This information I also passed on to various agents, jazz-club proprietors and people in the know. Some of these immediately became interested in the concept of a new-type jazz revival based on the late thirties, and in the rare spectacle of a leader being pulled along by the members of his own band. For it must be admitted in all honesty that most of the donkey-work of making contacts was undertaken by the men in my band, who could see from the start that to leave these things to me would have been sheer madness.

The first of my Jump Bands was very much a scratch team with a great many rough edges. It received some adverse criticism and probably deserved it. Even so, many writers found themselves able to say friendly things about this music that defied current fashions and went its own way. Critics, as distinct from pundits, had been well disposed towards my playing over the last few years. If I played badly, they usually said so, but if I blew anything worthwhile this was likely to get a mention too. The critics had been more than fair, and now there were those who rallied behind the Jump Band.

Right at the start we had an unexpected setback. We applied for some broadcasts and were immediately turned down by the BBC. A few days later, the musical papers carried the news: 'Bruce Turner fails BBC audition' – a ludicrous situation, since I had at that time been a well-known broadcasting musician for ten years.

One columnist, the late Maurice Burman, was incensed. He happened to know that I was feeling very disconsolate at the time, and that I needed to get the new band quickly under way. Maurice therefore weighed in with some colourful expletives in his weekly column. He wanted to know on what grounds a well-established pro musician and his chosen accompanists had been failed, at a time when there were some pretty dire 'trad' bands floundering about on the air. If I had been failed for musical reasons, what sort of standard was the BBC attempting to set up? Was the Jump Band being accused of musical incompetence – or simply not being in fashion?

Then Humphrey Lyttelton pitched in too. He queried in strong terms the BBC's policy of giving preference to very early 'trad' jazz, regardless of musical ability. The axing of my band seemed to have stirred up feeling on all sides.

Humph described some of these ultra-conservative musical directors as 'gorged like pythons in the aftermath of the trad boom' – which I thought was rather good. A spokesman from the BBC then explained that their action had in no way been intended to reflect on me personally. They simply felt that the band wasn't ready yet.

Maurice Burman was not to be put off lightly, however, and asked to be allowed to hear the audition tapes. The BBC willingly complied. In all honesty, it had to be admitted that the band did sound extremely rough and unsure of itself. There was some hesitant phrasing and a few nervous 'fluffed' notes. I began to feel I had been a little premature in taking my new band before the BBC, but Maurice now simply changed his line of approach. Every member of my band had already done many broadcasts for the BBC – in New Orleans-type bands. Surely it wasn't anybody's capabilities that were now in question – but *jump music*.

Maurice, now in full cry, badgered the BBC for a second audition, and the somewhat startled Beeb was only too willing to agree. With a slightly different line-up we took the second audition without any trouble, and I was aware that a big-hearted critic had proved himself to be a good friend.

For a while the band improved with every public appearance. Bobby Mickleborough came in on trumpet, switching from his main instrument, which was the trombone. Al Mead was on piano and Danny Haggerty on bass – two of my earlier associates from the Randall days. Mickleborough was (and still is) a consummate musician, but too nice a man to be able to compete successfully in the rat-race. In order to hide the fact that he was a soft touch, Bobby often assumed a hard, even abrasive attitude to frighten off any potential foes. This prickly, defensive armoury even had me fooled for a time. Another thing about Bob was that he liked to pretend that he was a slave to the written part, and had no spontaneous initiative.

Freddy Randall's band in the studio: Randall, Ronnie Gleaves, Bert Murray, Graham Beesley, Ruan O'Lochlan, Tony Allen, author (*left to right*)

Lytteltonians: author, John Picard,
Wally Fawkes, Johnny Parker, Stan
Greig (*left to right*)

Later Lyttelton band: Colin
Purbrook, Dave Green, Humphrey
Lyttelton, author, Kathy Stobart,
Tony Mann (*left to right*)

Henry 'Red' Allen with Pete
Strange and author

First Jump Band: Tommy Jones, Jim Bray, Al Mead, Terry Brown, author, Bobby Mickleborough (*left to right*)

Acker Bilk and the Paramount Jazz Band: Tucker Finlayson, Tony Pitt, author, Acker Bilk, Ron McKay (*holding cymbal*), John Mortimore, Colin Bates, Colin Smith (*left to right*)

**Eddie Condon, author, Wild Bill
Davison, Cutty Cutshall, George
Wettling** (*left to right*)

Author with Ben Webster

Author with Bill Coleman; Ke
Higgins and Tony Bayliss in
background

Author with Buck Clayton

**Author with Laura, April and Isle of
Man jazz promoter Alan Grubb**

Whenever I turned to him during a number and suggested we make up a simple background 'riff' he at once became a worried man.

'Bruce! Bruce, there ought to be *parts*. Where are the written *parts*?'

He was a fluent player and a fine soloist, but every simple instruction had to be written down.

On the way to one of our out-of-town dates, Bobby surprised me by declaring that he wished to remain anonymous when I announced the band's names over the mike. Would I mind very much if he did the gig under a fictitious name?

'I was here a few weeks ago,' explained Bobby, 'and had an awful row with the boss. I really rubbed him up the wrong way – we very nearly came to blows.'

I had to smile at the thought of Bobby Mickleborough coming to blows with anyone, but I promised to think of a good pseudonym for him when the time came.

We arrived at the jazz club, and I went into the promoter's office to arrange playing times. Almost at once the man went into a long rambling account of the unfortunate experience he had had with a former visiting band.

'Fellow called Mickleborough,' he growled, 'never want to set eyes on him again. Ever come across him, did you?'

'Well . . . er . . . um . . . er . . .'

'Played trombone. Looked something like your trumpet player. Couldn't be him, could it? Of course not – different instrument. All the same . . .'

All through the first set, the promoter stood staring at Bobby crouched behind his trumpet. During the interval he once again commented on the uncanny resemblance between my trumpeter and the detested Mickleborough. I made a non-committal choking noise, while I thought up a fictitious name for Bobby that I would use during the final announcements. At last it came time to beat the boys into our last number. With bass and drums playing a subdued rhythm, I grasped hold of the microphone to make the usual signing-off spiel. The man was glowering unpleasantly at Bobby, and my mind had gone almost a complete blank.

'Well,' said I, 'that's about it from the Jump Band. We hope you've enjoyed our kind of jazz, and now it's good night from myself on sax and clarinet, Al Mead on piano, Bobby Mickleborough on trumpet . . . WHOO-OO-OOPS!'

I don't recall that we ever went back to that particular club.

Around the time that I formed my first Jump Band, 'peace' had become a dirty word. Anyone who suggested that we should be talking things over with the Russians was thought to be either a left-wing fanatic or somebody with a very low IQ. My own view was that if we were planning to blow these people to bits one day, we might as well go and take a look at them first. The World Youth Festival was planning a cultural visit to Moscow, and I had already made up my mind to go along. Then it transpired that Ewan McColl was going to be there with a folk group, and that Ewan thought he could get the Jump Band there as part of the festival team. Thus I became the first British musician to take a jazz band to the Soviet Union. The Russian people hadn't heard much Western jazz, except for some celebration concerts during the final stages of the war, before things began to turn sour. Ewan spoke to some people on the festival committee and suddenly my Jump Band was booked.

In Moscow they didn't just hire a hall. The band's first concert took place in Gorky Park before a crowd of approximately one thousand noisily appreciative Muscovites. This, it should be noted, was several years before Benny Goodman took a band over, allegedly giving the Soviets their first taste of Western jazz.

In Russia, I had a strong impression that the people didn't want to be blown up, and that they didn't want to blow up anyone else, and there was a wonderful sense of well-being in the air, to say nothing of the strong desire to live in peace. That dirty word again! These people were crazy about jazz, in spite of Khrushchev having said scathing things about it in the press. Many people couldn't understand why their leaders were uneasy about this spirited working-class music with its message of brotherly love.

Jazz musicians are not as a rule politically minded. On my return from the Soviet Union I was full of all the interesting things I had seen, but all most of my friends wanted to know was how many jazz clubs there were in Moscow.

'Never mind about all that,' I replied, 'do you know that books and classical records cost about half the price that they do in the West. And most essentials are pretty cheap. Take canteen meals . . .'

But the response would invariably be that Russians know almost nothing about jazz and that this proves they have a pretty repressive regime. One of the hierarchy, I think it was Zhdanov, had referred contemptuously to jazz as 'fat man's music', which was one of the daftest remarks ever made by a jazz critic. Certainly no one was getting fat on the revival, not even the top bands, for quite a long time. My own group went on struggling for work, despite the Herculean efforts of Jim Godbolt, our agent.

Jim was lean, cynical and almost impossible to hold a quiet conversation with, but had the redeeming quality of being a staunch enthusiast of good jazz. He was not in it for the money, which was just as well because for years Jim and I just about managed to get by. Selling the Jump Band to these craven promoters of safe predictable British trad became something of a crusade. To most of these people, banjo bands had become a safe bet and there seemed no point in suddenly changing horses in main stream.

Then it became fashionable for some of these cautious businessmen to go in for what might be described as 'prestige' bookings. About once every three months they would try something out of the ordinary, just to show what devils they were. Then, instead of giving their support to what they had started, they would fly into a last-minute panic and start apologizing to the audience. At one club, my band had to stand in the wings and listen to a five-minute diatribe against jump music by the very man who had booked us, ending with the furtive admission: 'Personally, I quite like the stuff – and of course Bruce likes it. So give the boys a chance. They are doing what they believe in, and they're all really nice guys.'

In other words, before we had even played a note of our music the listeners were urged to look on it with suspicion, but to tolerate us if they could.

At other clubs, the man running the session would stand biting his fingernails during our opening numbers, or pleading with us to play more in the manner of his regular bands. When the audience started to applaud, and there was no mass walk-out, he would hardly be able to believe his senses. But Jim would still have to chase after him for a return booking.

The true situation was always that the kids were delighted to have a new sound to listen to, if only as a welcome change after the staple fare of commercialized 'trad'. About four-fifths of the fans would respond, but it only needed half a dozen die-hards to complain and then we might not get a return booking.

It was hard to see what was in the club promoters' minds. They fed their clientele on a stable diet of predictable 'trad', and then wondered why my band had the audience cheering for more. Evidently we offered something different, but all these promoters could see was that their 'trad' bands sold a handful of extra tickets and kept their regular customers happy.

If we played somewhere for the first time, we invariably arrived with a big ostentatious question mark against our name. These cautious businessmen were not prepared to take even the slightest risk. At one place where we were making a debut, there was nobody to meet my band when we arrived. We had showed up rather too early, so to while away the time I picked up John's trumpet and commenced to play a very simple tune – all on three notes. John grabbed my clarinet and made a few squeaky sounds, and soon everyone was making joke noises on each other's instruments. While all this was going on, the man who ran the club finally showed up. For a few moments, he stood in the shadows, listening. Then he came forward to introduce himself.

'Thank heavens!' he exclaimed, in a relieved sort of voice, 'I was so afraid you were going to be one of those dreadful *modern* bands.'

By this time we had a fixed personnel. They were all strong-willed, individualistic characters. The only thing that stopped us having clashes of personality was that we weren't together for long enough, due to the work situation not being what it could have been. Then Jim told us he had booked us for an entire summer season in Weymouth. We would be herded together for about three months.

By the time we got to Weymouth there was no cheap accommodation left, and we hadn't thought of booking anywhere. So we rented a cottage on the outskirts. All six of us were there in this cottage, slowly getting on each other's nerves. Call us a motley crew and that would just about be right. Johnny Chilton and trombonist John Mumford were about as unlike in character as two people could possibly be. The first was bluff and outspoken, given to playing outrageous practical jokes; the other was a dreamy sort of bloke, with a tendency to brood. Pianist Collin Bates had a stentorian voice. Plaster trickled from the ceiling while he was simply asking you to pass the mustard. Jim Bray, our bass player, and drummer Johnny Armatage differed considerably whenever music was the subject of discussion. Loud arguments started breaking out within minutes of our moving in. Perhaps there would have been more harmony if only I had been a rather more firm and decisive chap myself. I think everyone was in a state of jitters over the complete absence of leadership in the band. It was like going into battle and discovering that the general is one of Mr Spike Milligan's cardboard replicas. Not once, either before or after the Weymouth season, did I sense this feeling of great unease in the band. It all started after we had rented the cottage.

Take a man with an eccentric lifestyle, and lodge him under the same roof as five other recalcitrant misfits – and you are bound to have trouble. Soon there were loud complaints – relating to the smell of fatty bacon at mealtimes, the tendency for Chilton and Bates to stay up until all hours shouting at one another, and the sharp odour of unidentified blow-offs as a new day began. Everybody's nerves were on edge by the end of the second week, at which point Johnny Armatage had found himself alternative lodgings and hurriedly took himself off. It was like watching one of those prison movies, where someone goes 'over the wall'. I never saw such profound relief on anybody's face. None of us ever found out who John's mysterious benefactor was, but I know how much we all envied him. Life at the cottage was bringing out the worst in us all.

At this time, my marriage was slowly folding up, with the result that I wasn't my usual cheerful and accommodating self. It is the quiet, undemonstrative guys who often turn nasty over a comparatively minor issue, after they have been smouldering away for a long time. This happened to me, after we had a loud discussion about artificial stimulants. Some of the boys were laying down the law about food cranks, and I took it into my head that everybody was having a go at me. Voices were raised and there were some cutting remarks passed back and forth. John Chilton had invited a girl round on that occasion, and she sat in utter bewilderment as this battle raged – over some nonsense that she couldn't even begin to understand. Grown men shouting their heads off about nothing!

The argument reached fever-pitch, and then I sprung to my feet and shouted: 'Go ahead – take all the caffeine and tannin you want! It doesn't bother me. If you need your stimulants – fine – but don't ask *me* to drink all that muck.'

The girl became quite alarmed. She put a restraining hand on my shoulder and called out soothingly: 'Now, now, Bruce, nothing to get worked up about. You sit down here, and I'll go and make you a nice cup of tea.'

I shout like that only about once every five years, if I'm under a severe strain. My domestic life was in a turmoil and I knew it was my own fault. The boys in the band saw only that I was turning from my usual placid nature into a great big grizzly-bear, but there was no way they could have known the real reasons. In the end we blamed everything on the cottage. It was an immense relief when the Weymouth season came to an end.

As soon as we were back on one-night stands we were all good friends again. I cheered up considerably, we rehearsed some fresh material and everything was cool. We didn't all like the same music, but at least we agreed about the middle period. Small-band jazz, of the kind typified by Goodman and Basie, was a taste we could share in common, whatever else we happened to enjoy.

On some of the longer journeys we played jazz on a portable tape recorder connected to the car battery. Musicians find it hard to keep a good thing to themselves. After a while we were all preparing special 'coach tapes' from our respective record collections. There was no lack of good-humoured sarcasm, if a certain piece of music was too 'trad' or too 'boppish' for certain tastes. If a recorded item had tuba and banjo in the rhythm section, the cry of 'Pinketry' was set up by those of us who preferred the more modern sounds. Ward Pinkett was a good solid trumpet man who played with Morton and Chick Webb in a previous era. I don't know why he was singled out as exemplifying the corniest type of jazz, but there it is.

The Jump Band listened with respect to most recorded jazz from the Louis Hot Five onwards, but it was our policy to try and revive interest in the lesser-known swing arrangements and, where necessary, to adapt them to the requirements of a small band. Benny Carter's 'Swinging at Maida Vale', John Kirby's 'Opus Five' and Spike Hughes's 'Donegal Cradle Song' were wonderful classics which we liked to knock around.

The band's fortunes fluctuated alarmingly. There would be a lot of steady work and then, suddenly, a quiet spell. Alex Welsh offered me work during these quiet periods. His clarinettist, Archie Semple, was not a well man and I kept getting emergency calls to appear with the band on clarinet. I was thankful to have this work with Alex, but on one occasion he booked me for a job where my own band was due to appear the following week. I had never heard of the barring clause, but Jim Godbolt now spelled it out for me: 'Alex tells me you have agreed to go up there with his band. Forget it. Clearly you don't take the trouble to read the contracts I send you.'

I quickly phoned Alex, who told me I had left it rather late in the day: 'If you back out now,' he told me cheerfully, 'you put me in a bit of a tight spot, as there are no other clarinettists available now. I feel sure you will not let me down. Don't forget to wear a tie.'

I spent most of that night twisting and turning, with my mind on barring clauses. By early morning I had found the solution. What Mickleborough could do, I could do – I would go up there incognito.

I dialled Alex's number. 'Tell me,' I said hurriedly, 'have you put my name on any of the posters?'

'No – there wasn't time.'

'Great! In that case, I'm willing to come up and play for you under an assumed name. Americans do it all the time.'

'It wouldn't work – they'd spot you a mile away.'

'Not many people know it, Dad, but I once nearly became an actor.'

Alex agreed, and promised that on the night I would be introduced as Mal Colman, a visiting musician from out of town. He also told me I was wasting my time trying to disguise my identity, since I was one of a kind. The day finally arrived, and I climbed on to the Welsh bandwaggon looking like a stretched-out Pierre Laval. I had dyed my hair jet-black and plastered it all over my ears with Brylcreem. I had managed to grow a length of incipient moustache, accentuated with some eyebrow pencil. The foam rubber stuffed inside my shirt had been the difficult bit. In order to keep this in position it was necessary to adopt a peculiar crouching stance. Everyone thought the general effect was striking, if not exactly convincing.

When we reached the gig, nobody batted an eyelid – not even the promoter who greeted us at the stage door. Everything went well during the opening numbers and soon a crowd of Alex's fans had formed a semicircle around the front of the stage, nodding and swaying to the music. During a pause, one of them called up to Alex, asking if he would play a request.

'Of course. What would you like to hear?'

'Would you ask Bruce to play something on the saxophone?'

Apart from that, everything went off quite smoothly, and nobody so much as mentioned the barring clause.

Louis Armstrong came to this country for the second time, and Alex's band was booked to do a short tour with Louis's

All-Stars. Once again Archie Semple was incapacitated, so I was offered the job. The shows were a success, Louis said glowing things about 'Little Alick Walsh and his boys' and I was able to get closer to the fabulous trumpeter than I had done at the Empress Hall. What really knocked me out were the coach journeys. I occupied a seat not far behind Louis, so that during each long trip I was entranced by the back view of his neck and the throaty comments that issued from him from time to time. It was one of those salutary reminders that greatness is cased in perfectly simple forms. This man who, almost single-handedly, changed the course of twentieth-century music was one of the most earthy and unassuming individuals you could wish to meet.

On another occasion, I went to Vienna for a series of concerts with the Jazz Couriers. Ronnie Scott and Tubby Hayes were the greatest tenor saxists in Britain, and among the best in the world. Whoever selected me as an addition to the Couriers' line-up wasn't thinking very clearly about disparity of styles. There was no way I could have fitted in with their soaring two-part inventions and tightly-knit routines. In the end, it was agreed that I would come on as a guest soloist whenever Ron and Tubby needed a breather. This worked out well. Those few days in Vienna were notable for some fine music and pleasant times.

Vienna now had juke-boxes in the cafés, and some of the spacious boulevards had unsightly adverts on display, usually for Coca-Cola or 'pop' concerts that were to be held at the local Musikhalle. We had been booked into a boarding-house in the city centre. In answer to our knocking, a kindly old girl came to the door and ushered us in, informing us repeatedly: '*Ich bin nicht Frau Knakke.*'

What she was trying to say was that the lady of the house was out, but had left her temporarily in charge. Ever after, Tubby referred to our hostess as: 'Not Mrs Frog-nacker – the other one.'

The best thing that happened to me during that week in Vienna was the drumming of Phil Seaman. Phil had not played drums with me since about five years previously, but he had me sized up after the first few bars. He was a musician drummer, one of that rare species who listens carefully to what is going on and then provides exactly the right accompaniment. Phil and Tubby will be greatly missed. They were two of the most creative players we ever had, and marvellous guys.

These gaps in the Jump Band's date sheet were few and far between. Godbolt was able to provide us with month after month of regular work. At last we attracted the attention of one Jack Gold, a most talented and enterprising film director. Gold wanted to make a short documentary about the members of a typical jazz band. It wasn't easy to see why my band was chosen as the subject of such a film. But it was, and in 1961 *Living Jazz* was made and had its premiere at the National Film Theatre.

Now as far as I could make out, this film was intended to show how dull and unremarkable life could be in a typical touring band. We were portrayed as six ordinary people engaged in just another mundane travelling job. Jack Gold was a brilliant young director, but in this instance I believe he was attempting the impossible. It seemed to me at the time that he missed the whole point about the kind of music jazz is. You cannot make a documentary about it in the usual sense. Jazz musicians are *not* the same as transport drivers or travelling salesmen.

The end result, if a director really managed to get into a jazz musicians's mind, would be a zany comedy with perhaps overtones of the starkest tragedy. The movie tried to depict a life of monotonous routine, equating the level of boredom with any work normally involving travel and time schedules, until the point when the musician finally clambers on to the stand. Then suddenly it's all quite different from everything else.

This isn't so at all. In their private lives and daily routines, jazzmen are usually eccentric and nonconformist, which is why they turned to jazz in the first place. The film was in this sense self-defeating and unreal.

I find it mystifying that many writers speak of jazz as though it were a working-class music. This hasn't been the case for at least fifty years. Look in at any jazz club. You will find proletarians in the audience sure enough, but for the most part you will encounter students, professional people, middle-class social workers and maybe an aristocrat or two. The boys in the band will be as likely to come from safely petit-bourgeois homes as from working-class ones. All these people share one thing: they are at once the beneficiaries and also the victims of a mechanized world.

When I suggested rough scripts, the producers of *Living Jazz* smiled tolerantly. This was a documentary – a slice of real life. I remember one scene in which the band arrived at a transport café, supposedly a bit worried about whether we would make the gig on time. We sat around sipping tea and glancing anxiously at our watches. Our conversation was supposed to indicate what we would really have said under such circumstances and so, with cameras turning, drummer John Armatage leaned over to me and enquired: 'How much further is it to the place where we're playing?'

I shrugged my shoulders, gulped down a mouthful of cheesecake and mumbled: 'Gosh, Dad – don't know really. Don't know really. Couldn't say.'

Someone shouted 'Cut!' and Jack Gold wandered up to me and explained, with a kindly tolerance, that nobody spoke like that in real life. The appropriate answer should have been: 'Too ruddy far, mate,' or something along those lines. It was with difficulty that we finally got through the scene.

There is very little about the world of jazz which is commonplace, or typically working-class. A film about jazz musicians ought to be out to capture the curious atmosphere and its accompanying jargon. I'm not talking about the 'jazz' characters of romantic fiction, where musicians are portrayed as lunatics, spouting phrases like 'Real gone!' and working themselves into trance-like stupors. This would be equally remote from the truth.

The jazzman is not a prototype, but a particular manifestation of the person who cannot conform in an unfriendly environment. Possibly he was a duffer at school, quite hopeless at athletics, perhaps nearly expelled once or twice for flouting the accepted code, utterly miserable in the armed forces – very much a lone wolf at the various army or RAF camps. Back again in Civvy Street, he either made the supreme effort by carving a niche in the system, or else he continued to play jazz and carried on, refusing to conform.

Once I was asked to make a brief appearance on the television programme, 'This is Your Life'. The selected victim on that occasion happened to be Humphrey Lyttelton, so I had a phone call requesting my momentary presence on the show. As soon as I arrived at the TV studio, I was ushered into a small waiting-room.

'I'm afraid I will have to lock you in here for a moment,' I was told. 'We have to make sure Mr Lyttelton doesn't bump into any of the surprise guests.'

I sat there alone for a few moments, but then they shoved someone else into the room with me. It was John Dankworth. We argued for several minutes about modern jazz, until

Eamonn was ready to bring us on.

'John,' I said, 'this is the first time we have ever discussed music together. I think it is a shame if we have to wait for Divine Providence, or somebody working for Eamonn Andrews, before these matters can be thrashed out.'

John agreed with me that certain important points needed to be discussed. The jazz scene was not looking very encouraging just then. Somebody writing for the *Melody Maker* rang me to enquire whether I still had a band, since it hadn't been active for a long time. I blurted out something about bandleading being a precarious business, and that I was thinking of packing it all in one day. A week later Jim Godbolt rang me and wanted to know what I was playing at.

'It says here in the *Melody Maker* that you have disbanded. Am I to understand, Bruce, that I'm moving heaven and earth to find work for a band that doesn't even exist?'

I promised to go immediately and demand a retraction. It wasn't easy to locate the man who had printed this premature announcement. When I finally did, he made it quite plain that I was taking up far too much of his valuable time. Wasn't it enough that I had already had a mention in last week's issue? And now I was asking to receive yet another helping of publicity. Who did I think I was – Frankie Vaughan? The man didn't use these exact words, but by yawning and looking at his watch he managed to convey the fact that jazz wasn't news any longer. Soon after this, the *Melody Maker* had a big board meeting and decided to become a 'pop' newspaper. It is nice to know who your real friends are.

I never did get my retraction, and a few weeks later the Jump Band really did fold – though only for a matter of weeks. During this time, I played for Freddy Randall, who was attempting a comeback. Even the irrepressible Fred wasn't able to find regular work, although he had a star-studded band, including a dynamic vibes player called Ronnie Gleaves. When Gleaves left Freddy, I had a great longing for another Jump Band, one that would entice the kids back with a few wild arrangements in the manner of Goodman and Lionel Hampton. I told Ronnie I might be able to bring Ray Crane in on trumpet, also a good swinging rhythm section, if he cared to join. I was able to enlist Ray and Ron all right, but for the rhythm section, I just wasn't able to find anyone who would join on a permanent basis. Bass players came and went – pianists likewise. It was with this scrappy, makeshift of a Jump Band that I found myself accompanying some of the big names of pre-war jazz. Godbolt had put my name forward as the man who could provide swinging accompaniment for some top-class Americans on tour. Bill Coleman was to be the first.

Bill Coleman was almost too nice. He agreed with every suggestion that was made regarding playing times or the programme format, and if anyone played a wrong chord during one of his own specialities he would whisper something like: 'Don't you think that maybe an F minor seventh would be a better chord here?'

Many of us regarded Bill as a very important link between swing-era trumpet and the post-war modernists, very much on a par with Roy Eldridge, though not so well-known. This affable piece of jazz history settled in with my band almost without effort, and we had a most successful tour. At the end we all pitched in to buy him an inscribed silver cup, having taken the man completely to our hearts. The inscription was 'To the Guv'nor', which was the way we had all come to think of him by that time. He chuckled a lot when we explained to him that a 'Guv'nor', in the argot of British musicians, is a man who is absolutely tops, and that is the way all of us will remember Bill.

In contrast, the next assignment for my Jump Band was a difficult and ponderous one. Don Byas emerged as a very forward-looking tenor saxist in the Hawkins mould. After making his name with the Count Basie band, he found his way to a harder, more athletic musical approach. The later Byas played in a manner less decorative than before, using phrases that sounded thrusting and almost defiant. Meeting this man for the first time I found him to be a small, wiry, aggressive character with whom I was able to find almost nothing in common – except for my admiration for his playing, which it appears we both shared. Nothing went right for me on the Byas tour. No sense in apportioning the blame for this situation – we just didn't speak the same language, and that was that. After a few days, Godbolt complained that I wasn't keeping things under control. At one club, for example, the tenor man had started a loud argument with somebody in the front row of seats. This altercation had ended with Don springing down from the stage and challenging the other man to a bout of arm-wrestling at one of the tables. It all culminated in some breathless laughter and mutual back-slapping fortunately, but people had come to hear jazz and not to watch side-shows.

Throughout this whole tour, Don and I hardly exchanged a

dozen words. I am afraid I do not make friends until I can actually see the other person's outstretched hand, and as Don was not prepared to make the first move either, the thing soon became a wretched stalemate. The boys in the band were making a big fuss of the American and on coach journeys I would sit at the back, pretending to be asleep, so that I would not have to take part in the loud, strident back-chat. With Bill Coleman it had all been so quiet and peaceful. Then I began to suspect that Don was a little contemptuous of me because I would not become one of his drinking partners. Like so many musicians who enjoy themselves with the hard stuff, he seemed to be misinterpreting my abstemious ways. I believe he sensed some kind of silent disapproval in my manner, but I swear I wasn't disapproving in the least. The longer they kept Don at the bar, the better it was for me. I could sit alone in the band-room and enjoy my solitude for a moment or two. I now see that I was to blame for the atmosphere becoming increasingly tense. At one club, Don kept leaving the stand after his own solo, so that he could go off and replenish his glass at the bar. Each time he did this, he shot a glance at me – like John McEnroe squaring up to a recalcitrant linesman. Once he stayed away a long time, and was nowhere to be seen, so at last I signalled for the number we were playing to be brought to an end. We went into the last chorus of the tune – and then Don appeared out of the crowd. With four bars left to go he leapt on to the stage, picked up his tenor and went to the microphone to play.

'Carry on – keep going!' I said, in my normal voice. Anyone standing six or seven inches away might have heard me above the din, but as it was the band went into the final chord and the music stopped. Don was left standing there with the tenor in his mouth and looking undeniably rather foolish. He spun round on me, his eyes blazing indignation and wronged innocence.

'That was deliberate,' he said. 'See here, Bruce – you stick with your goddamn cream cakes and let me have *my* kicks. OK!'

From that moment until the end of the tour, Don and I played the sessions without even glancing in each other's direction, and any instructions had to be passed via Ray Crane standing in the intervening space. It was round about that time that I came to suspect that bandleading was not for me.

As already stated, the Jump Band wasn't at its best during this last period. I was able to acquire the services of truly first-rate musicians such as Dave Green or Ron Ruben for some of the time, but not as permanent fixtures, so the band was never able to play its best arrangements with anything like the required precision. I was to blame for the Don Byas fiasco, but bandleading was becoming so much of a strain that I was emotionally falling apart.

This was perhaps not the best time for me and my band to be offered the chance to tour with one of jazz's all-time greats. Our next assignment was a man called Ben Webster, and when Jim told me the news I clutched feebly at the hope that I might be allowed time to rehearse a first-rate band for this formidable task. Not a chance. Two weeks before Ben's arrival, I was still without drums and bass and it was suggested that Ron Gleaves would have to alternate between vibes and piano. Ben Webster! The most important tenor player to emerge since Hawkins and Lester Young, and a Titan of the jazz ballad!

It was also mentioned to me that Ben might have a drink problem. As it turned out, the problem wasn't Ben's at all, but other people's. He simply tilted his head back, and the stuff went down easily enough. It made him happy, and for some of the time it added a piquancy to his conversational flow.

At first, Ben played consistently well throughout each of our shows. Sometimes I noticed that his announcements became longer and more rambling as the evening wore on, indicating that he was struggling to get his breath back, but while it often looked as if the colossal frame was just about to come crashing to the ground, this never happened. The first appearances of Ben with my band were conspicuous for good music and a good relaxed atmosphere. Then the drinking increased noticeably and the announcements became longer, interspersed with heavy breathing. Jim Godbolt kept on at me, hoping that I would assert myself in some way.

'For God's sake, can't you keep things under control! Try hiding his bottle or something.'

We even gave this a try, but a grieved and resentful Ben was even more of a handful than one who was always slightly smashed. Personally, I didn't let it bother me, as long as the magnificent sounds kept coming out of Ben's horn, but one night things did get a little out of hand.

It was at the Dancing Slipper, Nottingham, that the enormous musician, swaying precariously after the intermission, finally did come toppling downwards, like some felled oak. That was Ben through for the evening, and so the Jump Band had to finish the show without him. The task of shovelling him off the stage and getting him out into the fresh air was given to two perspiring young policemen. Ray and I rushed forward to lend a hand. Halfway down the stairs, the boys in blue found that the enormous weight was too much for them, and the curious little trio was more or less jammed there together, so that nobody could come up or down. Taking advantage of the pause, Ben solemnly surveyed the two uniformed figures for a moment in silence. Then he enquired: 'You guys ever heard Tatum?'

He then went into a long, highly informative account of how Art Tatum had once visited a club where a very young Oscar Peterson was slowly making a name. Tatum went up and played something very fast and technical, just to show he was still boss around those parts, but then Peterson sat down and gave it everything he had. The two pianists battled it out for a long time, Peterson having insisted on continuing the struggle right into the small hours.

'Well,' concluded Ben, winking at the two policemen and spreading out his huge hands, 'there it is – I mean, *you know Oscar.*'

Next day, Ben received me and Ray at his hotel, saying that he very much hoped he hadn't embarrassed us in any way. Then he said he was pleased with the way things were going, but that some buildings didn't seem to be using the right kind of ventilation system. It was good to hear Ben speaking in praise of some British jazz he had recently heard, not only from my band but also some of the modern groups. He said some very encouraging things about my own playing, and then he added: 'You cats are going to eat a big meal with me, on the last evening, before we split up. You're gonna be my guests, and we are going to have a very special dish – spare ribs and black-eyed peas. I tell you, you never tasted anything like it in your life.'

All through the rest of the tour, Ben kept reminding us about the spare ribs and peas. I protested that I was a vegetarian, but Ben brushed this aside with an imperious wave of his hand. I would not remain a vegetarian, he assured me, after I had tasted spare ribs the way *he* knew they should be prepared.

When the time came, we all sat around a big table and feasted on this stuff, under Ben's watchful eye. Every time he looked in my direction I had to shovel another mouthful down, somehow managing to force a smile. I don't think I would have done it for anyone else but Ben Webster. He was the greatest jazz musician I ever worked with, the gentlest and sweetest of men, and one who holds a special place in my memory.

But I am forgetting the brief encounters with Earl Hines. I didn't so much *work* with Hines as accidentally brush up against him several times – and in the most unusual circumstances. The first time I blew with Hines was at the Manchester Sports Guild, in front of an audience composed mainly of devout Turner fans. All through the session, Earl was plagued with requests for tunes which I had written for the Jump Band, and which people seemed to assume that Earl Hines would be sure to know. In the interval, some characters came up and told Hines that he and Bruce Turner were about the two greatest jazzmen of all time. I was never so embarrassed in my life.

Some time elapsed, and then I had to work with Hines under the most trying circumstances, at a club in Hampstead. The idea was that Earl would be invited to an 'informal' jam session, and that one or two of our best players might drop in later for a number or two. It was all very casual and spontaneous, but it wasn't long before I could sense things slipping out of control. In a little while you couldn't move, for all the musicians on the stage. If anyone had come especially to see and hear Hines, they were out of luck, because he had been relegated to the background. Everyone and his best friend was at the microphone, trying to hog the show. Whenever my turn came to take a solo, I tried giving it to Hines, by stepping forward and then waving in the direction of the piano. All that happened was that someone else would barge his way forward, while the greatest jazz pianist of all time was pushed unceremoniously back into the shadows.

Now for some reason that I have never been able to divine, Jim Godbolt had put me in charge of this monstrous session, so at first I did try to exert some authority. But I am no sergeant major, and there is no way I can make myself heard in a roomful of feverish narcissists. In the end I walked off the stage and sat with the audience – an act of humility which Jim Godbolt was never able to forgive. In Jim's version of the story, I showed myself 'lacking in moral fibre' and I don't suppose anything I can say will alter his verdict. By this time, I knew I was through with bandleading of any kind. I simply wanted to play music – preferably my own.

It occurred to me that even the Jump Band hadn't been exactly what I wanted to do, but only a sort of prelude to what I really wanted. We had set the stage, so to speak, by reviving some things from the past – but now came a new, important, phase. How to bring all that inspiration to bear, and make one's *own* sounds?

Even in the recording studios, whenever I wanted to make a personal statement something or someone stood in my way. The first big opportunity I'd had for putting my *own* music on to a record had eventually come to nil. I had been selected, along with two other altoists, Joe Harriott and Bertie King, to make an LP spotlighting the alto sax in three contrasting styles. The first number was a medium-tempo blues. Joe went first and then Bertie, and by the time it was my turn I was oozing inspiration out of my ears. I came forward, closed my eyes and started to do the life-story bit. The next thing I knew was that the man in charge was tapping on the glass and waving his arms about. He shouted 'Hold it!' and then came in to explain what had gone wrong.

'No, no, Bruce,' he explained, keeping his temper with an effort, 'you don't seem to understand. I thought I had explained it over the phone. You see – *you're* supposed to be *Johnny Hodges*.'

Hodges, that very great Ellington sideman for so many years, is the altoist I was supposed to sound like sometimes. At first this had not been intentional, merely a logical outcome of my having saturated myself with Ellington's music for about thirty years. Later, whenever I committed the heinous crime of trying to express something of my own, there would always be someone complaining that I was not doing my Hodges impression. Critics and promoters, and others in positions of extraordinary power, could not resist the temptation to play at toy soldiers with their jazzmen.

Most of my recorded work of this period has pseudo-Hodges creeping in from time to time. It is a situation that was never of my own making. Sometimes I wondered if the men in charge of recording sessions had booked me to play *my* music or theirs. In September 1963 we went into the recording studio to make *Going Places*, an LP which was to showcase the best of our jump-style arrangements. The band was really sounding good at that time, and I had high hopes of a breakthrough and a wider acceptance of what the band was trying to do.

This wasn't to be. No sooner had I set foot inside the door of the recording studios than I was being given my instructions.

'Keep all solos down to a minimum, you fellows. What I want is short tracks. You never know – there might be a juke-box hit somewhere in this lot.'

I had written a simple little tune called 'The Two Two to Tooting', which I thought might have some commercial potential as well as being a swinger. I was living in Tooting at that time, and thought the title would be fairly apt.

The man supervising the recording thought differently. 'Nobody writes music about a place like Tooting,' he complained. 'There's no *glamour* in the name. And what's all that "Two Two Two" bit?'

I drew a couple of deep breaths, before replying. I told him, with only very thinly-veiled sarcasm, that this was an impressionist work depicting a tube train that left for the aforementioned station at two minutes past two o'clock.

'I see,' he replied thoughtfully, 'all the same – Tooting! I mean, really!'

After some discussion, it was agreed that the number should be recorded under the glamorous title of 'Night Train to Munich'. It didn't matter one way or the other, as by this time I was in such a state of jitters that I wasn't able to solo at anything like my best form. The LP contains some quite charming little arrangements for the sextet but, in my view, some of the most frustrated alto solos I have ever played.

'Jim,' I moaned, 'this is definitely the end. Everyone is leading this band except me. What's so bad about Tooting, anyway? I quite like the place.'

Godbolt told me to be more assertive in the future. It was shortly after this that we began touring with the American big names. As already stated, the tour with Bill Coleman went extremely well, but the tours with Byas and Ben Webster proved to be the very last straw. I told Godbolt I was about to be assertive for the first time in my life. I told him I was through with bandleading and that it was final. My long-suffering agent now had several premature grey hairs on account of me, and reluctantly admitted that perhaps it was the right decision after all. He had done just about everything a man could do, but it just hadn't been enough, considering my poor showing as a leader of men.

I don't regret any of those years with the Jump Band, for they put me in touch with some of the most talented performers in British jazz and there was often a kind of magic in what we played – although it never happened quite as I had originally planned. It was as if life's leaden metal was always about to be transmuted into gold, but we just never quite got around to it.

One outstanding commitment which I couldn't get out of was the tour with Ray Nance. This had been booked well in advance, and had to be seen through to its conclusion. I hoped fervently that this last series of concerts would be something the band could look back on with pride. Instead, it was the same old story as before. There was such a vast gulf between me and Nance that it was sheer heaven for me when the last session came to its end and I was able to get away. This story also has a rather unpleasant sequel.

Years later, when Ray Nance died, Peter Clayton decided to put on a programme dealing with some aspects of this ex-Ellington player. Peter thought it might not be a bad idea to hear from the two men whose bands had toured with him in this country – myself and Chris Barber. He felt that this would be more interesting than the usual cosy sort of obituary loaded with sanctimonious praise. I duly appeared on Peter's programme and said my say.

Two weeks later I was vehemently attacked in print, by a jazz critic in the Newcastle area. He accused me of having callously insulted and abused Nance on the Peter Clayton programme. The writer went on to describe my own music as absolutely worthless, picturing me as a player of no account who hadn't been able to feel at ease in the presence of 'greatness'.

Luckily for me, I had asked my wife to record the Peter Clayton interview, so I was able to play it back and find out what I had actually said. Peter had asked me how I had got on with Nance, and I'd replied: 'Not at all well' – adding that I believed it had been my own fault. Then Peter had asked what I thought of Nance's playing. My own opinion had been that the man was a very good player, but perhaps not a great one. I had been asked for my opinion and given it, but now I was being pilloried by this non-musician, in a way that was very nearly libellous. I wrote immediately to the paper in question, demanding a retraction, but I am not aware that they ever printed one. All that was left for me was to go somewhere and lick my wounds.

This sort of thing leaves an unpleasant taste in the mouth, but all in all I can say that the Jump Band period gave me some happy times. Why else would I have continued to lead a band for almost nine years?

10 'No Mass Hysteria, Please!'

In my younger days, I was naïve enough to think of great music as something pure and unsullied. The creative artist stood aloof from the mass and, seated on his Olympian mount, frowned down upon anything that whiffed even remotely of the tavern. I believed that jazz was 'sincere', other forms of dance music 'commercial', and that a great chasm lay in between.

But jazz grew up under the patronage of the entertainment industry. The transition from New Orleans music to a world music, from raw folk expression to high art, from plantation songs to Ellington's 'Black, Brown and Beige' and from the early marching bands to Lester Young – all this covers a period of little more than twenty years. And it was all done by compromise, by the performer accepting reality and 'putting on a show'.

Jazz musicians are not demigods. They are warm, vulnerable human beings with a desperate need to go on paying the rent. During the swing era, great music emerged out of the compromise that took place between creativity and the box-office. Flashy orchestration and some insipid vocalists were used as window-dressing, while improvised jazz evolved to a high peak. This having been said, it behoves us to study the real connection that exists between jazz and entertainment. There are certain spiders who, in the very act of copulation, devour their mates. We should make certain that jazz doesn't suffer a similar fate.

Certain writers thought that the earlier pundits had been much too solemn and long-winded in defining jazz. They protested that jazz was no more than a form of popular entertainment after all. The musician is a paid entertainer, and if the customer isn't applauding this shows that the music has failed. The man who sets out to please his audience is, perforce, a better jazzman than the one who plays for his own pleasure.

The main difficulty with this theory is that scarcely any jazz musicians are able to recognize this picture of themselves. It is clearly a case of wishful thinking on somebody's part. There are *some* jazzmen who are also great entertainers. Armstrong, Fats Waller and Lionel Hampton come immediately to mind, but they are the exception, not the rule. For the most part, those of us who play jazz for a living do not know any way of entertaining an audience other than by making the best music we are capable of, and that is surely the way it ought to be.

The audience is there, and is not to be ignored. The New Orleans revival bands were divided on this issue. A few of them, egged on by their personal agents, donned garish costumes and went in for extrovert clowning and a regimented hand-clapping, finger-snapping routine. The more they did this, the more philistine their regular following became. Others of the New Orleans persuasion, notably the doughty Ken Colyer, scorned this method of attracting attention. Ken's way was always to assume that the music contained its own appeal. Ken simply played the stuff he believed in, occasionally transfixing with a scowl any members of the public who did not seem to be paying attention.

Some would say that Ken's approach has been shown to be the correct one. For years the band had loyal support from a large section of this country's trad enthusiasts, and never had to depend on sales-pressure techniques.

Modern jazz, too, came to be appreciated on its own merits, regardless of whether its practitioners were standing motionless or leaping about the stage. Dizzy Gillespie's humour and occasional firework displays did not make him any *more* popular than the cool, withdrawn Mr Getz.

Most popular music clearly isn't popular at all – it is simply foisted on people. Truly popular music reflects the historic traditions of masses of ordinary people, but this hasn't been the case for a long time. Old-time music hall once spawned some fine songs and some fabulous artists who *belonged* to the rank and file. Even now, there are entertainers who remain close to the working-class tradition in which they learned their trade. Somehow they manage to remain steeped in its banalities and in some of its vitality and charm.

Acker Bilk was and is one of the natural entertainers in British trad. He is the same whether on or off stage, so no one could accuse him of setting out to 'please' an audience. He sings and plays in a certain way, which is perfectly natural to him, and the audience simply laps it all up. Even the outrageous bowler and striped waistcoat merely enhance, in a strange sort of way, what is already there. Not for Acker the suave Hollywood image of what a bandleader should be. He wears his West Country origins with a manifest pride, sings everything from negro blues to a whole range of Tin Pan Alley favourites in a thick, cidery West Country drawl, and holds aloof from the Americanization of British dance music. Acker probably never needed a band, or the jazz idiom. He could have gone in the halls and made himself a fortune. Except that the halls were no longer there, so in the changed world Acker got himself a band and made a fortune anyway. Vaudeville was dead by the time he had arrived on the scene, otherwise I am quite certain it would have benefited from the arrival of a powerful new force.

It's questionable whether Mr Bilk managed to do for jazz what he might have done for the world of light entertainment. Still, he provided work for at least one dispirited jazz musician.

Here is how I came to join Acker's band. There was nothing premeditated at all. I had made up my mind to disband, because I wasn't at all happy about my own bandleading capabilities. All that now lay between me and freedom were a few commitments I had signed for, and which had to be seen through. Meanwhile, on my evenings off, I had nowhere I could go and play. If only, I thought, someone *else* would start up a Jump Band, and then ask me to join. Then, one evening, I took my alto to 100 Oxford Street, not really intending to blow it but because it allowed me into most places free. I didn't know who was playing at the 100 Club, and didn't much care. Then, as I came in the door, I heard this jump number starting up.

It was like the stuff my own band had been playing over the past few years. A bit more frantic, perhaps. There was Colin Smith on trumpet, Stan Greig on piano and Tony Pitt on guitar, all steaming away. I asked if I could join in, and soon we were making some marvellous sounds. I then discovered that I had been sitting in with Acker's band on one of their club appearances.

'We do this for quite a lot of the time,' explained Ack. 'We start out playing the good old New Orleans tunes, and maybe one or two clarinet ballads, but soon everyone is dancing and making a hell of a lot of noise. After that, well, we just go *beresk*!'

Going 'beresk' was Ack's way of describing the loose jamming that went on for a lot of the time, after the band had played a few special requests in order to placate some of the regular fans. When Acker's brother sent me a letter, asking if I was interested in joining, I didn't take much persuading. My only outstanding commitment with the Jump Band was the short tour with Ray Nance. As soon as that was out of the way, I went in to augment the Bilk front line. I was now working, on average, about five nights a week and playing more jazz than I had played with my own band during its final months. The addition of an extra voice in the front line was immediately successful, and I stayed on with Acker for about four years.

We played to no special clique of enthusiasts, but to a motley crowd of fun-loving squares. People of all ages and from all walks of life came to see the funny man in the bowler hat, then stayed to enjoy the ribald music which had so much in common with some of America's best. The band played a fair amount of traditional New Orleans jazz, but this wasn't its selling-point. The best of Acker's music now stemmed from a different source, the jumpy, nose-thumbing, jazz-tinged humour of artists like Louis Prima, Louis Jordan and Slim Gaillard. Acker was the British equivalent, but precisely *because* it was so British, the critics kept away. They couldn't get it out of their heads that jazz was supposed to be an American music, and that the best we could aim for over here was a facsimile.

The band had already settled for a workable compromise between commercialism and an attractive jazz sound. At some places, the striped waistcoats had to be worn, and a great deal of comedy was expected; at other venues, notably the small provincial clubs, mainstream jazz was dished out for most of the evening – and nobody ever complained! For much of the time, we toured the provinces, playing mostly in cabaret spots on the northern circuit of working men's clubs, as they were then called.

Those working men's clubs! The name is, of course, totally misleading, for such places were frequented by small business-men, reps and minor executives for the most part. Members of the proletariat would probably not have been able to afford the cover charge. There was usually a small gambling casino in an adjacent wing and fruit machines everywhere, nestling in the alcoves. In the course of the evening, a comic would leap on to the stage and tell jokes about Pakistanis to an idiot roar of approval from the dimmer types in the crowd. Somewhere on the bill there would be a girl singer, and if she happened to sing almost a semitone flat, no one would notice. Tired tradesmen and their simpering spouses accepted the jazz along with the slapstick, since it was all being presented to them with the brazen effrontery of a music-hall act.

In jazz, entertainment is all a question of doing what comes naturally. The idiom is chock-full of built-in ribaldry, its own incorrigible jests, or else a subtler form of wit – the jazzman's 'in' humour. Either way, there is never any need to force the pace. Most musicians prefer to keep the humour low-key and implied, some others use a more direct approach. Acker is the epitome of a simple man, and knows how to communicate with others. He speaks directly to his public as an *equal*, never as a condescending professional showman. He does not set out to 'entertain' anybody. He is just himself.

When I first came into the band, I was a little nervous on account of my lifestyle being vastly different from everyone else's. The Bilk band's public image had been carefully fostered for years. Everyone staggered about, clasping half-empty whisky bottles in their hands and whistling at birds. It was a relief to find out that all this was only the way some journalists liked to portray the Bilk circus – in real life I found that the boys often remained sober for hours on end. During these moments, I discovered them to be lively and intelligent in spite of what one had been told. On our first jet flight across the world, I boarded the plane with a couple of heavy novels peeping out of my hand-luggage. Trombonist John Mortimer shook his head sadly. 'You'll never get past page one,' he told me. 'Tucker Finlayson has the seat next to you, and he tends to keel over, round about midday. If you can read *Jude the Obscure* with Finlayson draped all over you, you're a better man than I am.'

John Mortimer was never a man to say no to a drink, but I found him to be a man of considerable wit and intelligence, despite outward appearances. There is something almost sinister about John, when you meet him for the first time. He surveys you with a jaundiced eye, as if wondering where to insert the dagger. Under all this, an acute and gifted mind is skilfully hidden from view. The guy speaks fluent German, writes very good jazz tunes, plays the best genuine rhythm and blues music I have heard on this side of the Atlantic, and yet was never able to cash in on any of these gifts. One seldom hears his name mentioned any more, and yet he had so much potential that wasn't ever used to good effect.

By this time, Acker had probably passed the stage where he could be described as a superstar in Britain, though he was still very popular. It was in places such as Australia and Singapore that he remained a top attraction. In far-off lands, the band could always count on receiving the red-carpet treatment, time after time, so it can be imagined that we were kept pretty busy hopping on and off aeroplanes. I was really seeing the world. We visited Fiji, Singapore, Czechoslovakia, New Zealand and many other places I had always wanted to see. On the way back from New Zealand, we flew via San Francisco, where we stopped off and spent a whole afternoon sightseeing. We didn't get to play any jazz in San Francisco, but soon afterwards we had a tour of the Middle East. The band was booked to play at some US oil towns on the Gulf, and it was at one of these places that I landed myself in a spot of trouble, although things came out all right in the end.

Colin Smith and I had gone to a swimming pool, to cool off before a rather important concert. I could hardly swim at all, but I was flirting with danger by jumping in at the deep end and then quickly grabbing the nearest hand-rail.

After one of these jumps, I came up spluttering and in great distress. 'My front crowns!' I said to Colin. 'They must have been loose or something. I hit the water with my mouth open, and now they are floating about in there. It looks as though I won't be able to play sax tonight.'

The pool was absolutely full of people, flailing about. Colin ducked down a couple of times, but all he could see was other people's legs. Some American kids, armed with snorkels, asked us what we were searching for.

'Say, mister,' said one of these kids, 'if we manage to find your denture, do we get a reward?'

I turned pale, and said that the thing wasn't all that important. But Colin gave them the go-ahead, and in a few minutes almost everyone in that pool was ducking and peering about for the Englishman's missing crowns. It really was a fascinating sight. It was soon time to get changed, but still no one had found anything. Then Colin managed to borrow a snorkel. He disappeared for quite a long time. When he at last surfaced, he was holding something aloft.

'Could these be them?' enquired Colin, waving my teeth at me. About twenty American kids groaned at the news, as word was passed about that the Englishman had retrieved that which had been lost.

In Malaysia I had my first ride on a helicopter, and at Singapore we played every night in a luxury hotel which had an indoor swimming pool right next to the stage. After some of the jazz numbers, dancers fell into the pool just to cool off. One evening a Chinese millionaire invited us all to a banquet after the show. At table, each of us was seated next to a beautiful Malaysian woman. We took these haughty and bejewelled women to be some of the host's rich friends. Next morning, the man called on us, to find out how we had enjoyed the feast, and whether the prostitutes he'd hired for the night had been satisfactory.

All this was pretty hilarious, I have to admit, and helped to take my mind off certain domestic problems that were crowding in on me at home. My mother was now staying with me, in a large dilapidated maisonette which I had bought in West Dulwich. I had acquired an old piano, which was reasonably in tune. Mum still played the simpler Chopin studies from memory, but it was a lonely existence for the old girl, now that most of her friends and relations had either died or lost touch. When I was away on tour, she was quite alone, and could get up to all kinds of mischief, if my brother was not on hand.

A time came when I had to sell the Dulwich place, so that I could move to Buckingham and be close to my children. I had what the courts call 'reasonable access', but the journeys from south London to Buckingham could eat right into this precious time, and that was why I'd put the maisonette up for sale.

But now it emerged that my mother was going to be difficult about the move.

'I'm tired of being moved from place to place, like a stick of furniture,' she sobbed. 'I'm staying here, and that's final. This is my home.'

Even when the furniture van showed up, she still roared at me defiantly that she was staying. I put on one of my hard faces, and said: 'We've been on the move ever since I can remember. There never was any real home. Anyway, you must accept the facts. Contracts have been signed. There will be strange people coming here presently, with all their things and . . .'

'Don't forget to leave the paraffin heater. It's *mine*.'

She really had made up her mind to stay, squatting there when the purchasers came. I knew only too well that bitter taste of uncertainty, of solid familiar objects suddenly crumbling before one's eyes. But what was to be done? I went quickly to see if my brother could give me some advice. He promised to give it some thought.

'Have the car ready,' he said, 'I think I can persuade her to go.'

When Tren came to the maisonette, he was carrying a large bottle of whisky in one hand. Without even mentioning the move, he began pouring the whisky into two glasses, observing that it was the only way to keep warm in the cold winter months. While I was moving curtains and fittings into the car, I could hear their conversation becoming louder, at last culminating in bursts of song. By the time we had her out of the front door, one on each arm, she was executing a sprightly dance step, and before we were halfway to Buckingham she had passed out cold.

Buckingham was just another temporary address, as it turned out, but Mum was comfortable there and the two girls were able to visit their granny every weekend, which was nice. Not long ago, having time on my hands, I picked up a piece of paper and worked out the number of different addresses I have lived at during my lifetime, or at any rate, the ones which I can remember. Right up until my fiftieth birthday, if my calculations are right, I never stayed in one place for more than a couple of years. I wonder if this is some kind of a record!

Other domestic problems were now piling up. My oldest daughter, Caroline, was growing up to be very like me; in fact, the similarities were so marked that my ex-wife suggested that I might like to have full custody. She must have felt that bringing up Caroline herself was like having an unwanted ex-husband lurking about the place. She loved her daughter, but it was getting to the point where all the old vagaries and exasperating quirks were building up again in the person of young Caroline Turner. And we were happiest in each other's company, so when Pat asked if I thought I could give the girl a decent home I said 'Yes – no problem', and the thing was settled. But there was one obvious problem, and that was my busy schedule with the Bilk band.

In the end, it was arranged that Caroline would be sent to Summerhill, and come to me for her holidays. Summerhill is the well-known establishment which encourages children to find their own emotional and intellectual levels, without any of the usual compulsion from above. The kids are not compelled to attend lessons, although ultimately, they all do, being naturally inquisitive and inclined to learn. It sounds a bit idealistic at first, but when you meet the Summerhill kids for the first time, you honestly do find them happier and more relaxed than others. Things do go wrong, such as when the little kids are caught smoking, or an older boy becomes the school bully, but immediately this is put right by democratic means. The children hold meetings and pass laws against the offenders, while teachers and house-mothers remain tactfully in the background. I firmly believe that Summerhill gave Caroline some confidence again, after she had been deeply hurt by the divorce. I only regret that she had to leave the place so soon.

The first time I went up there, it was to give a record recital and talk about jazz. I hadn't expected the large crowd that turned up to listen. Most of these Summerhillians were between eight and twelve years old, but they were just about the most attentive audience I ever had – and I've given a few talks in my time. Only once did a few of the kids start to become restless, but then the others told them either to shut up or take themselves off to bed. After I had finished, there were some intelligent questions followed by an animated discussion. Then we had a jam session. At that time Summerhill boasted a trad band of its own, supervised by one of the house-mothers, Daphne Oliver, now retired. Daphne plays some of the hairiest tail-gate trombone you ever heard.

'This is *your* music,' I told the assembled children, at the end of my talk. 'There'll always be someone trying to tell you it's American, or African, or that you have to have a special education to play it. Don't you believe them. It's all about you yourselves, and the way you feel inside.'

This was also the way I felt about Acker's peculiar blend of 'funny-hat music' and good jazz. Almost none of the incidental horseplay was put on for the public's benefit. It arose out of thin air, so to speak, jazz musicians nearly always being endowed with a keen sense of the ludicrous. You just can't maintain a dead pan under certain conditions. When elderly ladies are trying to perform a Hawaiian tribal dance in front of the stage, it is clearly not a good time to lecture anybody about art. If you mentioned Bix at a time like that, people would think you were talking about a breakfast cereal. All you *can* do, in that kind of situation, is to carry on playing the appropriate form of music – and keep smiling.

The trad v. progressive argument had subsided a little by now. It was being replaced with the view that jazz is really a form of popular entertainment after all. They weren't talking, either, about the intense experience a great art work can hand out to a discerning mind. Nothing quite as corny as that. No, the new emphasis was upon the performer being willing to *sell* his product. It wasn't enough that jazz should be good music – it had to be 'entertaining' as well. It had got to the stage where jazz musicians had to think like vacuum-cleaner salesmen. Why do the pundits occasionally sink to these depths of banality? Isn't it because *they* are products of the entertainment business – disc jockeys, 'pop' critics, concert promoters and others who have a sleek vested interest in mass-produced sound? Jazz had become marketable in Britain. There were even modest profits to be made out of it. In this new situation, it became necessary that the performer should learn his place. He was, whether he liked it or not, an entertainer.

Of all the pundits' arguments, this is the most shabbily immoral. At least the old discussion between traditionalists and modernists had been about real artistic values. The 'jazz is entertainment' theory is only about money, when you boil it down. Jazz finds itself sponsored by the entertainments industry, and in return the latter feels entitled to demand its pound of flesh. Fair enough, but why in heaven's name confuse the issue? The distinction between what is done for love and what is done for quick cash is an obvious one. Jazz is what happens when city-dwellers search for personal and social expression in the machine age; 'pop' merely provides an anodyne which ensures that popular entertainment will remain acquiescent rather than militant, a dream-world rather than a world where masses of people awaken to a consciousness of their own problems.

On some of our cabaret appearances, Acker's band had to alternate with some rock singers who were very loud indeed. The man in charge would rhapsodize: 'Isn't it marvellous! All that crooning and sentimental ballad-singing is finished now. What the kids are into these days is blues. It's given popular music a real kick up the backside.'

I'd wonder if Bessie Smith would have recognized any authentic blues in what we had just heard. It was all so frenzied and over-amplified, and it didn't swing.

'Good ballad-singing,' I would point out, 'is an accepted part of our folklore. The troubador, serenading his love beneath flowered balconies . . .'

'*Love* songs – here! At this club! I'd be bankrupt within a week.'

Neither ballads nor blues was any longer about love, but about aggression. It all finally culminated in something called 'soul music', which the critics thought to be very fine, since it was putting the guts back into popular music and taking the place of those soppy, sentimental love songs. In my dictionary, the word 'soul' is defined as, among other things, 'the nobler feelings and capacities of the human mind'. It would be hard to think of an apter description of that quality which soul music particularly lacks.

There was once a television programme called 'What is Jazz?' A bunch of leading critics and one or two well-known players argued about jazz, and it afforded an opportunity for the old stereotyped arguments to come trotting out, one by one. We heard the usual obsessions with New Orleans, the innuendos against non-Americans, the dismissing of everything before Charlie Parker as old-fashioned. Up to that point I could hardly keep my eyes open, but then Derek Jewell got up and spoke his piece. After he was through, you could hardly hear anything through the hubbub. What Derek said, as I have the recorded evidence on cassette to remind me that it was not a dream, was: 'Most of the jazz musicians up to the period of Charlie Parker had thought of themselves primarily as entertainers playing for audiences – and the vast majority of jazz musicians since, who have not thought of themselves as playing and communicating with an audience *have failed, and deserved to.*'

Now I can think of very few jazz musicians who would recognize this picture of themselves, as painted for them by a non-playing critic. It's hard to think of such past jazz geniuses as Bix or Lester Young ever 'playing to an audience' in the sense here implied. When Lester occasionally went in for it, he played very badly, and when Bix found the audience crowding him he took to the bottle. What really astounds one about the Derek Jewell statement is that it seems to rest less on patient research than on clairvoyance. Jazzmen 'think of themselves' as entertainers. The critic is able to get into the musicians' *thoughts*.

In the heat of this discussion, one also heard the timid voice of jazz singer Norma Winstone trying to make itself heard. She did manage to cut in with just four words which, for me, constituted the most damning reply to Derek's quaint theory.

The words were: 'How does he *know*?'

It behoves me to add that I don't doubt Derek Jewell's sincerity for a moment, and I know him to be an intelligent and kind man. It is admirable, in a way, when pundits become deeply involved in discussions about jazz. It shows they care. The jazz musician rarely if ever gets himself involved in musical discussion. He cares about his own small corner of the idiom, but carefully ignores all the rest. This creates the intellectual vacuum into which the well-meaning pundit inevitably gropes his way.

Some of the best moments in jazz occur when you have a bunch of guys simply playing together 'for kicks'. I'm not suggesting that this is the way things ought to be, for only by becoming a working professional can any musician hope to speak the jazz language with any real fluency. The part-time player with money problems is going to find himself distracted and unable to give himself wholeheartedly to the music. He may also find himself succumbing to the very form of artistic blackmail I've been discussing previously, i.e. playing to 'entertain', whenever the rent becomes due. But even so, the quality of certain pub sessions is high, because the money isn't, and nobody would be there at all if it weren't for the musical pleasure involved.

I have been playing at the New Merlin's Cave for almost fifteen years. I have become something of a fixture there, in spite of the fact that no money is taken at the door and the musicians blow for what amounts to their expenses. The Merlin's is close to King's Cross and not far from Pentonville Prison, which in some ways it faintly resembles. Recently, a change of management has given the whole thing a facelift, but when I first went there it was memorable chiefly for the odd whiff of urine and antiseptic coming from the Gents'.

Thanks chiefly to some hard work put in by jazz connoisseur Graham Tayar, the pub quickly became the most important London venue of Sunday-lunchtime jazz. Some of the finest mainstream musicians in this country came to play at the Merlin's – not to entertain anybody except themselves. Word soon spread and large crowds came to listen to this music that was being played strictly for pleasure. Well-known Americans popped in occasionally to augment the sessions. Roy Eldridge, Ruby Braff, Milt Buckner, Bob Wilber and others made brief but notable appearances at the Merlin's. All the place needed was a thorough scrub-down, and it would have become this country's important centre and shop window for middle-period jazz.

Wally Fawkes lent his special kind of mystique to the earlier sessions. Wally no longer played jazz full-time, but was still remembered by the older fans with a great deal of respect. He had been an important figure in the New Orleans revival, and had come nearer to sounding like Sidney Bechet than perhaps any man alive.

Wally was always jazz's supreme amateur, in the very best sense of the word. He seemed to be at his ease only when the customers were chattering with one another and clinking their beer mugs. He was there to play clarinet and have a good time, not be a professional entertainer. When they started to set up a raised platform for the band, Wally refused to stand on it. He continued to operate at ground level, with the rest of us perched around him a couple of feet up off the ground. From a distance it looked as if Toulouse Lautrec had dropped in for a blow with the band.

I much preferred the safety of the platform, where there were fewer hazards. By hazards, I am thinking of things like spilled drinks, children brandishing lethal toys, and stray dogs sniffing ominously around the legs of the piano.

That piano! For years it became more and more out of tune, until one day we told the publican that he really would have to do something about it. He promised faithfully that he would, and a few days later he had the thing painted mauve.

When Wally drifted away, attendance fell off slightly. Then something happened which packed the crowds in as never before. George Melly was making a come-back as a singer of nostalgic and jazz-tinged popular songs. To see the superstar on his way, the Merlin's more or less offered itself as a convenient launching-pad. George made regular appearances at the club over a period of months. Soon you would have had to scrape the wallpaper off the walls in order to squeeze any more people in.

This revival of interest in George was inevitable, because he is what a certain type of inhibited fun-seeker evidently needs. He exudes from every pore the rich sap of bourgeois permissiveness. He encourages the timorous soul who once blushed at sex to snigger at it instead. There have been better singers than George, but no one that I can think of who could so coolly hold an audience in the palm of his hand. He is a great showman, and his continued success is more or less preordained.

Soon the crowds at the New Merlin's Cave were spilling out into the street as George's fans pushed their way in, to sit nudging one another and giggling at the suggestive lyrics. I appeared frequently with George, accompanying him on concerts, blowing behind him on certain LPs, and generally basking in his limelight. Then he became a very busy touring singer, which meant that his appearances at the Merlin's became infrequent. He still managed to show up there very seldom, on surprise visits, and it was probably for this reason that large crowds continued to surge into the Merlin's every Sunday, no doubt on the off-chance of seeing the big star. By this time, I had become a familiar figure at the pub in my own right, with a small hard core of fans, but some of the pub's recently acquired clientele had never heard of me, and probably didn't much want to. One Sunday, as I was testing one of the microphones at the start of the session, a middle-aged couple came up to me, and asked if I was going to sing a number entitled 'Nuts' some time during the programme.

'We think it is the best one of all your songs,' they enthused, 'do try and fit it in. We've come a long way this morning, just to hear it.'

'Listen, I think you may be mistaking me for someone else.'

'Does that mean you won't be singing it after all?'

For almost an hour, these two sat patiently, evidently half-expecting the request number to materialize, in spite of what I had said. At last it dawned on them that I wasn't going to oblige. They wandered off, about halfway through one of my solos, looking back reproachfully as they went out of the door.

I would like to entertain everybody who comes to hear me play, but can do only what I am cut out to do. It is no use anyone having a go at me for being too modern, not modern enough, too introvert, too extrovert, or simply for not being George Melly. I will go on playing the way I do, and hope that it will entertain some people for some of the time. It is all that should be expected of any man.

In mentioning the Merlin's sessions, I have gone a little ahead of my story. I started playing at the Islington pub shortly after leaving Bilk, and have continued to appear there regularly right up to the present day. The trouble with working in a name band for a number of years is that you become buried in it, especially if the musical policy is built around the leader's solo talents, whether trad or modern or whatever. No matter how much you may be enjoying yourself, you are playing another man's music – not your own. The temptation is to go on raking in the steady wage, adapting yourself to the other man's musical credo, and being thankful that it happens to coincide at certain points with your own. Then, one morning, you wake up and find that you are not known as an individual player any more. This happened when I left Acker. I had been quite an established figure in British jazz when I first joined the band. Now, it seemed, nobody wanted to know.

I went to one of the big agents, and he told me my own music wasn't saleable, because I didn't have a gimmick. Good music wasn't enough in itself. You had to wear a bowler hat, or use certain electronic devices so that the listener would be swept off his or her feet by the sheer volume of sound. Cool music didn't stand a chance – a jazz musician was expected to cavort and sweat in an ecstasy of 'free' expression, allowing the audience to glimpse the delights of pure, unrestrained self. Even our modern jazz musicians were now identifying themselves with the dissipated 'pop' scene. Amplifiers and synthesizers now dehumanized the beautiful natural sound of certain instruments. Groups began to call themselves by weird, nonsensical names, as if about to enter themselves for the Grand National.

Lennie Tristano visited this country almost unnoticed, except for the hard core of faithful admirers who had invited him here on a slender Arts Council grant. At about the time these beautiful concerts were taking place, more than one local 'pop' idol had become a cult figure heading towards his second million. I asked Lennie what he thought about it all, but he didn't seem worried. Perhaps people were not yet ready, was his only comment. We had to try and make truthful music whenever possible, and hope that it would be understood by and by.

I was pleased when I was given this opportunity of accompanying Lennie, in spite of the fact that I hadn't yet thrown off my bad habit of trying to sound exactly like Konitz. Bassist Peter Ind and I were, I think, able to give the great pianist some useful support, and the concerts produced some of the most creative sounds of that lamentable period.

Teenage 'pop' music was already elbowing jazz out of the clubs, but some pundits were not disposed to take a firm stand. Instead of glorying in the fact that some musicians were resisting the commercial pressures, instead of delighting in the attempts to change public taste rather than pander to it, they cried out for jazz to be more 'entertaining'. If this is good, honest criticism, then the kiss of Judas was sincere.

Lennie Tristano always saw himself as a musician, and the task of winning people over as a slow and painstaking one. As a popular entertainer he was not impressive – unless you happen to believe as I do that great music is in itself profoundly entertaining. We are too ready to accept the *illusion* of pleasure, rather than its substance. Entertainment becomes a multicoloured froth, but all this is nothing new. For most of her life, Billie Holiday sang with a penetrating truthfulness, a wholesome candour that has made her one of the timeless artists – but the system ensured that she would never become a star of the entertainment world. True genius does not know how to compete in the rat-race. She never really understood the formula for a prostituted music, or if she ever did, she turned from it in disgust. I guess some critics would have said that she 'failed', and that she deserved to.

History will no doubt offer a different verdict. Singers who have seen themselves as entertainers, rather than as artists with their roots in human society, don't tend to hang around in our memories for very long.

Acker Bilk and George Melly are both powerful entertainers who have carved a niche for themselves in the world of show business. They are also important offshoots of the kind of hedonistic 'good-time jazz' sound that came to absolute perfection in the music of Fats Waller, Cab Calloway and Louis Prima. They chose to walk along this road because they had exactly the temperament for it. It was their natural form of expression. I am pleased to have been associated with these two performers, with whom I very much enjoyed working, but in the end I had to admit that I am *not* that kind of performer myself. My inclination is to go along an entirely different road, so in the end we went our respective ways.

Acker used to have a favourite little catch-phrase, which he would come out with from time to time. If the applause for one of his numbers went on for too long, as it very often did, he would at last cut in with: 'Now, now, boys and girls – no mass hysteria, please!'

He, of course, meant it in fun, but sometimes I think that it sums up my own musical philosophy very neatly. Music, I feel, ought to be under control. Cool jazz, by the way, didn't start with Paul Desmond and Stan Getz, but way back in the twenties with Jelly Roll Morton, Artie Whetsol, Joe Smith, Bix, Miff Mole and many others. Even the more impassioned players were skilful in the use of light and shade, starting gently and then working up to a climax. A supreme example of this would be Louis Armstrong's two choruses in 'Knocking a Jug'.

I don't know what prompted popular music to start shouting its head off, in the past ten or fifteen years especially. Maybe it is the insane arms race, with its feverish scramble towards nuclear war, that is reflected in the way musicians currently play. Jazz and 'pop' both get louder every day and the sound of jazz isn't always cool or charged with human warmth and genuine feeling, any more. Today, some jazz instrumentation doesn't so much talk as snarl at you. It may not be mass hysteria, but they're blowing a lot of awfully nervous music these days.

11 'Turner Returns'

In adult life, I have hardly ever had bad dreams. Bogeymen don't bother me – but a few weeks after my departure from Acker's band I did spend one particularly rough night. I was drowning, somewhere in the middle of a vast ocean, with nothing I could cling to and nobody around for thousands of miles. The water was getting into my lungs and freezing my feebly threshing limbs. I woke up feeling terribly depressed and with the last theme of Debussy's 'La Mer' pounding away in my head.

This wasn't caused by anything I'd had for supper. I couldn't *afford* to eat supper. The evening before, I had clambered into bed with the dismal realization that I wasn't getting any work now that I was a freelance jazz musician once again. For about six weeks, I had learned all about what it is like to be an out of work. It had never happened to me before, in all my years of professional playing. Always I had passed easily from one name jazz band into another, but now the whole situation had changed. My kind of music was no longer being played in the clubs, or featured on radio or television. Or so it seemed. Many of the old venues now presented American artists, or local musicians who were dedicated to something called free form. I sat around by the phone, hoping someone would ring me up and ask me to join their band. Every time it did ring, it was the estate agent telling me he hadn't been able to sell my house for me, and would I consider lowering the figure. I finally did sell, at a slight loss, and a few months later house prices soared into the stratosphere.

It was almost, but not quite, funny when a headline appeared in one of the jazz weeklies, which read: 'TURNER RE-TURNS'. Underneath there was a short paragraph to the effect that I had 'forsaken' jazz a few years ago to play 'funny-hat' music. Not a word about the swing sessions Acker had been featuring almost every night of the week, in addition to the comedy and 'trad'. The writer now welcomed me back into the fold, stating magnanimously that the past was over and done with. I had perhaps learned my lesson, and everything was all right now.

Some writers were not happy unless their favourite jazzmen were in rags and queueing at soup kitchens, thus proving their loyalty to the one true sound. In contrast, some people who *didn't* like my playing were even more delighted that I had left Acker. To these characters, I had always been the 'dirty bopper' who went around contaminating pure traditional jazz with my unwanted presence. One promoter had hardly waited until I was out of the band before having some special posters set up, blazoning forth the good news: 'AT LAST! ACKER'S BAND IN ITS ORIGINAL AND UNEXPURGATED FORM' ran one of these promoters' hand-outs, 'GENUINE TRADITIONAL JAZZ – DEFINITELY NO SAXOPHONE'.

It was nice to know that I was making someone happy, just by simply not being around. I had to keep reminding myself that some of the top musicians in jazz had praised my playing, either in recorded interviews or in the jazz press (Basie, Buck Clayton, Ruby Braff and others). If it hadn't been for this, I would probably have ended up dangling from a beam. Those five or six weeks without any public appearances nearly destroyed all the self-confidence I had been building up for years.

Then I remembered that Humphrey Lyttelton occasionally used guest soloists with his band. I searched out his phone number and reminded him that I was around.

'Where is all the work nowadays?' I enquired of him. 'Nobody rings me any more to play in their clubs. It's racial persecution, that's what it is.'

'I'll let you in on a little secret. You're supposed to ring *them*. Otherwise, people lose track of you. I certainly did.'

'Can't stand telephones – everyone sounds like Donald Duck.'

Humph didn't reply right away, and I thought I heard a deep breath being drawn. Then he told me to come to a rehearsal in a couple of weeks' time, if I was interested in joining his latest band. I gulped several times, and said I was interested. He then imparted the details of time and place.

'You remember how to get to 100 Oxford Street, don't you?' he began carefully, 'You come out of the station and turn right . . .'

'Oh, that's all right, Dad – I drive a car now . . .'

'Oh, God . . .'

On the appointed day, I showed up on time and all in one piece, to the evident relief of both Humph and Kathy Stobart. When this band was finally launched upon the public, I would be in it, and the wolf would just have to find another door. What a tremendous line-up of first-class musicians! Kathy on baritone sax, Colin Purbrook on piano, Dave Green on bass, Tony Mann on drums. Colin didn't stay with us for long, but then Mick Pyne came in on piano. This has to be one of the finest bands ever brought together by the maestro.

More weeks would elapse before the band had been rehearsed, publicized and then unleashed upon the public.

Times had changed since I last turned my back on the competitive world of freelance music. The Permissive Society had arrived at a final impasse. Sex and violence had become the legal right of all citizens, glossy porn stared down at us from the bookshelves, and gutter urchins filled their lungs with nicotine in full view of the adult population. Red-blooded youths who beat up old ladies for their small change were whisked off to psychiatric wards for tea and sympathy, while their victims were left wondering when the next attack would come.

There was much talk about the 'freedom of the individual'. This was what the Establishment held in the very highest esteem, as against the wicked notion that human beings ought to be working together as one huge family, towards the ultimate betterment of all.

Laissez-faire then began to take a strong grip upon the jazz critic and so, inevitably, upon the sound of jazz. Labels became suspect. The word 'jazz' was no longer held to possess a clear, specific meaning. It was now used to describe almost any collection of random sounds made by young, experimental musicians. Some of Britain's finest jazz soloists were forced to take a back seat, while preferential treatment was given to ultra-modernists who tried to graft jazz and folk influences on to the techniques of Stockhausen and John Cage. This jazz-tinged 'free' music is often very fine, but it is questionable whether jazz programmes are quite the right place for it. If a radio programme is advertised under the heading: 'China Today', we are entitled to complain if it turns out to be a summary on world affairs, in which China is mentioned only very briefly in passing.

Nobody was busy defining jazz during the seventies, but what seemed clear was that seasoned and established players were not getting a fair deal. Such superb musicians as Tommy Whittle and Kenny Baker were not receiving the acclaim that their enormous talents deserved, although they have always been kept very busy in the sphere of commercial 'session' work. Those of us who were not brilliant sight-readers found things increasingly difficult. Colin Smith, regarded by many of our top players as the best jazz trumpet in Britain, was virtually unemployed for a time. Others took shelter under the 'umbrellas' provided by the name bands. Roy Williams and John Barnes blossomed into fine, mature players during their long stay with the Alex Welsh band. So did that excellent but self-effacing tenorist, Al Gay. The Humphrey Lyttelton band gave sanctuary to such class musicians as Dave Green, Kathy Stobart and Mick Pyne. Collin Bates went on tour with George Melly, while Pete Strange and Alan Elsden survived somehow, seeming to grow in stature with every passing day.

'Free' music is something of a hybrid and, by definition, a departure from established jazz rather than a development of it. By 1970, it was cropping up everywhere, often where one least expected to find it. On one occasion, I agreed to blow with a rhythm section whose names were not familiar to me. These boys claimed to be 'modernists', and I was looking forward to having a go at 'Confirmation' and 'I Remember Clifford'. I should have known that I was being hopelessly naïve. Just before our opening number, the piano man told me that he had come to jazz through listening to me and Humph in the early days.

'I am fond of those Johnny Hodges tunes,' he explained. 'Why don't we warm up on "Squatty Roo"?'

I was reassured. 'Squatty Roo' is a nice safe thing to open with. I mean, what could possibly go wrong?

Everything went along nicely in that opening tune – for at least three minutes. I established the theme and then started to build up a few ideas. Then my luck gave out. A rending dissonance assailed my ears. At first I couldn't imagine what was making all that noise. It sounded a bit like a piano, only louder. It was as if the pianist had succumbed to a nervous fit, pulled the whole framework down on top of him, and was there twitching amongst a pile of hammers and bits of wire. The noise now took on a more insidious shape – 'like sweet bells jangled, out of tune and harsh', as Ophelia might have described it. I wish she had been there instead of me.

What had happened was that the musician in question had

suddenly decided to 'freak out'. You are allowed to do this sort of thing in free form. The performer is impelled to a personal statement, often regardless of what happens to be going on at the time. If anyone else feels like joining in – fine. This withdrawal into some primordial subconscious can produce interesting music if it is based on a central discipline, but young musicians often indulge in musical tantrums and imagine that this is creative art. On this occasion, I'm afraid that my perverse sense of humour got the better of me. Adopting a swashbuckling stance, I gave out with some weird sound effects of my own. By the end of the set, I was perspiring freely and the other three musicians were staring at me with their mouths open. There was some wild applause as I left the stand, but all I could discern was the face of the man who had booked me for the job. It was contorted in a curious expression. I wondered if I was about to be booted off the premises and hoped it would be possible to collect my fee on the way out.

'That was really splendid,' said the man, excitedly, 'I didn't realize you were into all that modern stuff.'

At that moment I think I came dangerously near to dashing my saxophone against a wall and sobbing like a child. Later the pianist came up and congratulated me on my daring innovations, chiding me for having pretended to be an old-fashioned player when I first arrived. I could not find the heart to reply that 'free' expression left me cold. It actually restricted musical invention – to the grunts and incoherent animal cries which humanity left behind it, when it at last emerged from the cave.

The Lyttelton date sheet was soon looking good, so that I no longer needed to look around for solo dates. Audiences everywhere were responding to our judicious mixture of traditional and mildly explorative sounds. Humphrey wasn't interested in placating any of the small élitist factions that were darting backwards or forwards in time. The band brought present-day jazz to the widest possible audience, taking as its starting-point the timeless music of Armstrong, Ellington and other veterans whose music could by no stretch of the imagination be described as passé. To many of the pundits, our music fell somewhere untidily between the fixed categories of 'trad' and 'mod', but Humphrey had the obstinacy and the persistence to barge his way through any adverse criticism levelled against him or the band. He was like a horse brushing away flies, an attitude which some critics have found it very hard to forgive.

One thing that continued to worry me was my chronic state of absent-mindedness. I had tried to pull myself together over the years, but there were occasional relapses. Once I had to find my own way to a jazz concert that was being held in a large provincial town. The instructions were sketchy, but I arrived at the theatre somehow – or at least, I thought I had. I had arrived early and the place was in darkness. I groped my way on to a raised platform, then took out my clarinet and proceeded to warm up on a slow blues. After a few minutes, I was able to see better, when an enormous screen of light appeared behind me. This light flickered occasionally, but I was too engrossed to pay much attention. Then voices and bursts of dramatic music impinged on my consciousness. Someone has their radio up too loud, I thought, and responded with a few defiant high notes. Then someone discovered me, and explained that I was sitting right behind the screen at the local cinema, and that I had been providing part of the musical accompaniment to a suspense movie.

Every touring band has a road manager, one of whose jobs it is to keep a very watchful eye upon scatter-brained sidemen. There's no getting away from it – we have a higher proportion of 'absent-minded professors' in the jazz business than in just about any other walk of life. I am widely reputed to be the vaguest man in British jazz, but if this is so I can think of a few challengers for the title. At any rate, we are the 'roadie's' nightmare, and it is most important that we should be kept under close surveillance all of the time. This way, catastrophe is going to strike only once in a blue moon.

Humphrey Lyttelton has somehow managed to stave off these disasters ever since 1953, when I first joined his band. This is a long time, and speaks well for his ability to bring some order out of chaos. Apart from everything else, each of us has his own firm convictions with regard to music and life, stubbornly held and always in danger of coming into collision during moments of stress. Some friends of mine recently asked me how on earth I had managed to work so well with Humph over such a long period of time, in view of the differences in our temperament. My reply is usually that he likes the way I play alto and I like the way he plays trumpet. He is the best around, in his chosen idiom, with a sensitive understanding of this enormously exciting music which we share. Louis Armstrong and Buck Clayton are two of my very favourite trumpet players; Humph has absorbed a great deal from them and is able to rouse the listener in much the same way. This musical affinity is not the only thing we have in common, but I guess we both believe that it is the most important thing.

Morecambe and Wise once remarked that they have very little to do with one another in private life since, in a satisfactory working arrangement, the duologue says everything that needs to be said. Probably the same thing applies to a couple of jazz musicians who work well together, but might not get on too well if plagued with one another's company outside working hours. On tour, I know I tend to be morose and rather homesick, killing the time by reading a lot or listening to symphonic music in my hotel room. It's downright unsociable, and I know it – but I've been getting away with it for years now, and I hope I manage not to bring anybody down.

It isn't easy to be a good mixer if you don't drink. A large part of the jazz musician's social life is built around drinking. This is not to say that musicians are habitual drunks, or anything like that. But before going on stage, and then in the intermission, they like to chatter to each other over a drink or two. This is where I find myself stranded on unfamiliar territory. Jim Godbolt, when agenting my Jump Band, insisted that I once primly denounced 'the false camaraderie of the saloon bar'. Put this way, it sounds terribly po-faced, but I suppose I do have a thing about conversations in bars. It seems to me that as soon as two or more jazz musicians are facing each other with pints in their hands, the chat becomes about as profound as a front-page article in the *Sun*.

I am not much good at small-talk. Whenever I feel that some light badinage is expected of me, I lapse into the most inane drivel. This is me trying to be sociable, but I can see where it might get on other people's nerves after a while.

In order not to appear *too* serious, I often give the impression of being not serious enough. When it comes to frivolous conversation, I have taught myself to become the greatest of them all.

Take spoonerisms. Legend has it that the first great spoonerism came from a radio announcer who had to read out the title of Delius's 'First Cuckoo'. The poor man became tongue-tied, and it came out as: 'On Cooking the First Hero in Spring'. I can't explain why I find this immensely funny, but I do. When Freddy Randall and I went to see *Arsenic and Old Lace*, Fred referred to it as 'Lace Knicks and Old Arse', and I have toted this one around with me ever since. Nowadays, I spoonerize all the time, especially when I am trapped in a bar with a tomato juice and nothing of importance to contribute to the general chatter. It is a good way of appearing to communicate without actually doing so. Someone mentions the Buck Clayton Jam Sessions, and I immediately twist it round into 'Jack Clayton's Bum Sessions', and it gets a laugh. Kenny Baker's Dozen quickly becomes 'Denny Baker's Cousin' – not such a big laugh this time, but the thing has served its purpose. It has edged me into the prevailing back-chat, without quite pulling me out of the reverie I'm nearly always in during these intervals. I don't like intervals. I would just as soon go on playing, without any half-time break, but please don't tell the Musicians' Union I said so.

Touring around Britain can be dull, unless one takes plenty of reading matter and some good music on cassette. Luckily Humphrey has been able to avoid all the depressing chores involved when bands go on tour. We do strings of one-nighters, usually managing to return home on the following day. If we are away from home for a week or two, it is to visit foreign climes, and some of the places we've visited recently have been anything but dull.

A few years ago we spent some time in Poland, already a bankrupt nation and certainly not the vigorous, optimistic place I had visited in 1956. There was prostitution in Warsaw, black-marketeering, drug-traffic and some of the direst 'pop' groups I've ever heard. People seemed to spend their leisure hours either praying or listening to the latest hit singles – just as in Palermo or Syracuse. The record shop near our hotel had a large, framed photo of Elvis Presley hanging over the counter. I asked the man whether he sold any records of Chopin, but he seemed to think I was making a bad joke. The kids didn't listen to that old stuff any more.

Our music went down very well in Poland and even better, a few years later, in the Lebanon. Here I had the impression of a kind, friendly people oppressed by the most wretched poverty. Soon after we ended our tour, Israeli jets swooped down on Beirut and demolished parts of the town which we had all been admiring so much. Then came the appalling Beirut massacre. This was a very beautiful place once, which we were able to take a last look at, just before the death sentence was passed.

In Northern Ireland there were barbed-wire barricades, with armed soldiers at checkpoints, and shopkeepers only unlocked their doors after they had taken a good look at you through the steel shutters. We gave more successful jazz concerts and then went back to the airport at Belfast. An official told me I wouldn't be able to take my sax with me as hand-luggage.

'But it *has* to be hand-luggage,' I explained. 'Look, it's a soft case.'

'I'm sorry. Regulations. Don't worry – it will be handled with care.'

Dave Green and I took our seats in the plane, and glanced out of the window, to watch our cases being taken off the trolley and handed into the plane. The first thing we saw was my soft, plastic saxophone case, with the zip broken and no saxophone inside. The porter slung these pathetic remains into the plane and, a few seconds later, flung my saxophone after it. I have seen dustmen handle my week's refuse with infinitely more care. At Heathrow I filled in a form, and was able to have myself a new Yamaha without any trouble. Roll on that next flight to Belfast! I could do with a new saxophone round about now.

The way we see other people often comes into sharp conflict with the way they prefer to see themselves. If I now find it extremely difficult to set down my impressions of Humphrey Lyttelton, it is because there are so many facets to the man. What I have come to regard as the real Humph may well turn out to be a figment of my imagination, or nothing more reliable than a crude identikit drawing supplied by somebody in a state of shock. Having said that – well, I am ready to have a go. Who is this fellow I have been standing next to, on and off since 1953, on bandstands and concert platforms throughout the world?

Herewith, then, a brief pen portrait of the man I have slowly come to think of as Hurricane Humph. Unlike the rest of us, who tend to become more languorous over the years, Humphrey's lifestyle has increased in intensity. His music, too, is far more vigorous now than it was twenty or thirty years ago. The man simply refuses to turn his engine off, or even to switch into a lower gear. No half measures – the curtain must always be going up on the show to end all shows. Each performance is a kind of explosion, and it doesn't matter what obstacles are put in his way. No microphones? Then we'll just have to blow louder, won't we! No sleep the night before? Don't let the audience see this, whatever happens. They paid to hear good music, not to extend their sympathy.

If you are well enough to stand up, then you are well enough to play. Once he failed to turn up at the start of one of our concerts, and word came through that he was hospitalized and that the doctor had told him he mustn't on any account go to work. The concert looked as though it would have to be cancelled but then at the last minute a dishevelled Humph appeared in the wings, to lead us all on stage. He would announce the numbers and possibly blow one or two notes here and there, he told us in a whispered aside. What finally did happen was that he blew lustily throughout the entire concert, although I think he must have been near to collapsing at the end of it all. Not once did he even mention his state of health to the audience. Those people don't want to hear about our physical problems, he commented. They paid to hear *music*.

All this was rather like watching Brian Close facing up to a battery of West Indian fast bowlers on a wearing pitch. Personally, I have never been able to think of music-making as if it were an endurance test. The human frame can stand just so much punishment, although I am all for getting as much mileage as possible out of mine. I may be fairly stoical about pain, but I can't help feeling that if something is hurting somewhere, Mother Nature is trying to tell me something.

One evening Humph and I appeared on the same concert bill as guest soloists. I was in radiant health until the morning of the concert, and then started to feel an old back trouble coming on. Oh no, not that slipped disc again! Whenever the twinges come back, I know immediately that I have to lie on a hard flat surface for a day or two, but now there was no time. What was I to do? So there I was in the wings, waiting to be announced on stage for two solo feature numbers. My spinal column felt as if it had been surreptitiously removed and replaced by foam rubber. I would be lucky if I made it as far as the microphone without falling over.

I heard my name being announced to the audience, and started to move forward, but my legs began to get other ideas. By the time I had reached the mike, I was giving a remarkably good impression of John Cleese doing one of his silly walks. Someone in the stalls began to laugh, and it was then that I made my first mistake. I picked up the microphone and explained about my back trouble. My act was not supposed to be funny, and I simply wanted to make the point.

From that moment, I became the star of the show. Everything I did received frantic applause. Everybody must have had the impression that I was playing in spite of the most fearful agony. After the show, while Humph and I were putting our instruments back in their cases, the dressing-room was besieged by people wanting to know how I had managed to survive my 'ordeal', and to tell me what a brave fellow I was. I didn't dare to look in Humphrey's direction while all this was happening. He would have bounced up from an operating table to do the show, blowing all out until he finally keeled over. And he would have blamed *that* on a loose floorboard.

The present Humph band has endured for many years now, through sunshine and rain, in spite of the difficulties which confront British jazz musicians these days. The problems are very real ones, and it is no use musicians trying to look the other way. Critics, promoters and the media have turned away from local talents, to cast their adoring gaze upon the Americans. Big names have become more important than good music. Let's be quite clear about this. Most of the big American names *do* play good music, but the US no longer holds a monopoly. In fact, as the great veteran players have started to pass away, or merely to repeat themselves, Britain's top players have begun to show that they can more than hold their own. All through the 1970s, Humph had to cope with the problem of presenting British musicians as stars in their own right, and not merely as pallid substitutes for an American 'real thing'. And it *was* such a problem precisely because it was *we* – the jazz enthusiasts of this country – who initially clamoured for the American greats to be brought over. But in those days, 'greats' meant Duke Ellington, Louis Armstrong, Johnny Hodges, Sidney Bechet and Ben Webster. This top stratum almost disappeared, during the decade, and now the situation is completely changed. There are some fine, creative musicians in the US, who will always be cordially welcomed here, and there are some fine, creative musicians in Britain. Is it too much to expect that the two should now be accepted on equal terms?

Our own bands have had to face other problems, too. Free music usurping the jazz musician's already limited air-space; blues-oriented 'pop' music crowding us out of the clubs; and radio and TV 'jazz' programmes continuing to be run by isolated pundits, and not by representative committees of jazz musicians – which would surely be the only democratic way of going about things.

In spite of all these pressures, H.L. has succeeded in keeping a band afloat, and not just any old band, one might add. The personnel nearly always includes some illustrious names – the best in this country's modern and mid-period jazz. It is handy if you have managed to build up a reputation under your own name as well as within the Lyttelton fold. This means that if things become quiet and there is not a great deal happening on the Humph date sheet, you can work around the clubs as a guest star. A few years ago, I accepted an offer to play at the Nice Festival, in the company of the world's best. For part of the time, I would be blowing with a hastily-assembled group calling itself the British All-Stars, and the rest of the time I would be in sessions with American players of stature. Nice promised to be a thrill a minute, but from the moment I arrived everything seemed to go wrong.

The British All-Stars were all well-known players, but it is as if they had been picked out of a hat, by someone not even faintly connected with this country's jazz scene. Some of the players were incompatible with one another, but that wasn't the main problem. All of us were front-line musicians – there was no rhythm section in this all-star band! Before each of our appearances in Nice, we had to wait around while someone tried to find a drummer and a bassist who might be kind enough to lend a hand. This meant that a bunch of top-ranking players were unable to find anything like their best form throughout the entire Nice period. Kathy Stobart and Roy Williams, both wonderful musicians, never quite found their true form in Nice, and neither did I.

All this was bad enough, but then came the fateful day when I was called out to play in a big band. Up until that moment I had never even considered working in any area other than small-band jazz – and why? Because I can't read music, that's why! And what is more, I haven't the least desire to learn. Well, yes, I suppose I read just a little – just a *very* little. But on account of having a very good memory, I have always found that sufficient, and if anybody shoves music in front of me nowadays I can muddle through it somehow – given time. But in this instance, time was the very thing I didn't have. Sheets of music were being handed around, and there I was, sitting in a saxophone section next to some of the finest sight-readers in the business.

I hissed into the ear of Bob Wilber, who was placed next to me: 'Listen, Bob, there's been a stupid mistake. I can't read this stuff. Someone had better go and find Tony Coe.'

'Quit worrying,' said Wilbur, soothingly, 'it's all simple and straightforward. You won't have any trouble.'

I looked down at the lead alto parts Dick Hyman had just placed in front of me, and searched in vain for the simple bits. As soon as Hyman beat us in, I would be exposed in front of the whole festival as a fraud and a charlatan. If musicians can't read music, what the hell *can* they do?

While the crowds were coming in, I was able to commit some of the first page of music to memory. This way, I was able to scramble through that first number – but then I looked down at the second one. It was all speckles as far as I could see. There must have been more notes on that page than in a cashier's safe – but not so neatly stacked. I groaned inwardly, preparing for the inevitable. The man beat us in, and after the first bar I had dropped out of the race. I just sat there in a kind of stupor, waiting for the axe to fall on my playing career. I could see Dick Hyman ambling towards me, wearing a look of concern. I wondered if I could persuade him that I'd suddenly been taken ill.

And then a wonderful thing happened.

It started to rain – very hard. The stuff came down in great torrents, swamping the open-air platform and its assembled bandsmen. Someone shouted, 'Grab those charts', and then we were all scampering for cover. This doesn't often happen in the South of France in midsummer, as far as I am aware. Anyway, the big-band concert was washed out, and my honour was saved. The timing had all been so incredibly perfect that I looked up involuntarily towards the heavens. I think I half expected to hear the rumblings of some omniscient being who had just decided to let me off the hook. He would have been amused at my brief, pathetic incursion into big-band jazz.

The Nice Festival gave me a chance to blow with some of jazz's biggest names. It was nice to be in a couple of sessions with the great Earl Hines once again. Barney Bigard played clarinet on one of these, but was not staying the pace as well as Hines. He looked and sounded like a sedate old man, which is fair enough, I suppose. The marvel is that a man like Hines, entering the final phase of his life, could go on vitalizing jazz up to the very end.

Then they put me into a session with Zoot Sims.

I might have known I would become tongue-tied, coming face to face with Zoot at long last. Ever since 1950, when I met him briefly in New York, I have thought of Zoot as the greatest jazz musician since Parker. He embodied everything I wanted to be myself, but I knew I wasn't that sort of player in any case.

Even if I played at the peak of my *own* capabilities, I would never be able to capture what this man had, and it was no use thinking I ever could.

In short, even the mention of Zoot Sims's name was enough to give me an inferiority complex – and now here I was, seated in between Zoot and Clark Terry on a raised platform at Nice. Of course I played as well as I was able, but somehow my breath wasn't coming in and out in the normal way, and I must have sounded as if I was blowing through several layers of thick carpeting. To make matters worse, I hadn't even opened my mouth to say 'Hello', and at the end of the session I simply faded out of sight.

Later on, Zoot and I were waiting for the coach that took the performers back to their hotels. He was scowling, taking furtive sidelong glances at me and then looking away. I don't know if it was my bad playing that had annoyed him, or the fact that I hadn't said a word in all the time we were seated together. All I knew was that I had to break the silence somehow, while I still had a chance. Zoot's tenor case was leaning against a wall, in between us. I leaned over it and prepared to make conversation.

Immediately there was a snort of rage from Zoot Sims. 'Say, you're a musician, ain't yuh?' he called out.

'Yes – sort of.'

'Then why the hell you walkin' all over my saxophone?'

I gave up after that, and after a mumbled apology I never had a chance of speaking to Zoot again. He is not, by all accounts, a difficult man to get on with, but once again (as so often before in my life) I had found it very hard to communicate. I returned from my adventures in Nice very much the worse for wear.

Let it not be imagined that I close up like an oyster whenever the top-line American players are around. Humphrey worked closely with some of my favourite musicians during the seventies, and on each occasion I was able to rise to the occasion and show everyone what I could do. Buck Clayton, the marvellous ex-Basie trumpeter and arranger, gave me a lot of encouragement when he came here. Coming from Buck, any words of praise have to be taken as reflecting the man's real opinions, because he just doesn't fool around. If Buck thinks you are good he says so, and conversely he would not hesitate to point out any weak or unstable elements in the music he is connected with. Buck is a perfectionist, an impeccable performer who has had a lot to do with the training of young players in this country and in Europe. His influence on jazz outside the US hasn't yet been clearly understood. Both he and tenorist Buddy Tate have worked with Humph and stamped their personalities upon the band.

A word about this remarkable band of Humph's, and some of the people I have been working with over the past thirteen years. When Roy Williams and John Barnes came in from the Alex Welsh band, we had a four-piece front line of real quality. Roy has to be one of the world'd finest jazz trombones, as well as being an engaging character and irrepressible humorist. For years Roy and I commuted to Humphrey's gigs from our respective homes in Bedfordshire, which meant that we occasionally shared the same car and split the petrol expenses. On these journeys we either talked about cricket, or listened to Sims–Brookmeyer recordings on my portable cassette player. For such a volatile man, Roy was unusually prone to take sudden cat-naps – sometimes in the middle of a conversation. If I was driving to London, he could fall into a deep sleep somewhere between Luton and Hemel Hempstead.

John Barnes plays all the saxophones, in addition to clarinet and flute. In concerts, John's part of the stage is littered with instruments and you have to be careful where you walk. Multi-instrumentalists are never easy to assess, the talents being dispersed over a wide range, but I would say that on baritone sax and flute he has few equals in this country. On clarinet, he and I are about as different as chalk and cheese. John prefers a clean, orthodox approach, while I use a lot of vibrato and bend some of the notes out of shape. If we are both playing clarinet in the same number, there is a competitive atmosphere on stage. From a seat in the stalls, it might look as though friendly words of encouragement were being exchanged, but nearly always we are hissing insults into each other's ears.

'Ready for your first lesson?'

'Oh no – not more Reginald Kell!'

'As a kid, you always wanted to play the clarinet badly . . .'

'They used to call you Little Jazz, because that's what you play – little jazz.'

Very mature, we musicians.

Like Humphrey, John Barnes seems intent on draining the cup of life to the dregs. There is no keeping him under control. In Istanbul we all went into a restaurant for a meal. There were some young Turkish men at a nearby table, singing folk airs. Not to be outdone, John gave out with an old music-hall ditty he had learned by heart. Then he beamed across at the other table, inviting a reply. The young men responded with another of their national songs, and then John capped it with some more vaudeville. It had become a battle between their music and ours, and I half expected to hear knives whistling through the air. At long last both tables had exhausted their repertoires and were willing to call it a draw.

'You are nothing but a piss artist,' I told him afterwards, 'and a Lancastrian piss artist at that.'

John and Roy were both from the Manchester area, while Mick Pyne and I were Yorkshiremen. When Adrian Macintosh came into the band on drums, the 'tykes' outnumbered the 'hot-pots' by three to two. Adrian was from York, so it looked as though Humphrey would soon be the only southerner in the band.

H.L. has always fronted a line-up which includes world-class players. Dave Green had so many offers of tours with American musicians, that in the end he had to hand in his notice with Humph. Roy Williams also had important solo bookings which were beginning to clash with the band's engagements, so in the end he had to leave too. I suppose this is what a leader has to expect, if he insists on using only the best available players. Humphrey has never been satisfied with second best, but a star-studded line-up will always have its problems.

There is bound to be a conflict between the sideman wishing to stretch himself by finding as many solo engagements as possible, and the bandleader striving to present a stable and unchanging personnel. It isn't only a question of a man wishing to make extra money on his days off. An improvising musician knows that he has to keep on blowing, or else he will simply rust. Theme and variations, played over an entire evening by a horn and three rhythm, offers the soloist a chance to extend himself in a way he could not do on an all-star jazz concert, with everyone waiting his turn. In this respect, guest appearances at jazz clubs, although they may not always be adequately paid, are vital to most jazz musicians.

For a very long time, I was so well pleased with myself as a member of Humph's band that I didn't notice my technique deteriorating and my sound losing much of its bite. I had only myself to blame, since I had made no attempt to retain my old connections with the club circuit. I'd been silent for so long that large sections of the jazz fraternity had assumed that I wasn't available for solo work. When anyone *did* manage to book me for an appearance at their club, it was after they had gone to great trouble to find my latest address, and to ascertain that I might be free. As for me taking the trouble to *enquire* about solo work, I hadn't done anything like that for ten years.

Pretty soon I had even forgotten how to play a slow ballad, as I hadn't been featured on one for such a long time. That does it, I thought after a particularly rough session, I will just have to get back on the circuit – even if it means writing to someone. I found as many club addresses as I could, and sent off circulars to them on headed notepaper. I told everyone I was available, and raring to go. Then I waited for the replies to come flooding in.

Nothing happened for about three weeks. Some clubs had their programmes already booked up well in advance. Others, I guess, simply didn't want to know. I had hidden myself away for all these years, and now I was paying the price.

Then I had a call from Lennie Felix, to whom I had sent one of the circulars almost as an afterthought. I hadn't seen Lennie for a while. He told me he was playing solo piano at the Pizza Express, on a regular basis. He occasionally booked a guest soloist to appear with him, and would I care to be the next one? Not everyone could feel comfortable blowing in front of Lennie's wayward and unpredictable piano, but I knew that man's playing better than I knew my own. My appearance at the Pizza Express was so successful that Lennie wanted me to blow with him there on a permanent basis. He told me he would see the management about it as soon as possible.

Shortly after this, word came through that Lennie had been knocked over by a car, while halfway across a pedestrian crossing. He remained in a coma for several days. He never really came out of it before he died.

12   The Endangered Species

It is a dull, wintry morning in 1984. The sound of incandescent Chopin still drifts up through the walls of my home. My mother died several years ago, but my ten-year-old daughter is taking piano lessons. She is building up quite an enviable technique, with those small hands, and looks likely to follow in the footsteps of her intense, piano-happy grandparent.

Then there is my seven-year-old, who also likes to have a go when nobody else is on the keys. This one refuses to take lessons, preferring to fumble away on her own. I guess it is the way I have been making music over the past fifty years.

When the older girl was born, we had already decided to call her April, after the well-known month. It then occurred to us that children do not necessarily like the name that was chosen for them at birth. It is always advisable to throw in a couple of spares, just in case.

'How about April Lynn Paris?' I suggested, with my mind on the Artie Shaw version.

Sandy thought that perhaps April Lynn would suffice. A girl might not want to spend the rest of her life bearing the name of a popular ballad. Three years later we had our second daughter, and gave her the name Laura. I don't think either of us was thinking of the Charlie Parker record.

Sandy had been a singer and a dancer before I knew her. We had so many things in common, it was almost uncanny. Her father was a schoolteacher who came from Northern Ireland, just across the water from my dad's home. Her mother was a Durham woman, just like mine. Sandy was already turned on by the music of Stan Getz, Johnny Hodges and Claude Debussy, even before I met her.

When we first met, I was having trouble with my oldest daughter Caroline. The girl was at that time passing through her rebellious-teenager phase. Her room looked like the city dump and was usually filled with shrieking school chums who spent a lot of time drawing rude murals on the walls and ceiling. As soon as there was no more space, they ran a soapy cloth over some of it, and started again.

Sandy took one look and gasped in astonishment. She wanted to know why I had let the situation get so out of hand.

'Not my fault, really,' I stammered. 'Difficult situation. Had to take Caroline away from Summerhill after only a few terms. With no work coming in, I couldn't afford the fees.'

'So?'

'Well, then I had to send her to this rather tough comprehensive. It's overcrowded and understaffed. Kids are always being screamed at and clouted with rolled-up newspapers. Poor old Caroline, she's now completely mixed up, and I can't say I blame her.'

This was putting it mildly. When I first took Caroline to the new school, I explained things carefully to the headmaster. I told him my daughter had just left a place where enforced education didn't exist, but was replaced by kindness and understanding. He looked at me as though I had shifted into a foreign tongue, but did promise that there would be no rough stuff. Children were beaten up only if they had committed serious crimes. A few days later Caroline arrived home with a red mark on her hand, where she had been caned for not doing a lesson properly. I think I must have broken some Olympic records for short distances, by the time I was at the school, demanding to see the head man. I don't recall just what I shouted at him in my rage, but his face was a strange chalky colour by the time I'd finished. After that she was left alone by the staff.

Caroline became a different person. The noisy kids stopped coming round, having been superseded by one steady boyfriend, and one day Caroline and I spent an entire Sunday repapering the walls of her room.

My own life became completely altered after I met Sandy. She was loving wife and personal manager rolled into one. Most of my early problems, which had been caused by my timidity and indecision, simply melted away. Things started to come out right for a change, and at last I was able to feel secure. We moved to the attractive village of Toddington, in Bedfordshire, where I was able to wallow in the delights of a home life – which I'd never really had before. One of the good things that came out of all this was that my playing improved quite a lot. I have always been my own harshest critic, but over the past few years

I have felt that everything is clicking into place. I am playing better now than ever before. Not that this has had the slightest effect on my work situation.

I never intended to become a jazz musician, and for a long time I would much rather have been in the acting profession. In 1972 I flew to Bangalore to spend some time with my dad, shortly before he died. He presented me with copies of *Hamlet* and *Othello*, which contained pages of his own copious notes and explanations. Something about those two weeks with Dad must have set fire to my imagination. When I left him, I was even more infatuated with the stage than before. My father absolutely lived for Shakespeare. He used to sit up in bed during the night, and declaim loudly: ' 'Tis now the very witching time of night, when churchyards yawn . . .'

Anxious mutterings would issue from the servants' quarters, and lights would be turned on.

'. . . and Hell itself breathes out contagion to this world . . .'

Lights would be turned off again, followed by a relieved silence. It was only the white Sahib having one of his fits of Shakespeare.

Back in England, I started to work my way through the great tragedies, one after the other. I was no intellectual snob, or anything like that. I just wanted to act, or at least to watch actors. When I wasn't reading the plays, I was goggling at television. *Any* good, crisp TV series would do.

One day, a lantern-jawed young man came into the Merlin's and seated himself in front of the band.

'It's Norman Bowler!' I whispered fervently at Colin Smith, who was standing next to me up there.

'Norman *who*?'

'You know – the star of "Softly, Softly".'

'Oh, that television series. Don't tell me you watch all that stuff!'

But the awful truth is that I *do* watch all that stuff, and after all these years I am still hooked on actors and acting. I can't help feeling that, even if I hadn't made it on the stage, I would at least have made an interesting failure. Norman came to the Merlin's frequently and I got to know him quite well. He assured me the profession wasn't as glamorous as I had led myself to believe. It was very hard work, not always artistically fulfilling, and the level of unemployment was higher than just about anywhere else.

John Turner and Barbara Jefford also payed a visit to the

Merlin's, and to some of Humphrey's concerts. It was a curious feeling, being listened to and applauded by a couple of consummate Shakespearian actors, and a pleasure for me to become better acquainted with this delightful pair.

One evening I went to see them in *The Merchant of Venice* at a theatre in Oxford. Shylock was played by that splendid actor, Leo McKern. All three of them gave powerful, audacious performances, while I sat there bewitched by it all. And to think that I had once hoped to become an actor! Jazz had been the poor second best – but now I understood that my drifting into a life of music-making hadn't been such a fortuitous thing after all. Either I would make it in music, or I wouldn't make it at all, but in any case I had to keep on trying until the end.

Before going to see the *The Merchant of Venice*, I had spent the day with my number-two daughter, Jackie. After my ex-wife had moved out to Farringdon, it had only been possible to see Jackie fleetingly, whenever Caroline and I could motor there for a few hours. We three sat on park benches in Oxford and Swindon, scoffing doughnuts and chattering the time away. Jackie is now a tall, vivacious woman who attracts many an admiring glance, when I walk into a jazz club with her. It makes me feel like somebody.

I'm aware that my status as a jazz musician is reasonably high, and that I needn't feel unsure of myself any more. The problem now is that jazz itself is going through a rather lean period. At one time, only the two extremes of ancient and ultra-modern were bringing in the crowds, but now most of us are finding it tough. Banjo trad thrived on a wave of nostalgia that was sweeping through the entertainment world. At its worst, it became a genial form of escapism, the musical equivalent to a piss-up at the local pub, and with about the same degree of social content.

The avant-garde lived precariously for a time, getting by on Arts Council grants and on the patronage of some BBC programme chiefs. At its lowest level, it could boast no real, mass following, having rather the adverse effect of turning some horrified listeners off jazz for life.

I am absolutely convinced that jazz could enjoy a wide acceptance, but that it is up to musicians to publicize their wares. A performer should be able to explain, in simple terms, what he is trying to do. It is no use hoping that the music will in some magical way 'explain itself', and that if people don't respond to it they are just being dense. This seems to me to be a very defeatist attitude indeed.

Understandably, some of us feel helpless before the literary man with his command of words. We are not prepared to enter the arena of discussion, for fear of being torn into shreds by someone with a better command of language – so the intellectual writer is presented with a clear field. Very occasionally, a dissenting voice is heard. Peter Ind, an important musician but one who has had to struggle for recognition ever since his return from the States some years ago, has this to say: 'I believe,' says Peter, 'that most professional writers are misrepresenting the development of jazz. I also feel that my work situation would be easier if this were not so. I realize that I have gradually accumulated a reputation, but a grudging one as far as the critics are concerned.'

He then goes on to make the point that the critics are not entirely to blame. In Britain there is 'such an inferiority complex about creative musical talent – it's built into the very fabric of social life'.

Some years ago, another musician introduced him with the apology: 'You probably won't like what he's doing, but I can assure you it's good.'

'To me,' concludes Peter, 'that just about sums up the malaise.'

Peter often ran private sessions at his home in Ickenham, and he invited me to bring my sax along. I had a shock when I first arrived. There was no piano, no drums, and the rhythm section consisted of two guitarists and two bass players. There were further shocks in store. One of the guitarists was a young man from Newcastle, whom I'd never heard of before. He played so much guitar I couldn't understand why he wasn't world-famous and naming his own fees. From that moment, Dave Cliff became my favourite guitarist.

At these same sessions I came to know the marvellous tenor player Chas Birchall, whose cool introspective phrases remind one of Warne Marsh and Stan Getz, but who has very original ideas as well. Chas works in an office in the daytime, blowing occasionally in the evenings for his own pleasure. He is treated by our critics as if he didn't exist. If the latter ever decide to wrench their gaze away from the Americans, even for just a moment, they might notice this array of local talent which lies under their noses.

It would be a laughable situation if it were not so completely insane. But are British musicians tackling these problems and shouting them from the house-tops? Not so as you'd notice.

'I explain myself through my music,' mutters the average muso, pulling out his tired trump card. 'All I'm interested in is my sounds. What's the point in using all those long words?'

The idea that jazz is a mysterious force which can never be adequately explained is a cliché of the dime novel and the pre-war Hollywood musical. In a movie supposedly about jazz, pop-eyed janitors sweep the floors of hotel lobbies to a boogie beat, and grinning shoe-shiners perform their chores in a series of strange jerking movements as though suffering from a nervous twitch. Say what you like about these people, you have to admit they've got *rhythm*, goes the argument. This is the unaccountable magic, the elusive quality that only a few are blessed with. The rest of us can only stand and stare.

To define jazz in this way, as something ineffable, is a very convenient and easy way out. The writers have fallen for it, and they sometimes talk us into believing it, too. We may think it absolves us of the need to talk in clearly defined terms.

We came to this pass somewhat abruptly, when the rhythm clubs ceased to function at the end of the war. Heaven knows, discussion at the rhythm clubs had been limited enough, but at least there had been some. Then came the jazz clubs, with their fixed combos. Everyone was handed their helpings of standard-ized real jazz, and nobody argued any more. The pundits had said all there was to say.

Traditionalists and modernists now tolerate one another, and smile when they recall the old heated arguments, but this does not mean that the problems will simply disappear. I would love to hear a discussion on the radio between, say, Ken Colyer and John Dankworth on the origins of jazz. And it isn't a question of music being regarded in isolation. There are outside pressures to be considered, pressures which impinge on the professional musician at every turn. As an instance, there are clubs in this country which are no longer interested in booking British players, preferring to display the imported American product. When they *do* book a British player, as I have found to my cost, he is presented almost apologetically, without much advance publicity, and not even with an introductory announce-ment. We must get rid of the fiction that British jazz is nothing more than American jazz played by Britons. This simply isn't true any more.

With a little encouragement, and a lot of much-needed publicity, some of our players could be international stars. Mick

Pyne is now a master of the jazz piano in all its forms. In technique, feeling and sheer versatility he compares favourably with Ralph Sutton and Dick Wellstood, but the Americans are presented and publicized far more efficiently than our players. Collin Bates is another pianist who comes to mind, whose brilliant inventions rank him among the very best.

We can't really blame the critics for this lack of acceptance for British players. Critics have worked hard for a music in which they believe, and it isn't their fault that our musicians have been too reticent for too long. We have turned our backs on a great debate that has been going on for half a century now – the debate about jazz, and its place in our lives. We never really tried to explain our own music in words. We thought that the music would speak for itself, but in the end masses of people wanted to know more about the new sound, and so it was left to the professional writer to do the best he could.

The jazzman was seen as an engaging simpleton. He could sing, or play an instrument, but he wasn't very good with words. The pundit then tried out one theory after another. Jazz was 'the music of the Deep South'. That rather left Django Reinhardt out in the cold. Then it was 'collective improvisation' – but somehow this didn't account for Duke Ellington. It was described as a 'serious art form', with a reproving glance in the direction of Fats Waller, and then as 'popular entertainment' in despite of Charlie Parker, for whom the mass audience might scarcely have existed at all.

Then, when the many-sided idiom refused to be pinned down, it was protested that jazz was being 'betrayed'.

Now, jazz criticism passes from one extreme to the other. The old labels just wouldn't stick, so why not abolish labels altogether? Music is – just music. There are only two kinds, good and bad. The word 'jazz' is no longer held to have a clear, specific meaning. All manner of rude noises are now presented on radio programmes under the banner of 'jazz'.

The pundit has only tried to do the job which musicians have shirked for so long, the job of defining jazz. It isn't easy, but I believe it can be done only by musicians getting together and talking about their own art. Unless this happens, listeners will drift away, possibly to become enthusiasts of punk rock, country and western, or anything else that has a persuasive sales campaign.

It would help a great deal if jazz musicians were allowed to present their own music on radio. At present, 'live' performances are introduced by professional announcers, and records are played and commented on by disc jockeys (Humph's weekly programme being a notable exception). Peter Clayton has always tried to bring the views of musicians on to his programme, but there is a limit to what one man can do. A 'Musician's Choice', presented by a different jazz performer each week, would be of enormous interest to this country's enthusiasts, and would give musicians a chance to express their views.

At the start of the eighties, it wasn't easy to predict what jazz would sould like by the end of the decade. Hawkins, Hodges, Webster, Condon, Armstrong, Bigard, Ellington and Hines checked out rather abruptly, all within the space of a few years. Buck Clayton had to give up playing, and Benny Goodman no longer made regular public appearances. Then we looked around and discovered that there were no young players to follow in the footsteps of these great men. Most of the young virtuoso musicians were now espousing free form. When Scott Hamilton emerged, as a tenor player rather in the Hawkins mould, everyone gasped with astonishment because this was such an unusual case.

The theorists are now talking about 'cultural overlapping'. It is now considered rather passé for anyone to confine himself to the jazz idiom alone. Music is 'all one'. The new musician is influenced by 'sounds in general', and dabbles in this and that. There is Afro-Asian tribal music, the atonal system of Webern, even the computerized sound of electronic 'pop'. But there is also, ever so occasionally, the influence of classic jazz. It may only be a mere sprinkle of flavouring, dropped as an after-thought into the amorphous mess, but still it is there – playing its small part in the music that is 'all one'. It appears for a brief moment, and then is gone – like a face in the crowd.

Or like the ghost of some departed friend.

Discography

compiled by Michael N. Clutten

Grateful thanks are due to many people who have freely given their help to make this work possible, and especially to the following: Gerard Bielderman, Peter Carr, John Chilton, Clark's Shoes Ltd, Reg Cooper (*Jazz Journal*), Susan da Costa, Maurice Fleming, Syd Gallichan, Ralph M. Laing (*Jazz Catalogue*), Leicester City Libraries, Humphrey Lyttelton, Notley Advertising Ltd, Ross Russell, Peggy Seeger, Keith Smith, Barry Witherden (*British Institute of Jazz Studies*) and of course Bruce himself.

Abbreviations

alt	alto saxophone	sop	soprano saxophone
arr	arranger	tbn	trombone
bar	baritone saxophone	tpt	trumpet
bjo	banjo	vcl	vocalist (e)
bs	string bass	vib	vibraphone
c	circa	wbd	washboard
clt	clarinet	xyl	xylophone
cnt	cornet	ten	tenor saxophone
d	drums	Am	American
flt	flute	PaE	English Parlophone
fl-h	flugel horn	Esq	Esquire
fr-h	french horn	Met	Metronome
g	guitar	Col	Columbia
p	pianoforte		

FREDDY RANDALL & HIS BAND

Freddy Randall (tpt), Eddie Harvey (tbn/vcl -1), Bruce Turner (clt), Al Mead (p), Bob Coram (g), Jack Surridge (bs), Harry Miller (d)
London, 26 June 1948

3277/1/1M	**Wolverine Blues**	Cleveland FR 2
3277/2/1M	**Viper Mad**	Cleveland FR 3
3277/3/3M	**If I Could be with You** -1	Cleveland FR 4
3277/4/1M	**Tin Roof Blues**	Cleveland FR 1

BRUCE TURNER QUINTET

Bruce Turner (alt), Al Mead (p), Bob Coram (g), Jack Surridge (bs), Harry Miller (d)
London, 31 July 1948

Sweet Georgia Brown	unissued

FREDDY RANDALL & HIS BAND

Freddy Randall (tpt, vcl -1), Eddie Harvey (tbn), Bruce Turner (clt), Al Mead (p), Bob Coram (g), Danny Haggerty (bs), Harry Miller (d), Beryl Bryden (vcl -2)

London, 18 September 1948

1003/1	**At the Jazz Band Ball**	Cleveland FR 7
1003/2	**Hurry on Down** -2	Cleveland FR 5
1003/3	**Lonesome Road** -1	Cleveland FR 8
1003/4	**Cooks Ferry Parade**	Cleveland FR 6

MARK WHITE PRESENTS THE JAZZ CLUB

Freddy Randall (tpt), Geoff Love (tbn), Bruce Turner (clt), Freddie Gardner (bar), Dill Jones (p), Vic Lewis (g), Hank Hobson (bs), Max Abrams (d)

London, 24 February 1949

DR 13266	**Barefoot Blues**	Decca F 9158, LF 1047
		London (Am) LPB 344,
		LL1337

Freddie Gardner, Cliff Townshend, Bruce Turner (clt), Dill Jones (p), Vic Lewis (g), Hank Hobson (bs), Max Abrams (d)

London, same date

DR 13264	**Clarinet Blues**	Decca F 9190, LF 1047,
		ACL 1121
		London (Am) PLB 344,
		LL 1337

FREDDY RANDALL & HIS BAND

Freddy Randall (tpt), Eddie Harvey (tbn), Bruce Turner (clt), Pat Rose (bar/clt -1), Al Mead (p), Danny Haggerty (bs), Harry Miller (d).

London, 22 September 1949

TRS 51	**Washington and**	
	Lee Swing	Tempo A 45, EXA 2
TRS 52	**Dark Night Blues**	Tempo A 45, EXA 2
TRS 53	**Georgia Cake Walk**	Tempo A 55, EXA 2
TRS 54	**Sugar Foot Strut**	Tempo A 55, EXA 2
TRS 55	**Riverside Blues** -1	Tempo A49
TRS 56	**Jazz Club Stomp**	Tempo A49

as last, plus Bob Coram (g), Pat Rose plays bar on both tracks
London, 1949/1950

| DT 1 | **Honey** | New Jazz 400 |
| DT 2 | **Georgia Cake Walk** | New Jazz 400 |

FREDDY RANDALL & HIS BAND

Freddy Randall (tpt), Norman Cave (tbn), Bruce Turner (clt), Stan Butcher (p), Don Cooper (g), Ted Palmer (bs), Lennie Hastings (d)

London, 15 October 1951

CE 13469	**Tight Lines**	PaE R 3494, GEP8515
CE 13615	**Sensation Rag**	PaE R 3469, GEP8515
CE 13616	**Won't You Come**	
	Home Bill Bailey?	PaE R 3469, GEP8515
CE 13617	**Baby Won't You**	
	Please Come Home?	PaE R 3494, GEP8515

as last, except Lennie Felix (p), Lew Green (g/bjo) replace Butcher and Cooper
London, 30 January 1952

CE 13839/2	**IAGGYNOT Jelly Roll**	PaE R3525
CE 13840/1	**Dark Night Blues**	PaE R3525
CE 13841	**Swannee**	unissued
CE 13842	**Sugar**	unissued

as last, except Art Staddon (p) replaces Felix
London, 24 April 1952

| CE 13957 | **Clarinet Marmalade** | PaE R3573, GEP8661, MSP6007 |
| CE 13958 | **Original Dixieland One-Step** | PaE R3573, MSP6007 |

BILLY BANKS, acc. by FREDDY RANDALL & HIS BAND
Billy Banks (vcl), Freddy Randall (tpt), Norman Cave (tbn), Bruce Turner (clt), Art Staddon (p), Bob Coram (g), Ron Stone (bs), Lennie Hastings (d)
London, 14 May 1952

| CE 14002 | **Tishomingo Blues** | PaE R3545 |
| CE 14003 | **Walkin' the Dog** | PaE R3545 |

FREDDY RANDALL & HIS BAND
Freddy Randall (tpt), Norman Cave (tbn), Bruce Turner (alt/clt), Dave Frazer (p), Bob Coram (g/bjo), Ron Stone (bs), Lennie Hastings (d)
London, 8 October 1952

| CE 14255/2A | **Smokey Mokes** | PaE R3603 |
| CE 14256/2A | **Sheik of Araby** | PaE R3603, GEP8661 |

as last
London, 23 November 1952

CE 14366	**At the Jazz Band Ball**	PaE R3681, PMC1067, MSP6030
CE 14367	**Sunday**	PaE GEP8533
CE 14368	**All Change Boogie**	PaE unissued

HUMPHREY LYTTELTON & HIS BAND
Humphrey Lyttelton (tpt), Wally Fawkes (clt), Bruce Turner (alt), Johnny Parker (p), Freddy Legon (g), Micky Ashman (bs), George Hopkinson (d)
London, 24 February 1953

| CE 14433/1A | **Shake It and Break It** | PaE R3667, MSP6034, GEP8734, Angel 60008 |
| CE 14434/4A | **Jail Break** -1 | R3667, MSP6034 |

-1 Lyttelton (tpt & clt), Fawkes (clt & bs-clt), Turner (sop & clt); add Iris Grimes (vcl)

as last, except Lyttelton (clt) -2. Archie Semple (clt), added on -3. Neva Raphaello (vcl) -1. Legon out
London, 16 March 1953

CA 97	**Revolutionary Blues**	
CA 98	**Texas Moaner Blues**	
CA 99	**Shake It and Break It**	

CA 100	**On Treasure Island**
CA 101	**Coal Cart Blues**
CA 102	**Chicago Buzz** -2
CA 103	**Mahogany Hall Stomp**
CA 104	**That Da Da Strain**
CA 105	**Apex Blues**
CA 106	**Jive at Five**
CA 107	**Farewell Blues** -3
CA 110	**St Louis Blues** -1
CA 111	**Doctor Jazz** -1
CA 112	**Baby Won't You Please Come Home** -1

recorded by Chris Albertson at 100 Oxford Street

SAM WALKER
Bruce Turner (alt), Sam Walker (ten), Mike McKenzie (p), Dennis Evelyn
(vib), Joe Sampson (bs), Leslie Weekes (d), Fitzroy Coleman (g)
London, 17 April 1953

| PL 1039 | **Makin' Whoopee** | Lyragon J 715 |

BRUCE TURNER
as last
same date

| PL 1040 | **I Cried for You** | Lyragon J 714 |
| PL 1041 | **The Piccolino** | Lyragon J 714 |

HUMPHREY LYTTELTON & HIS BAND
Humphrey Lyttelton (tpt), Wally Fawkes (clt), Bruce Turner (alt/clt) -1,
Johnny Parker (p), Freddy Legon (g), Micky Ashman (bs), George Hopkinson
(d)
London, 28 April 1953

| CE 14583/5A | **Maryland My Maryland** -1 | PaE R3700, MSP6033, PMC1067 |
| CE 14584/3A | **Blue for Waterloo** | PaE R3700, MSP6033, PMC1067, PMC7147, Angel 60008 |

as last, except Turner (sop) -1
London, 3 June 1953

| CE 14651/3A | **Red for Piccadilly** | PaE R3734, MSP6045, GEP8700 |
| CE 14652/3A | **Kater Street Rag** -1 | PaE R3734, MSP6045, GEP8734 |

as last, plus Al Fairweather (tpt), Sandy Brown (clt), Legon (bjo)
London, 17 September 1953

| CE 14702/7A | **Four's Company** | PaE R3773, GEP8734 |
| CE 14703/5A | **Forty and Tight** | rejected |

as last, but omit Fairweather and Brown. Legon (g)
London, 27 October 1953

| CE 14755/2A | **Ain't Cha Got Music** | PaE R3787, MSP6061 |

CE 14756/2A	**Just Once for All Time**	PaE R3851, MSP6093,
		Angel 60008
CE 14757/3A	**Texas Moaner**	rejected

as last. Turner (clt) -2
London, 29 December 1953

CE 14849/1A	**Joshua Fit de Battle of**	PaE R3851, MSP6093,
	Jericho	PMC1067
CE 14851/3A	**Breeze (Blow My Baby**	
	Back to Me) -2	PaE R3819, MSP6076

JAZZ TODAY UNIT
Dickie Hawdon (tpt), Keith Christie (tbn), Bruce Turner (alt), Jimmy
Skidmore (ten), Dill Jones (p), Jack Fallon (bs), Alan Ganley (d)
R.F. Hall, London, 28 February 1954

	Going to Minton's	Esquire 32-005
	I'm Beginning to see	
	the Light	Esquire 32-005

MELODY MAKER ALL STARS
Humphrey Lyttelton (tpt), George Chisholn (tbn), Wally Fawkes (clt), Bruce
Turner (alt), Mike McKenzie (p), Fitzroy Coleman (g), Joe Muddel (bs), Eric
Delany (d)
London, 7 April 1954

| CE 14925/2A | **Mainly Traditional** | PaE R3846, MSP6079, |
| | | Ang 60008 |

as last, except Micky Ashman (bs), replaces Muddel. Omit
Fawkes
same date

| CE 14926/4A | **Oh! Dad** | PaE R3846, MSP6079, |
| | | Ang 60008 |

MELODY MAKER MODERN GROUP
Kenny Baker (tpt/fl-h), Jimmy Deuchar (tpt/fr-h), Bruce Turner (alt), Tommy
Whittle (ten), Vic Feldman (vib), Dill Jones (p), Sammy Stokes (bs), Tony
Kinsey (d)
London, 7 April 1954

491-2	**If I Could be with You**	Esq. 20-030
491-3	**If I Could be with You**	Esq. 20-020, 10-362
492-2	**Young and Healthy**	Esq. 20-030, 10-362
492-3	**Young and Healthy**	Esq. 20-030
493	**A Long K.B. Blues**	Esq. 20-030

HUMPHREY LYTTELTON & HIS BAND
Humphrey Lyttelton (tpt), Wally Fawkes (clt), Bruce Turner (alt/clt) -1,
Johnny Parker (p), Freddy Legon (g/bjo)-2/(vcl)-3, Micky Ashman (bs),
George Hopkinson (d)
London, 9 June 1954

CE 15045	**Coal Black Shine**	unissued
CE 15046/1B	**Mezz's Tune -1**	PaE R3917, MSP6128,
		Ang 60008

CE15047/2B	**Jelly Bean Blues** -2	PaE R3917, MSP6128, GEP8645
CE 15048	**Ace in the Hole** -3	rejected

BRUCE TURNER with GEORGE BROWNE

Bruce Turner (sop), with group led by George Browne (vcl). Personnel unknown
London, c. 1954

CEE 15/1A	**One at a Time**	PaE MP 130
CEE 16/2A	**Acapulco Joe**	PaE MP 130

BRUCE TURNER with Mike McKENZIE

Bruce Turner (sop)-1/(alt)-2, Mike McKenzie (p), Jack Fallon (bs), Phil Seamen (d)
London, 27 July 1954

CM 305/2A	**Moonlight in Vermont**	Col: DC 671
CM 306/1A	**My Old Flame**	Col: DC 671
CM 307/3A	**I Wished on the Moon** -1	Col: DC 676, SCMC 9
CM 308/3A	**Falling Leaves** -2	Col: DC 676, SCMC 9

THE FAWKES TURNER SEXTET

Wally Fawkes (clt), Bruce Turner (alt), Johnny Parker (p), Freddy Legon (g), Micky Ashman (bs), Ron Bowden (d)
London, 3 August 1954

DR 19328	**The Sheik of Araby**	Decca DFE6193, LF1214
DR 19329	**Fishmouth** – Take 1	Decca DFE6192
DR 19330	**Fishmouth** – Take 2	Decca DFE6193, LF1214
DR 19331	**Exactly Like You**	Decca DFE 6193, LF1214
DR 19332	**Summertime**	Decca DFE6192, LF1214
DR 19333	**That's What It's All About**	Decca LF 1214
DR 19334	**Oh Baby**	Decca DFE6193, LF1214
DR 19335	**My Monday Date**	Decca DFE6192, LF1214

All titles from LF1214 also on London (Am) LB1122; reissued on DeG DS3274/1

NOTE: From about this point E.M.I. recordings were made on tape. Master numbers were allocated only for titles issued on 78s, for original 78 releases and 78 reissues from previous LPs. (This also applies to numbers given to 45 single releases.) This means that master numbers will now only refer to release date, and not recording date

HUMPHREY LYTTELTON & HIS BAND

Humphrey Lyttelton (tpt/vcl)-3, Wally Fawkes (clt), Bruce Turner (alt/sop)-1, Johnny Parker (p), Freddy Legon (g/bjo)-2, Micky Ashman (bs), George

Hopkinson (d), announcements Lyttelton
Conway Hall Concert, London, 2 September 1954

Texas Moaner -1	PaE PMC1012, ENC164
Coal Black Shine	PaE PMC1012, ENC164
Last Smile Blues	PaE PMC1012, ENC164
Elephant Stomp	Angel 60008, PaE PMC1012, ENC164
Bucket's Got a Hole in It -2	PaE PMC1012, ENC164
I Double Dare You	PaE PMC1012, ENC164
That's the Blues Old Man	PaE PMC1012, ENC164
St James Infirmary	PaE PMC1012, ENC164
Memphis Shake -2	PaE PMC1012, ENC164
Mo Pas Lemme Cas -3	PaE PMC1012, ENC164

as last, plus John Picard (tbn) -1 spoken introduction by Lyttelton -2 vcl. by front line. -3 vcl. by audience. Legon (bjo) -4
Concert, Royal Festival Hall, 28 November 1954

	Introductory Blues -1	PaE PMD 1032
	High Society -4	PaE PMD 1032
	I Wish I Could Shimmy Like My Sister Kate -2	PaE PMD 1032
	The Onions -3	PMD 1032
	When the Saints -4	PMD 1032
CE 15246/1A	**I Love Paris**	R3996, GEP8534

as last, Turner (clt) -2, Legon (vcl) -2
London, 2 December 1954

CE 15171/4A	**Ace in the Hole** -1	PaE R3967, GEP8514
CE 15172/3A	**Coffee Grinder** -2	PaE R3967, GEP8514

BRUCE TURNER with MIKE McKENZIE
Bruce Turner (sop)-1/(alt)-2, with group led by Mike McKenzie (p), personnel unknown
London, 1 February 1955

CM 365/1	**Heavenly Music** -2	Col. DC693, SEGC6
CM 366/1	**I've Got the World on a String** -1	Col. DC693, SEGC6
	It Could Happen to You	SEGC6
	Lazy Afternoon	SEGC6

JAZZ TODAY UNIT
Kenny Baker (tpt), Keith Christie (tbn), Bruce Turner (alt), Jimmy Skidmore

(ten), Harry Klein (bar), Dill Jones (p), Ike Isaacs (g), Frank Clarke (bs), Benny Goodman (d)
London, 16 February 1955

| PA 007 | **Farewell Blues** | Polygon/Nixa JTL2 |
| | **Blue Feeling** | Polygon/Nixa JTL2 |

as last, but Cedric West (g), and Eric Delaney (d), replace Isaacs and Goodman
London, 21 February 1955

| | **That's the Blues, Dad** | Polygon/Nixa JTL2 |

as last, plus Joe Harriott and Bertie King (alt)
same date

| | **Blues in Threes** | Polygon/Nixa JTL1 |

BRUCE TURNER QUARTET
Bruce Turner (alt), Cedric West (g), Dill Jones (p), Frank Clarke (bs), Benny Goodman (d)
London, 25 February 1955

PA 008	**I've Got to Sing a**	
	Torch Song	Nixa NJS2003, JTL2
	You're a Heavenly	
	Thing	Nixa NJS2003, JTL2
	Imagination	Nixa NJS2003, JTL2
	Love is Just Around	
	the Corner	Nixa NJS2003, JTL2

HUMPHREY LYTTELTON & HIS BAND
Humphrey Lyttelton (tpt), John Picard (tbn), Wally Fawkes (clt), Bruce Turner (alt/clt) -1, Johnny Parker (p), Freddy Legon (g), Micky Ashman (bs), George Hopkinson (d)
London, 8 March 1955

	Lastic -1	rejected
	Fisher Seller	rejected
	Ce Mossieu Qui Parle	rejected

as last
London, 24 March 1955

CE 15291/4A	**Fisher Seller** -1	PaE R4032, GEP8543,
		PMC7147
CE 15292/2A	**The Glory of Love**	PaE R4032, GEP8543
	Heat Wave	rejected
	Ce Mossieu Qui	
	Parle -1	rejected
	Lastic -1	rejected
	My Gal Sal	rejected

KENNY BAKER ENSEMBLE
Kenny Baker (tpt), Bruce Turner (alt/clt) -1, Dill Jones (p), Frank Clarke (bs), Eddie Taylor (d)
London, 11 May 1955

PL 324/1   **I'm a Ding Dong**   Polygon JTL4,
                  Daddy   JTS1503
                                               Nixa NJS2010,
                                               Marble Arch
                                               MALS1167

                  Oh, Baby   Polygon JTL4
                  Apex Blues -1   Polygon JTL4

BRUCE TURNER QUINTET

Johnny Steiner (tpt), Bruce Turner (clt/alt) -1, Johnny Parker (p), Jim Bray
(bs), Jeff Ellison (d)
Warsaw, August 1955

Queen Bess -1	Muza 2722
I've Found a New Baby	Muza 272 N0082
June is Jumping -1	Muza 2738
London Boogie	Muza 2738
After You've Gone	Muza 2745
Jumping with **Symphony Sid** -1	Muza 2764 N0082
What is this Thing **Called Love**	Muza 2807
Shine	Muza 2807 N0082
Memphis Blues	Muza 2812 N0082
Out of Nowhere (omit Turner)	Muza 2812
Honeysuckle Rose (omit Turner)	Muza 2812

HUMPHREY LYTTELTON & HIS BAND

Humphrey Lyttelton (tpt), John Picard (tbn), Wally Fawkes (clt), Bruce Turner
(alt), Johnny Parker (p), Freddy Legon (g), Micky Ashman (bs), Stan Greig (d)
-1, George Hopkinson (d)
London, 4 August 1955

CE 15335/3A	**P.T.Q. Rag** -1	PaE R4060, GEP8546
CE 15336/2A	**Heat Wave** -2	PaE R4060, GEP8546

at last, except Jim Bray (bs), and Stan Greig (d), replace Ashman &
Hopkinson, Turner (alt) -1. Invited studio audience
London, 25 August 1955

CE 15399/1A	**Ce Mossieu Qui** **Parle** -1	PaE R4092, GEP8546
CE 15400/1A	**C'es Filon** -1	PaE R4092, GEP8546
	Beale Street Blues	PMD1035
	Blues Excursion	PMD1035
	Sweet Muscatel	unissued

FAWKES-TURNER SEXTET

Wally Fawkes (clt), Bruce Turner (alt), Lennie Felix (p), Fitzroy Coleman (g),
Jim Bray (bs), Stan Greig (d)
London, 27 September 1955

New Orleans Hop	Nixa NJE1004,
Scop Blues	Met. MEP1091

Viper Mad	Nixa NJE1004,
	Met. MEP1091
Roses of Picardy	Nixa NJE1004,
	Met. MEP1091

HUMPHREY LYTTELTON FIVE
Humphrey Lyttelton (tpt), Bruce Turner (alt), Johnny Parker (p), Jim Bray (bs), Stan Greig (d)
London, 29 September 1955

Slippery Horn	rejected
Squeeze Me	PaE GEP8580
Handful of Keys	rejected
Lightly and Politely	PaE GEP8580
It's a Thing	PaE GEP8580

as last
London, 20 October 1955

Slippery Horn	PaE PMD1035
Handful of Keys	GEP8580

BIG BILL BROONZY
Big Bill Broonzy (vcl/g), acc by Leslie Hutchinson (tpt), Bruce Turner (alt), Kenny Graham (ten), Benny Green (bar), Dill Jones (p), Jack Fallon (bs), Phil Seamen (d)
London, 26 October 1955

It Feels So Good	Nixa NJ2016, NJE1005, NJL16
Southbound Train	Nixa NJ2016, NJE1005, NJL16
Trouble in Mind	Rejected
Whiskey Head Man	rejected

HUMPHREY LYTTELTON & HIS BAND
Humphrey Lyttelton (tp), John Picard (tbn), Wally Fawkes (clt), Bruce Turner (alt), Johnny Parker (p), Freddy Legon (g), Jim Bray (bs), Stan Greig (d)
London, 13 December 1955

CE 15464/3A	**She's Crying for Me**	PaE R4128, GEP8572
CE 15465/3A	**The Lady in Red**	PaE R4128, GEP8572

ALBERT NICHOLAS
Albert Nicholas (clt), with Humphrey Lyttelton (tpt), Wally Fawkes (clt), Keith Christie (tbn), Bruce Turner (alt), Paul Simpson (bar), John Parker (p), Jim Bray (bs), Stan Greig (d)
Richardson's Recording Rooms, 4 January 1956

High Society	unissued
Royal Garden Blues	unissued
Ain't Misbehavin'	unissued
Indiana	unissued

MIDNIGHT AT NIXA
Kenny Baker (tpt), Bruce Turner (alt), Derek Smith (p), Frank Clarke (bs), Phil Seamen (d)

London, 16 January 1956

Bugle Blues	Nixa NJL 3
Truckin'	Nixa NJL 3
Jive at Five -1	Nixa NJL 3
Sidewalks of Cuba	Nixa NJL 501

MAINSTREAM AT NIXA

Kenny Baker (tpt), Keith Christie (tbn), Bruce Turner (alt), Jimmy Skidmore (ten), Fred Hartz (bar), Dill Jones (p), Ike Isaacs (g), Jack Fallon (bs), Phil Seamen (d)
London, 18 January 1956

LL 1001/A	**Time's a Wastin'**	Nixa NJT501
	Three Little Words -1	Nixa NJT501
LL 1001/B	**Blues for John** -2	Nixa NJT501

add Martin Slavin (vib) -1, (xyl) -2

HUMPHREY LYTTELTON & HIS BAND

Humphrey Lyttelton (tpt), John Picard (tbn), Wally Fawkes (clt), Bruce Turner (alt), Johnny Parker (p), Freddy Legon (g), Jim Bray (bs), Stan Greig (d)
London, 24 January 1956

CE 15495/1	**Pagin' Mr Fagin**	PaE R4149, GEP8572
CE 15496/1	**Skeleton in the Cupboard**	PaE R4149, GEP8572

MIDNIGHT AT NIXA

Bruce Turner, Bertie King (alt), Derek Smith (p), Frank Clarke (bs), Phil Seamen (d)
London, 20 February 1956

Tea for Two	Nixa NJL 3

Kenny Baker (tpt), Bruce Turner (alt), Derek Smith (p), Major Holley (bs), Don Lawson (d)
London, 23 March 1956

Don't Worry 'bout Me	Nixa NJL 3
Blues Any Friday	Nixa NJL 3
It Don't Mean a Thing	Nixa NJL 3

HUMPHREY LYTTELTON & HIS BAND

Humphrey Lyttelton (tpt), John Picard (tbn), Wally Fawkes (clt), Bruce Turner (alt), Johnny Parker (p), Freddy Legon (g), Jim Bray (bs), Stan Greig (d)
London, 29 March 1956

CE 15567/1	**Close Your Eyes**	PaE R4184

as last, without Picard, Fawkes and Legon
London, 20 April 1956

Waiting for Picard	PaE GEP8609
Sugar Rose	PaE GEP8609

FAWKES-TURNER SEXTET

Wally Fawkes (clt), Bruce Turner (alt), Dill Jones (p), Major Holley (bs), Don Lawson (d)
London, 28 May 1956

Creole Love Call	Nixa NJT510

| | **Blue Turning Grey** | |
| | **Over You** | Nixa NJT510 |

Phil Seamen (d), replaces Lawson
London, 26 June 1956

	Mandy	Nixa NJT503
	Blue Berry Hill	Nixa NJT503
	Blues Gone Away	Nixa NJT510

HUMPHREY LYTTELTON & HIS BAND

Humphrey Lyttelton (tpt), John Picard (tbn), Bruce Turner (alt), Johnny Parker (p), Freddy Legon (g), Jim Bray (bs), Stan Greig (d)
London, 30 July 1956

| CE 15644/1 | **Love, Love, Love** | PaE R4212, 45R4212 |
| CE 15645/1 | **Echoing the Blues** | PaE R4212, 45R4212, GEP8645 |

as last, except Eddie Taylor (d) -1, and Tommy Jones (d) -2, replace Greig
London, 27 August 1956

	Christopher Columbus	
	-1	PaE PMD 1044
	That's My Home -1	PaE PMD 1044
	Swing Out -2	PaE PMD 1044

as last, but Stan Greig (d) -3
London, 29 August 1956

	Just One of Those	
	Blues -1	PMD 1044
	Why Was I Born -1	PMD 1044
	Glad Rag Doll -3	PMD 1044

as last, but Turner (clt) -1, Eddie Taylor (d), Legon out
London, 7 December 1956

| CE 15731/1 | **It's Mardi Gras** -1 | PaE R4262, GEP8668 |
| CE 15732/1 | **Sweet and Sour** | PaE R4262 |

as last
London, 14 January 1957

| CE 15757/1 | **Baby Doll** | PaE 4277, CMSP41 |
| CE 15758/1 | **Red Beans and Rice** -1 | PaE R4277, GEP8668 |

as last
London, 17 April 1957

| CE 15850/1 | **Early Call** | PaE R4333, 45R4333 |
| CE 15851/1 | **Creole Serenade** -1* | PaE R4333, 45R4333, GEP8668 |

* It has been suggested that Jimmy Skidmore (ten), is present on this track. Jepson gives the recording date as 25 May 1957

as last
London, 26 April 1957

| | **Apex Blues** | PaE PMD 1049 |

You Brought a New	
Kind of Love	PaE PMD 1049
Someone Stole	
Gabriel's Horn	PaE PMD 1049
Just Squeeze Me -1	PaE PMD 1049

BRUCE TURNER'S JUMP BAND
personnel unknown, but prob. Terry Brown (tpt), from the sixth title
London, 29 August 1957

Broadway	unissued
In a Mellotone	unissued
Topsy	unissued
Softly as in a Morning	
Sunrise	unissued
Northwest Passage	
– two takes	unissued
Terry's Blues	unissued
Ballad Melody	unissued

recorded by John R.T. Davis, probably for Ristic

ILENE DAY (vcl) acc. by:
Bruce Turner (alt/clt), Martin Slavin (vib), Dave Lee (p), Roy Plummer (g),
Sammy Stokes (bs), Phil Seamen (d)
London, 9 September 1957

| Hey Baby | Nixa NJT512 |
| Mood Indigo | Nixa NJT512 |

KENNY BAKER'S HALF DOZEN
Kenny Baker (tpt), George Chisholm (tbn), Bruce Turner (alt), Eddie
Thompson (p), Lennie Bush (bs), Phil Seamen (d)
London, October 1957

| LL 1009B | Act One, Scene One | Nixa NJT509 |

DICK HECKSTALL-SMITH QUINTET
Dick Heckstall-Smith (sop), Bruce Turner (alt/clt), Harry Smith (p), Brian
Brocklehurst (bs), Eddie Taylor (d)
London, 30 October 1957

| Lover Man | Nixa NJL 20 |
| Russian Lullaby | Nixa NJT 10 |

BRUCE TURNER'S JUMP BAND
Terry Brown (tpt), Bruce Turner (alt/clt) -1, Al Mead (p), Danny Haggerty
(bs), Billy Loch (d)
London, 11 November 1957

Your Eyes -1	Nixa NJE 1051
Stop, Look and	
Listen -1	Nixa NJE 1051

ILENE DAY (vcl) acc. by:
Bruce Turner (alt-clt), Martin Slavin (vib), Dill Jones (p), Dave Goldberg
(g), Sammy Stokes (bs), Don Lawson (d)
London, 12 December 1957

Something to Live for	Nixa NJT 512
I Ain't Got Nothing	
but the Blues	Nixa NJT 512
I'm Beginning to See	
the Light	Nixa NJT 512

as last
London, 31 December 1957

It Don't Mean a Thing	Nixa NJT 512
Just Squeeze Me	Nixa NJT 512
In a Mellow Tone	Nixa NJT 512

The following single was also made by Ilene Day, details unknown, *1957*

Beat up the Town	Nixa NJ 2019
Come by Sunday	Nixa NJ 2019

KEN SYKORA GUITAR CLUB

unknown personnel but includes Bruce Turner (alt/clt) -1, Ken Sykora, Ike Isaacs (g), Reg Wale (marimba)
London, 1957/58

Little Black Dog/Here	
Lies Love -1	Saga ESAG 7001
Junior Bolero/Rangoon	Saga ESAG 7002
Garden in Versailles/	
Zenara	Saga ESAG 7003

as session on 11 November 1957
London, 13 January 1958

Jumpin' at the	
Woodside	Nixa NJE 1051
Donegal Cradle Song	Nixa NJE 1051

KENNY BAKER & HIS RHYTHM

Kenny Baker (tpt), Bruce Turner (alt), Johnny Scott (flt), Harry Smith (p), Jack Fallon (bs), Lennie Hastings (d)
London, 20 May 1958

Baby	Nixa NJT 517

MELODY MAKER ALL STARS

Kenny Baker (tpt), George Chisholm (tbn), Bruce Turner, Tony Coe (alt), Dill Jones (p), Lennie Bush (bs), Eddie Taylor (d)
London, Nov/Dec 1958

Poll Winners	Nixa NJT 518

BRUCE TURNER'S JUMP BAND

John Chilton (tpt), John Mumford (tbn), Bruce Turner (alt/clt), Stan Greig (p), Tony Goffe (bs), Johnny Armatage (d)
London, 18 March 1959

Accent on Swing	Int. Jazz Club: AJZ/4/LP
Cream Puff	Int. Jazz Club: AJZ/4/LP
Opus Five	Int. Jazz Club: AJZ/4/LP

Don't Get around Much any More	Int. Jazz Club: AJZ/4/LP
Stop! Look and Listen	Int. Jazz Club: AJZ/4/LP
Christopher Columbus	Int. Jazz Club: AJZ/4/LP
Queen Bess	Int. Jazz Club: AJZ/4/LP
Honeysuckle Rose	Int. Jazz Club: AJZ/4/LP
Nuages	Int. Jazz Club: AJZ/4/LP
Jump for Me	Int. Jazz Club: AJZ/4/LP
Blues for Lester	Int. Jazz Club: AJZ/4/LP

BRUCE TURNER SARATOGA JUMP BAND

Troels Knudsen (tpt), Hugo Hjulmand (clt), Bruce Turner (alt), Mogens Rusenfeldt (p), Niels Baumbach (bs), Flemming Kirkholt (d)
Concert Aarhus, 29 May 1959

I'm in the Mood for Swing	Debut DL-104
Things ain't what They Used to be	Debut DL-104
Queen Bess	Debut DL-104
Jumpin' at the Woodside	Debut DL-104

KENNY BALL – 'MADE TO MEASURE'

Kenny Ball, Al Fairweather (tpt), John Picard (tbn), Bruce Turner (alt/clt/ten), Dick Heckstall-Smith (ten), Ian Armit (p), Tim Mahn (bs), Alan Ganley (d)
London, 10 June 1959

By the Fireside	Ristic LP 21
The Music Goes Round and Round	Ristic LP 21
Sue's Blues	Ristic LP 21
Exactly Like You	Ristic LP 21

as last, except 'Red' Price (ten), and Stan Greig (d), replace Heckstall-Smith and Ganley
London, 17 June 1959

Goody Goody	Ristic LP 21
Easy to Love	Ristic LP 21
Sometimes I'm Happy	Ristic LP 21
Tin Roof Blues	Ristic LP 21

This record was rereleased in 1971 by Amalgamated Record Supplies

AL FAIRWEATHER'S ALL STARS

Al Fairweather (tpt), George Chisholm (tbn), Bruce Turner (alt), Tony Coe (alt), Stan Greig (p), Jack Fallon (bs), Lennie Hastings (d)
London, 13 October 1959

Love is All	Columbia 33SX 1221
Jump for Me	Columbia 33SX 1221
Rosetta	Columbia 33SX 1221
Let the Zoomers Drool	Columbia 33SX 1221

BRUCE TURNER'S JUMP BAND
John Chilton (tpt), John Mumford (tbn), Bruce Turner (alt/clt), Collin Bates
(p), Bill Bramwell (g), Jim Bray (bs), John Armatage (d)
London, prob. spring 1960

Nuages	Melodisc 45-1551
My Guy's Come Back	Melodisc 45-1551

BRUCE TURNER'S JUMP BAND
John Chilton (tpt), John Mumford (tbn), Bruce Turner (alt/clt) -1, Collin Bates
(p), Jim Bray (bs), Johnny Armatage (d)
London, 16/17 February 1961

Hyde Park	77-LEU-12/2
Cherry	77-LEU-12/2
Watch the Birdie -1	77-LEU-12/2
Coldwater Canyon	77-LEU-12/2
Opus Five	77-LEU-12/2, 77EPEU-1
Jump	77-LEU-12/2, 77EPEU-1
Knickerbocker Glory	77-LEU-12/2
Roses of Picardy -1	77-LEU-12/2
Stormy Weather	77-LEU-12/2
Clutterbuck	77-LEU-12/2, 77EPEU-1

as last, but John Picard (tbn), replaces Mumford
same date

Willie the Weeper	77-LEU-12/2

as last, but Mumford (tbn), added
same date

Morning Glories	77-LEU-12/2

BRUCE TURNER'S JUMP BAND
Bruce Turner (alt), John Chilton (tpt), Pete Strange (tbn), Collin Bates (p), Ike
Isaacs (g), Jim Bray (bs), John Armatage (d), Bill Shepherd (arr)
Chiselhurst Caves, 17 September 1961

Cave Girl	rejected
Charlie-My Darling	rejected

These tracks were made for an advertising film for Clark's Shoes Ltd, but were
rejected for bad sound quality. They were remade (below) and -1 was also used
in a film (*Cave Girl*) for the same company

as last, but unknown (g) replaces Isaacs
London, 23 October 1961

LYN 208	**Cave Girl** -1
LYN 209	**Charlie-My Darling**

as last, but omit unknown g
Copenhagen, 21 January 1962

Cushionfoot Stomp	Storyville SXP 2025
Accent on Swing	Storyville SXP 2025

Gone with what Draft	Storyville SXP 2025
How Long Blues	Storyville SXP 2025
A Little Bit	
Independent	unissued
Carioca	unissued

as last, but Long John Baldry (vcl) -1, John Chilton (vcl) -2
London, 21 February 1962

Big Noise from	
Winnetka	C.R.D. CRD 1000
Jamaica Jump	C.R.D. CRD 1000
New How Long Blues -1	C.R.D. CRD 1001
Four or Five Times -2	C.R.D. CRD 1001

as last
Six Bells Jazz Club London, 2 July 1962

DR 29562	**Ain't Misbehavin'**	Decca: LK(S) 4512
DR 29563	**Mood Indigo**	Decca: LK(S) 4512
DR 29564	**One o'Clock Jump**	Decca: LK(S) 4512

as last
London, 11–12 July 1962

Johnny Come Lately	Philips: 433627 BE
Donegal Cradle Song	Philips: 433627 BE
Lafayette	Philips: 433627 BE
Don't Get around	
Much any More	Philips: 433628 BE
Cherry Red	Philips: 433628 BE
A Flat to C -1	Philips: 433628 BE
Whisky Sour	Philips: 433628 BE
Indian Summer -2	Philips: 433628 BE

-1 omit Chilton and Bates, -2 omit Chilton and Strange

BRUCE TURNER'S JUMP BAND
Ray Crane (tpt), Pete Strange (tbn), Bruce Turner (alt/sop), Collin Bates (p),
Jim Bray (bs), Johnny Armatage (d)
London, 23 and 25 September 1963

Going Places	Philips: BL 7590
Nagasaki	Philips: BL 7590
Plastered in Paris	Philips: BL 7590
Donegal Cradle Song	Philips: BL 7590
Istanbul	Philips: BL 7590
Hong Kong Blues	Philips: BL 7590
Helsinki	Philips: BL 7590
Chicago	Philips: BL 7590
Night Train to Munich	Philips: BL 7590
St Louis Blues	Philips: BL 7590
Chinatown, My	
Chinatown	Philips: BL 7590
Copenhagen	Philips: BL 7590
The Snake Charmer	Philips: BL 7590

230

Big Noise from	
Winnetka	Philips: BL 7590
Russian Lullaby	Philips: BL 7590
Westminster	Philips: BL 7590

WILD BILL DAVISON & THE FREDDY RANDALL BAND

Wild Bill Davison (cnt), Freddy Randall (tpt), George Chisholm (tbn), Bruce Turner (clt/alt), Lennie Felix (p), Dave Markee (bs), Tony Allen (d), Ronnie Gleaves (vib) -1

London, February 1965

Royal Garden Blues	World Sound T 552
Memories of You -1	World Sound T 552
Hindustan	World Sound T 552
If I Had You	World Sound T 552
All of Me	World Sound T 552
Wolverine Blues	World Sound T 552
Ghost of a Chance -1	World Sound T 552
Struttin' with Some	
Barbecue	World Sound T 552
Tin Roof Blues -1	World Sound T 552

ACKER BILK & HIS PARAMOUNT JAZZ BAND

Colin Smith (tpt), John Mortimer (tbn), Acker Bilk (clt), Bruce Turner (alt/sop) -1, Stan Greig (p), Tony Pitt (g), Tucker Finlayson (bs), Ron McKay (d)

London, 4 January 1966

Dow de Dow Dow Dow	Columbia: TWO 154
Maori Farewell	Columbia: TWO 154
Acka Raga -1 -2	Columbia: TWO 154
The Swinging Hussar	Columbia: TWO 154

-2 Smith and Mortimer out

DON BYAS with BRUCE TURNER'S JUMP BAND

Don Byas (ten), Ray Crane (tpt), Bruce Turner (alt), Ronnie Gleaves (d), et al

March 1966

Lady Bird	Vantage LP 504
I Remember Clifford	Vantage LP 504
I'll Remember April	Vantage LP 504

ACKER BILK & HIS PARAMOUNT JAZZ BAND

as 4 January, but Ian Hunter-Randall (tpt), replaces Smith
London, c. May/June 1966

Stranger in New	
Orleans	Columbia: TWO 154
Fancy Pants	Columbia: TWO 154
Adios Mi Chaparita	Columbia: TWO 154
Volare	Columbia: TWO 154

as last, but Al Fairweather (tpt), replaces Hunter-Randall
London, July 1966

Kassian	Columbia: TWO 154
The Wild Colonial Boy	Columbia: TWO 154

Hong Kong Rose	Columbia: TWO 154

as last, but Pitt (bjo) -1
Concert New Zealand, c. October 1966

Tiger Rag -1	Columbia: SX/SCX 6241
Undecided	Columbia: SX/SCX 6241
Bugle Call Rag	Columbia: SX/SCX 6241
Front Seat Driver	Columbia: SX/SCX 6241

as last, with Ronnie Ross (bar)
London, 1967

Acker's Personal Jungle	Columbia: SX/SCX 6241, Met. B1670
Caravan	Columbia: SX/SCX 6241, Met. B1670
The Hucklebuck	Columbia: SX/SCX 6241,
Tarzan's March	Columbia: SX/SCX 6241, Met. B1670

ACKER BILK & HIS PARAMOUNT JAZZ BAND
Colin Smith (tpt), John Mortimer (tbn), Acker Bilk (clt), Bruce Turner (alt), Colin Bates (p), Tony Pitt (g), Tucker Finlayson (bs), Ron McKay (d, vcl) -2)
Kongresshalle, Leipzig, 14 January 1969

Undecided	Amiga: 8 55 180 8 55 252
Dinah -2	Amiga: 8 55 180 8 55 252
Stranger on the Shore	Amiga: 8 55 180 8 55 252
Bula-Bula	Amiga: 8 55 180
Creole Jazz	Amiga: 8 55 180
After You've Gone -1	Amiga: 8 55 180
Dardanella -3	Amiga: 8 55 180
Persian Market	Amiga: 8 55 180

-3 Smith and Mortimer out, -1 Bilk (vcl)

as last, but John Richardson (d), replaces McKay
London, 19 March 1970

Drop Me off in Harlem	Regal: SRS 5028
Big Bill	Regal: SRS 5028
Jazz Me Blues	Regal: SRS 5028
The Whiffenpoof Song -1	Regal: SRS 5028
Savoy Blues	Regal: SRS 5028
Opus 5	Regal: SRS 5028
L'il Darling	Regal: SRS 5028
At Sundown	Regal: SRS 5028
C'est Si Bon -1	Regal: SRS 5028
Lover Come back to Me	Regal: SRS 5028

-1 Bilk (vcl)

ADELAIDE HALL
Adelaide Hall (vcl), Humphrey Lyttelton (tpt), Bruce Turner (alt/clt), Danny Moss (ten), Brian Lemon (p, arr), Arthur Watts (bs), Tony Kinsey (d)
London, early 1970

Creole Love Call	Columbia: SCX 6422
I Must Have that Man	Columbia: SCX 6422
Diga Diga Doo	Columbia: SCX 6422
Porgy	Columbia: SCX 6422
I Can't Give You	
Anything but Love	Columbia: SCX 6422

BRIAN LEMON ENSEMBLE

Ray Crane (tpt), John Picard (tbn), Sandy Brown (clt), Bruce Turner (alt/ten/sop), Tony Coe (ten), Brian Lemon (p), Dave Green (bs), Bobby Orr (d)
London, 30 June 1970

Straighten up and Fly	
Right	77-LEU-12/38
Gentlemen of the Bar	77-LEU-12/38

as last, but Lemon and Orr out
same date

Sandy's Blues	77-LEU-12/38
When My Sugar Walks	
Down the Street	77-LEU-12/38

as last, but Lemon and Orr return, Coe out
same date

I'm Comin' Virginia	77-LEU-12/38
After Supper	77-LEU-12/38

as last, but Crane and Picard out
same date

Strike up the Band	77-LEU-12/38

MELODY MAKER TRIBUTE to LOUIS ARMSTRONG

The Fawkes-Chilton Feetwarmers: John Chilton (tpt), Wally Fawkes (clt, sop), Bruce Turner (alt), Colin Parnell (p), Steve Fagg (bs), Chuck Smith (d)
Q.E. Hall, London, 4 July 1970

Willie the Weeper	Polydor Select 2460 124
2.19 Blues	Polydor Select 2460 124
Big Butter and Egg	
Man	Polydor Select 2460 124

Guests with the Alex Welsh Band: Humphrey Lyttelton (tpt), George Chisholm (tbn), Bruce Turner (alt), Beryl Bryden (wbd), Alex Welsh (tpt), Roy Williams (tbn), John Barnes (alt/bar), Al Gay (ten), Fred Hunt (p), Jim Douglas (g), Harvey Weston (bs), Lennie Hastings (d)
same date

I'm a Ding Dong	
Daddy	Polydor Select 2460 125
When It's Sleepy Time	
Down South	Polydor Select 2460 125

ALEX WELSH & HIS BAND with guests

Alex Welsh (tpt), Roy Williams (tbn), John Barnes (clt/bar), Fred Hunt (p), Jim Douglas (g), Harvey Weston (bs), Lennie Hastings (d), *plus* Bruce Turner

(clt)-1/(alt)-2, Humphrey Lyttelton (tpt) -3, George Chisholm (tbn) -4
Q.E. Hall, London, 28 November 1971

Rockin' Chair -1	Polydor Select 2460 179 -1
Royal Garden Blues -	
2 3 4	Polydor Select 2460 180 -2
I Double Dare You -	
2 3 4 5	Polydor Select 2460 180
When You're Smiling -	
2 3 4	Polydor Select 2460 180
Sleep Time Down South	
- 2 3 4	Polydor Select 2460 180

Record -1 also on Black Lion BLP 12112 and Intercord Black Lion 127020
Record -2 also on Black Lion BLP 12113 and Intercord Black Lion (G) 157002
NB Polydor 2460 124/5 also on Intercord/Black Lion (G) 28777-1Z/1 - 3

HUMPHREY LYTTELTON & HIS BAND
Humphrey Lyttelton (tpt/clt), Bruce Turner (clt/alt), Kathy Stobart (ten/bar),
Colin Purbrook (p), Dave Green (bs), Tony Mann (d)
Hamburg, 12 March 1972

Cracked	WAM MLP 15433
Ev'ntide	WAM MLP 15433
Sonny Boy	WAM MLP 15433
They Can't Take that	
away from Me	WAM MLP 15433
Slippery Horn	WAM MLP 15433
Creole Love Call	WAM MLP 15433
Doggin' Around	WAM MLP 15433

GEORGE MELLY with the FAWKES-CHILTON FEETWARMERS
George Melly (vcl), John Chilton (tpt), Wally Fawkes (sop/clt), Bruce Turner
(alt/clt) -1, Collin Bates (p), John 'Chuck' Smith (d), Steve Fagg (bs)
Ronnie Scott's Club, London, 18 June 1972

Tain't Nobody's Business
Sam Jones Blues -2
Viper Mad
There'll be Some Changes
   Made -1
Nobody Knows You When
   You're Down and Out

-2 Melly, acc. by rhythm section only

MELLY/CHILTON The following tracks were rejected from the June session
and remade in the studio with dubbed-in audience effects
London, 24 July 1972

Doctor Jazz	W B K 46188, K 36005
Sugar	W B K 46188, K 36005
I Want a Little Girl	W B K 46188, K 36005
If You'se a Viper	W B K 46188, K 36005
Nuts	W B K 46188, K 36005

GEORGE MELLY with the FEETWARMERS
George Melly (vcl), John Chilton (tpt), Bruce Turner (clt/alt), Collin Bates (p),

Steve Fagg (bs), Chuck Smith (d)
New Merlin's Cave, London, 4 September 1973

Old Fashioned Love	W B K 46269, K 36006
I Need a Little Sugar	
in My Bowl	W B K 46269, K 36006
Good Time George	W B K 46269, K 36006
Winin' Boy	W B K 46269, K 36006
Joint is Jumpin'	W B K 46269, K 36006
Buddy Bolden's Blues	W B K 46269, K 36006
Heebie Jeebies	W B K 46269, K 36006
Kitchen Man	W B K 46269, K 36006
Roll 'em Pete	W B K 46269, K 36006
Young Woman's Blues	W B K 46269, K 36006
Show Me the Way to	
Go Home	W B K 46269, K 36006

HUMPHREY LYTTELTON & HIS BAND
Humphrey Lyttelton (tpt/clt), Bruce Turner (alt/clt), Kathy Stobart (ten), Mike Pyne (p), Dave Green (bs), Tony Mann (d)
Q.E. Hall, London, 5 September 1973

Let's Get in	Bl Lion 2460 233, Int B L (G) 162009
Late Night Final	Bl Lion 2460 233, Int B L (G) 162009
P.T.Q. Rag	Bl Lion 2460 233, Int B L (G) 162009
Dadbo	Bl Lion 2460 233, Int B L (G) 162009
The Comet	Bl Lion 2460 233, Int B L (G) 162009
Blues at Dawn	Bl Lion 2460 233, Int B L (G) 162009
Let's Get out	Bl Lion 2460 233, Int B L (G) 162009

as last
Hamburg, 9 May 1974

In Swinger	Happy Bird ST HB 5009
Toot'n in Karmen	Happy Bird ST HB 5009
Talk of the Town	Happy Bird ST HB 5009
One for Buck	Happy Bird ST HB 5009
Harry Looyah	Happy Bird ST HB 5009
St Louis Blues	Happy Bird ST HB 5009
New Bad Penny Blues	Happy Bird ST HB 5009
Georgia Mae	Happy Bird ST HB 5009

HUMPHREY LYTTELTON & HIS BAND with Buddy Tate
Humphrey Lyttelton (tpt/clt), Buddy Tate (clt/ten), Bruce Turner (clt/alt), Kathy Stobart (ten/bar/clt), Mike Pyne (p), Dave Green (bs), Tony Mann (d)
Pye Studios London, 3 July 1974

Kansas City Woman	Bl Lion BLP 30163, B L/Int (G) 162005

The One for Me	Bl Lion BLP 30163, B L/Int (G) 162005
Pamela	Bl Lion BLP 30163, B L/Int (G) 162005
Candyville	Bl Lion BLP 30163, B L/Int (G) 162005
Steevos	Bl Lion BLP 30163, B L/Int (G) 162005
Clarinet Lemonade	Bl Lion BLP 30163, B L/Int (G) 162005
Swinging Scorpio	Bl Lion BLP 30163, B L/Int (G) 162005
Outswinger	Bl Lion BLP 30163, B L/Int (G) 162005

SPACE
John Chilton (tpt), Chris Pyne (tbn), Bruce Turner (clt), recorded over existing tape by 'Space' (unk. gg, fender-bs, p, d)
London, 21 July 1974

Sweet Bird of Youth	unissued (?)

Bruce has also recorded other pop sessions with Keith Christie and Brian Lemon, no details

GEORGE MELLY with the FEETWARMERS & OTHER FRIENDS
Melly (vcl), John Chilton (tpt/arr), Roy Williams (tbn), Bruce Turner (clt), Collin Bates (p), Steve Fagg (bs), Chuck Smith (d)
London, 17/27 September 1974

All the Whores Go Crazy	W B K 56087
Tain't No Sin	W B K 56087

as last, plus John Barnes (bar), Turner (clt)

It Don't Mean a Thing	W B K 56087

as last, plus Tommy Whittle (ten)

Rosetta	W B K 56087
Gee Baby ain't I Good to You	W B K 56087

as last, except all three reeds play clt

Trouble in Mind	WB K 56087

Melly (vcl), John Chilton (tpt), Bruce Turner (alt), Harry Klein (bar), Collin Bates (p), Eric Ford (g), Steve Fagg (bs), Chuck Smith (d)

The Food of Love	W B K 56087

THE DIXIELAND ALL STARS
Colin Smith (tpt/ldr), Roy Williams (tbn), Bruce Turner (clt/alt)-2, Al Gay (clt)-2/(ten), Stan Greig (p), Cliff Wren (bs), Lennie Hastings (d)
London, 22 September 1974

Struttin' with some Barbecue	Line 2004
Squeeze Me	Line 2004

Chicago	Line 2004
Jamaica Jump - 1, 2	Line 2004
Basin Street Blues - 1, 2	Line 2004
Ja Da	Line 2004
That Da Da Strain	Line 2004
Beale Street Blues	Line 2004
Chinatown My	
Chinatown -2	Line 2004
Since You First Came	
My Way - 1	Line 2004
Jazz Me Blues	Line 2004
Way Down Yonder in	
New Orleans	Line 2004

JOHN CHILTON'S FEETWARMERS
John Chilton (tpt), Bruce Turner (clt), Collin Bates (p), Steve Fagg (bs), Chuck Smith (d)
Trident Studios, London, 15 November 1974

Walking in the Park	
with Eloise	unissued

THE DIXIELAND ALL STARS
as above, except Ron Rubin (bs), replaces Wren
London, 15 March 1975

At the Jazz Band Ball	Line 2025
Tin Roof Blues -2	Line 2025
Louisiana	Line 2025
Sundown Lowdown -1	Line 2025
I've Got a Feeling I'm	
Falling	Line 2025
Dippermouth Blues	
- 1 2	Line 2025
That's a Plenty	Line 2025
Sweet Lorraine	Line 2025
Wolverine Blues - 2	Line 2025
Frame up - 2	Line 2025
Nice Work if You Can	
Get It	Line 2025
Hindustan	Line 2025

HUMPHREY LYTTELTON & HIS BAND
Humphrey Lyttelton (tpt), Bruce Turner (alt/clt), Kathy Stobart (ten/bar/sop), Mike Pyne (p), Dave Green (bs), Tony Mann (d), Elkie Brooks (vcl) - 1
London, 23 June 1975

Take It from the Top	Black Lion BLP 12134/ Intercord/Bl Lion (G) 162024
Madly	Black Lion BLP 12134/ Intercord/Bl Lion (G) 162024

Big Ol' Tears	Black Lion BLP 12134/
	Intercord/Bl Lion (G)
	162024
Sprauncy	Black Lion BLP 12134/
	Intercord/Bl Lion (G)
	162024
Lion Rampant	Black Lion BLP 12134/
	Intercord/Bl Lion (G)
	162024
Very First Kiss -1	Black Lion BLP 12134/
	Intercord/Bl Lion (G)
	162024
Oh Baby, Maybe	Black Lion BLP 12134/
Someday -1	Intercord/Bl Lion (G)
	162024
We Fell out of love- 1	Black Lion BLP 12134/
	Intercord/Bl Lion (G)
	162024
Rain	Black Lion BLP 12134/
	Intercord/Bl Lion (G)
	162024
Don't Get around	Black Lion BLP 12134/
Much any More/	Intercord/Bl Lion (G)
I Let a Song - 1	162024

WILD BILL DAVISON with TED EASTON'S JAZZ BAND
Wild Bill Davison (cnt), Roy Williams (tbn), Bruce Turner (clt/alt), Pim Hogervorst (bjo), Jacques Kingma (bs), Theo van Est (Ted Easton) (- d)
Leiden, 8 October 1975

You're Lucky to Me	Riff 659 005
Memories of You	Riff 659 005
Thou Swell	Riff 659 005
Singin' the Blues	Riff 659 005
Just a Gigolo	Riff 659 005
Just You, Just Me	Riff 659 005
But Beautiful	Riff 659 005
Blue Again	Riff 659 005
Keepin' out of Mischief	
Now - vcl TE	Riff 659 005

THE BRUCE TURNER-JOHN BARNES JAZZ MASTERS
Colin Smith (tpt), Bruce Turner (alt/clt), John Barnes (clt/bar/flt), Keith Ingham (p), Harvey Weston (bs), John Armatage (d)
St Pancras Town Hall, London, 16 October 1975

Hiya	Cadillac SGC 1005
Boke's Blues (omit	
Smith)	Cadillac SGC 1005
The King	Cadillac SGC 1005
Amazon	Cadillac SGC 1005
Stormy Weather (omit	
Smith and Barnes)	Cadillac SGC 1005
Perdido	Cadillac SGC 1005

238

BUD FREEMAN – SONG OF THE TENOR

Bud Freeman (ten), Bob Wilber (sop/clt), Bruce Turner (alt/clt), Roy Williams
(tbn) -1, Keith Ingham (p), Peter Ind (bs), Bobby Orr (d)
London, 4/5 November 1957

Song of the Tenor	Philips 6308 254
That D Minor Thing	Philips 6308 254
Madam Dynamite -1	Philips 6308 254
Blue Room	Philips 6308 254
Keep Smiling at Trouble	Philips 6308 254
As Long as I Live	Philips 6308 254
Stop Look and Listen	Philips 6308 254
Roy Hits the Road -1	Philips 6308 254
Nobody's Sweetheart -1	Philips 6308 254
Easy to Love -1	Philips 6308 254
The Eel's Nephew -1	Philips 6308 254
Blues in Double C Flat -1	Philips 6308 254

SUSANNAH McCORKLE

Susannah McCorkle (vcl), Bruce Turner (alt/clt), Keith Ingham (p), Len Skeat
(bs), John Richardson (d)
London, 23/29 August 1976

Lullaby of Broadway	World Records WRS 1001
About a Quarter to Nine	World Records WRS 1001
With Plenty of Money and You	World Records WRS 1001
Girl Friend of the Whirling Dervish	World Records WRS 1001
I Take to You	World Records WRS 1001
Remember the Forgotten Man	World Records WRS 1001
The Gold Digger's Song	World Records WRS 1001

HUMPHREY LYTTELTON & HIS BAND

Humphrey Lyttelton (tpt), Bruce Turner (alt/clt), Kathy Stobart (reeds), Mike
Pyne (p), Dave Green (bs), Tony Mann (d)
London, 13 May 1976

Mo Pas Lemme Ca	Black Lion BLP 12160/ Intercord 147005
Triple Exposure: Hazy, Crazy, Blue	Black Lion BLP 12160/ Intercord 147005
Ory's Story	Black Lion BLP 12160/ Intercord 147005
Vive Le Roy	Black Lion BLP 12160/ Intercord 147005
Blues in Bolero	Black Lion BLP 12160/ Intercord 147005
You're Lucky to Me	Black Lion BLP 12160/ Intercord 147005
Mezzrow	Black Lion BLP 12160/ Intercord 147005

KEITH SMITH & FRIENDS
Keith Smith (tpt), Roy Williams (tbn), Alan Cooper (clt), Bruce Turner (alt/clt), Stan Greig (p), Jack Fallon (bs), Lennie Hastings (d)
London, November 1976

No details	recorded for Riff

HUMPHREY LYTTELTON & HIS BAND
Humphrey Lyttelton (tpt), Roy Williams (tbn), Bruce Turner, Malcolm Everson (reeds), Mike Pyne (p), Dave Green (bs), Alan Jackson (d)
London, 18 October 1978

Spreadin' Joy	Black Lion BLP 12173
Tishomingo Blues	Black Lion BLP 12173
Mabel's Dream	Black Lion BLP 12173
A Hundred Years	
from Today	Black Lion BLP 12173
Ugly Duckling	Black Lion BLP 12173
Black and Blue	Black Lion BLP 12173
Blues My Naughty	
Sweetie Gives to Me	Black Lion BLP 12173
East St Louis Toodle-oo	Black Lion BLP 12173
When Your Lover	
Has Gone	Black Lion BLP 12173
Honeysuckle Rose	Black Lion BLP 12173
James/If I Could be	
with You	Black Lion BLP 12173
Fish Seller	Black Lion BLP 12173

HUMPHREY LYTTELTON & HIS BAND with BUD FREEMAN
(a) personnel as above
(b) as (a), except Mike Pyne (cnt), omit Green and Jackson
(c) as (a), except add Bud Freeman (ten)
(d) as (c), Turner (alto), Everson (ten)

Chichester Festival, October 1978

Memphis Blues - (a)	Magnus 1
On Treasure Island	
- (b)	Magnus 1
East St Louis	
Toodle-oo - (a)	Magnus 1
I've Found a New Baby	
- (c)	Magnus 1
My Monday Date - (c)	Magnus 1
Crazy Rhythm - (d)	Magnus 1

KEITH SMITH'S CHOSEN FIVE with BENNY WATERS
Keith Smith (tpt/vcl), John Mortimer (tbn/vcl), Bruce Turner (alt/clt), Benny Waters (ten), Stan Greig (p/arr), Peter Ind (bs), John Cox (d)
Porcupine Studios, Elton, 20 November 1978

Chicken	Hefty Jazz HJ 105
Patrol Wagon Blues	Hefty Jazz HJ 105
Up Jumped the Blues	Hefty Jazz HJ 105
Blues Amore	Hefty Jazz HJ 105

Undecided	Hefty Jazz HJ 105
Just a Sittin' and	
a Rockin'	Hefty Jazz HJ 105
Perdido Street Blues	Hefty Jazz HJ 105
Sweet Marijuana	
Brown	Hefty Jazz HJ 105
Caldonia	Hefty Jazz HJ 105

RADIO BALLADS etc.
Bruce Turner also appears on *The World of Ewan McColl and Peggy Seeger* on Argo SPA 102, and on *Hot Blast* with Ewan McColl and Peggy Seeger on Blackthorne BR 1059 (track 3)

FINGERS
Bruce Turner (alt/clt) -1, Lol Coxhill (sop/ten) -1, Michael Garrick (p), Dave Green (bs), Alan Jackson (d)
Forum Theatre, Hatfield, Hertfordshire, 29 May 1979

Anthropology	Spotlite SPJ 521
Mood Indigo -1	Spotlite SPJ 521
Remember Mingus	Spotlite SPJ 521
Tears Inside	Spotlite SPJ 521
Alice's Wonderland	Spotlite SPJ 521

HUMPHREY LYTTELTON & HIS BAND
Humphrey Lyttelton (tpt/cnt), Roy Williams (tbn), Bruce Turner (alt/clt) -1, Malcolm Everson (clt)-2/(bar), Mike Pyne (p/cnt), Dave Green (bs), Alan Jackson (d)
Radio Luxembourg Studios, London, 24 July 1979

Panama Rag	Black Lion BLP 12188,
	BLM 51002
Toot Sweet	Black Lion BLP 12188
Buddy's Habits -1	Black Lion BLP 12188
I'm Old Fashioned	Black Lion BLP 12188
Sir Humph's Delight	Black Lion BLP 12188
Small Hour Fantasy -1	Black Lion BLP 12188
Ficklefanny Strikes	
Again	Black Lion BLP 12188
Cakewalkin' Babies	
-1, 2, HL, clt.	Black Lion BLP 12188

HUMPHREY LYTTELTON & HIS BAND
Humphrey Lyttelton (tpt), Roy Williams (tbn), Bruce Turner (alt/clt) -1, John Barnes (bar), Mike Pyne (p/cnt), Dave Green (bs), Alan Jackson (d)
R.G. Jones Studios, London, 20 February 1980

Play Boy	Black Lion BLP 12199
Ladyless and	
Lachrymose	Black Lion BLP 12199
It's a Thing	Black Lion BLP 12199
Blues in the Afternoon	
(Takes 1 and 2)	Black Lion BLP 12199
One Day I Met an	
African	Black Lion BLP 12199

Hop Frog -1	Black Lion BLP 12199
Hot House	Black Lion BLP 12199
Sirrumph	Black Lion BLP 12199

HUMPHREY LYTTELTON & HIS BAND
as last, except Mike Paxton (d), replaces Jackson
Private recording, Hamburg, 10 January 1981

Ficklefanny Strikes	
Again	Pinorrekk HB P 7003
Ladyless and	
Lachrymose	Pinorrekk HB P 7003

Note: To clear up some confusion over names, there are two Colin (Collin) Bates included in records in this discography. I understand that their Christian names are spelt as I have given them, and I hope that I have always included them in the right context. M.N.C.

Supplement: Radio Ballads.

Bruce Turner has taken part in a number of 'Radio Ballads' broadcast by the BBC and issued on record. While these are outside the scope of a Jazz Discography they are worth including in this supplement.

THE BALLAD OF JOHN AXON   *Argo*: DA 139

Transmitted: 1958

The Instrumentalists: Terry Brown (tpt), Bobby Mickleburgh (tbn), Bruce Turner (clt), Alf Edwards (concertina), John Cole (harmonica), Fitzroy Coleman (g), Peggy Seeger (bjo), Jim Bray (bs), Billy Loch (d), Brian Daly (g)
The Singers: Ewan McColl, A.L. Lloyd, Isla Cameron, Dominic Behan, Stan Kelly, Dick Loveless, Charles Mayo, Colin Dunn

SONG OF A ROAD   *Transmitted: 5 November 1959*

The Instrumentalists: John Chilton (tpt), Bobby Mickleburgh (tbn), Bruce Turner (clt), Alf Edwards (conc/ocarina), Francis McPeake (vileann pipes), Fitzroy Coleman (g), Peggy Seeger (bjo/auto/harp), Jim Bray (bs), Johnny Armatage (d)
The Singers: Ewan McColl, Isla Cameron, John Clarence, Seamus Ennis, Lou Killen, A.L. Lloyd, Jimmy McGreggor, Francis McPeake, Isabel Sutherland, Cyril Tawney, William V. Thomas

SINGING THE FISHING   *Argo*: DA 142

Transmitted: 16 August 1960

The Instrumentalists: Bruce Turner (alt/clt), Kay Graham (fiddle), Alf Edwards (conc/ocar), Fitzroy Coleman (g), Peggy Seeger (bjo/g/a-harp), Jim Bray (bs)
The Singers: Ewan McColl, A.L. Lloyd, John Clarence, Elizabeth Stewart, Jane Stewart, Ian Campbell, Sam Larner, Ronnie Balls, and Chorus directed by Katherine Thomson

THE TRAVELLING PEOPLE   *Argo*: DA 133

Transmitted: 17 April 1964

The Instrumentalists: Bruce Turner (clt/alt), Alfie Kahn (clt/piccolo/harmonica/flt), Dinah Demuth (oboe), Danny Levan (fiddle), Alf Edwards (conc), Bryan Daly (g), Peggy Seeger (bjo/g), Jim Bray (bs)

The Singers: Ewan McColl, Peggy Seeger, Belle Stewart, Jane Stewart, John Feaney, John Faulkener

The above were produced by Charles Parker of the BBC Birmingham, and grateful thanks are due to his department for these details.

A selection from the above has been reissued on *Argo*: SPA 102 & 216.

Supplement: Private Recordings

THE MAL TURNER TRIO

Malcolm Bruce Turner (clt/C-Mel. sax), Bob Farran (p), Jack Mould (d)
London, 3 May 1941

LT 1A	**Someday Sweetheart**
LT 1B	**Sugar**
LT 2A	**Bond Street Blues**
LT 2B	**Honeysuckle Rose**

as last, except Turner (clt)
London, 5 June 1941

	Poor Butterfly
	There'll be Some Changes Made

THE BILLY KAYE TRIO

Bruce Turner (clt/ten), Michael Grant (p), Rodney Crump (d)
c. 1946/7

C/211/1	**You Go to My Head**
C/211/2	**Wrap Your Troubles in Dreams**
C/211/3	**Taking a Chance on Love**
C/211/4	**Liza**

Index